Caylie Jeffery is a Brisbane writer and educator, with a passion for people and their stories.

A former nurse and counsellor, Caylie has lived an adventurous life, filled with incredible experiences, projects and people who have helped make her journey so memorable.

Caylie's first book, *Bedtime Stories for Busy Mothers*, was her gift to people experiencing the highs and lows of parenting. She shared her personal experiences for the benefit of others, with poignant, amusing and heart-warming tales of life with her ever-evolving but wonderful family.

The *Under the Lino Project* has catapulted Caylie's local community into her life in ways she'd never have predicted. She attributes its success to the relationship she has built with the friends and colleagues who have worked tirelessly alongside her for its duration.

Caylie currently lives in Milton with her husband, David, and their two beautiful children, Will and Kitty. They are still renovating their Heussler Terrace house after 23 years...

Under the Lino

The Mystery The History The Community

Caylie Jeffery

First Published 2018 by Caylie Jeffery
Milton, Queensland, 4064 Australia

www.underthelino.com.au
underthelino@hotmail.com.au

© 2018 Caylie Jeffery

© 2019 Caylie Jeffery second edition

This book is copyright. Except for private study, research, comments by the members of the Old Brisbane Album Facebook page and the Under the Lino Facebook page, newspaper articles, documents and photographs which have been permitted under the Copyright Act, or with permission of the owners. No part of this book may be reproduced, stored in a retrieval system or transmitted in any form or by any means without prior written permission. Enquiries should be made to the above e-mail address.

Cover Design and Graphic Art by Daniel Jarick and Caren Crawford
Cover Photograph by Natalie Jeffcott
Printed by Paradigm Print Media
Proof-readers/Beta-readers/Editors: Perry Morcombe, Claire Faulkner, Cheryl Palmer, Lyn Cox, Michelle Hill, Brenda Koster, Bronwyn Wallman, Sue Fernandes, Virginia McMillan, Daphne and Dom Gonzalvez
Back Cover Photograph thanks to Emily Harper
Author Photograph by Amie Neil
Artwork by Sue Fernandes

All attempts have been made to contact copyright licensees for permission to reproduce material.

Permission has been generously granted by members of the extended Webster and Murphy families to include excerpts and photographs from their respective family histories.

National Library of Australia cataloguing-in-publication data is available at http://catalogue.nla.gov.au

Under the Lino/Caylie Jeffery

Com-mun-ity
[kuh-myoo-ni-tee]
1. ***A social group of any size whose members reside in a specific locality, share government, and often have a common cultural and historical heritage***

Taken from a sign opposite Brisbane State High School. Had I not attended my 30th reunion there in 2017, what you're about to read may never have occurred.

I dedicate this book to *my* Community…
David, Will and Kitty; my Mum, Sue; my wonderful family ranging from Banyo to Oslo; my dearest friends in every corner of the world; and the entire Under the Lino team. Their belief in me has never wavered, and I stand strong within the enormous circle of their arms.

Praise for the Under the Lino Project

Robyn *I can honestly say that it has been the most amazing experience to be part of this not-so-small community of like-minded super-sleuths and history lovers, watching it all unfold. It's truly heartening, in this day and age, to witness hundreds of complete strangers come together in friendship and co-operation in a united effort to discover the truth about what happened so long ago. For me, personally, it has renewed my passion for getting back to unravelling my own family's stories. And to think it all started with a photo!*

Shar *Throughout this journey, I have been in awe of the research and researchers. The information that had been dug up, the mysteries that have unravelled, the theories developed, followed up and given solutions to, have been inspiring. I am so glad I caught this story from its earliest stages, because when it took off, it was like wildfire. I've enjoyed that ideas and thoughts (regardless of whether supported by fact or not) have been valued as possibilities. I am not an historian and have no experience in genealogy or ancestry, but I have a vivid and creative imagination. Each time I've put an idea forward, it has been considered, measured and respected. That in itself, gives everyone, regardless of being a novice or experienced, a place in the research... that's collaboration in its best example.*

Gwen *From the start, there was a sense of close involvement with this story and group. Like we had a personal stake in getting the truth behind the bank books and the Websters' lives, then laying old 'ghosts' to rest.*

Heidi *The energy and time Caylie has put into the project, giving her gift to the community and inviting everyone into her world, has created a very positive online community that is difficult not to want to be a part of. Even time-poor people have been able to connect easily and take part in a way that fits into their lives.*

Louise *The name of the group was a call to my childhood; to the times we found old newspapers under the floor coverings. I thought Under the Lino was another group like Lost Brisbane or Australian Social History, and, in a way, it is, but when I read about the bankbooks and cash, it became a story I wanted to keep reading. I didn't do a lot of research, only poking here and there at interesting looking rocks and gobbling up the information others found; querying some assumptions and making some wild leaps of faith myself. When I read Caylie's teaser, the quality of her writing kept me hanging on for the completed project.*

Leanne *I was hooked from the first post. Caylie shared her find and asked for help in such a genuine, honest, inviting way. People reacted and it has grown from then. Caylie's whole attitude of allowing and welcoming us is what has made it the best journey EVER. Thankyou.*

Belinda *It is like reading a great mystery novel, where you could do your own research and add to the collective knowledge, helping to discover the story.*

Caren *I have always had a passion for Brisbane of old. The '40s, '50s and '60s are times I always wished I knew more about. With my family history entwined in Brisbane with my grandfather's business, Olsen & Goodchap furniture store at Woolloongabba, I have always sought out Brisbane history from that time. Local author, Hugh Lunn, is one of my favourites, but now I have another author's book that I am anxious to read – Caylie Jeffery and her interesting tale of "Under the Lino". This book will also take pride of place upon my bookshelf. She has also inspired me to take up the challenge to research and write about my own family history.*

Forewords

Dr Glenn Davies

The collaborative community historical investigation, shepherded by Caylie Jeffery, has had hundreds of Brisbane's amateur historians researching day and night to unravel a mystery that has brought to life an intriguing local story. It is a great example of how 21st-century history skills can be used to bring to life a community.

History is about change. It is the subject that contributes most to the broadening out of the imagination. One of the purposes of historical study is to help transcend our own immediate experience and gain an understanding of how humanity has evolved and developed. History teaches critical thinking. It examines people over time in different societies, noting and explaining their attitudes, beliefs and behaviours, as well as interpreting their reactions to the various pressures, conditions and events that induce change.

People often think history is a dry, academic subject that you study at school, but of course, it's the complete opposite. History is all around us – national competitions, commemorations of special events, historic homes, heritage walks, antiques, vintage cars, history theme parks, historical drama, television documentaries and historical movies are increasingly entertaining and informing Australians about what it was like in the 'old days'. Genealogy is hugely popular these days – people are swabbing their mouths and getting their DNA tested so they can connect with fifth cousins they've never heard of. We're awash in our community with the study of history.

When Eleanor Webster decided to hide her family's bank books and cash, totalling over £2,000, under the linoleum flooring of her 1912 Queenslander during, and after, the Second World War, little did she know that 75 years later, over a thousand people in the new digital age would join an incredible historical hunt to find the heirs of her legacy. It's rare these days that people can become actively involved in solving a mystery and take some ownership of the tangible final results.

This community historical project, managed though social media participation, has really hit a bit of a zeitgeist.

'Historical crack' is how I described the *Under the Lino Project* to journalist, Leanne Edmistone. It has intoxicated a community and snared its members in an addiction unlike any other. Throughout the entire investigation, Caylie has not only collaborated with the community but has also been teaching history. She and her team have used 21st Century digital technology to tap into an older need to express our connection with our local area.

More than anything else, the *Under the Lino Project* shows the value that the incredible community of Brisbane, and Queensland, gives to their history of place.

Councillor Peter Matic

Mark Twain once said, "Truth is stranger than fiction, but it is because fiction is obliged to stick to possibilities; truth isn't". Although this book may seem fictitious, the story is very real.

Under the Lino is a gripping account of times past and the thrill of discovering where that past corresponds with the present.

As Local Councillor, Caylie's graphic account of this particular area of Brisbane has allowed me to escape into the streets of Milton, Paddington and surrounds, and to imagine being present in the Old Bishopsbourne and its Chapel.

I'm sure the greater Brisbane community will thoroughly enjoy reading this book and that they, too, will be captured by the twists and turns throughout Caylie's stories.

History, like our beautiful Brisbane River, snakes and twines through our lives, intersecting where we least expect it...

Cheryl Palmer

Introduction

My mother once told me that if I ever had a genuine need, to ask the Universe and it would provide, in some way or another. I had reason to believe her, because despite often being at the lower end of the socio-economic scale, we always had good food on the table, clean clothes on our backs, a quality education and the bills managed to get paid just in the nick of time. As a result, the Universe, and my Mum, have always been trusted and undeniable forces in my life.

Elizabeth Gilbert, in her book, *Big Magic*, refers to a Universe where ideas float freely all around us waiting for the right person to rest upon – the person who will grab hold of the idea and give birth to it, creating something truly remarkable and unique. If the idea settles upon the right person at the wrong time, however, it will only wait for so long, before drifting off to find a more worthy creator, one who is not quite as distracted by life's vicissitudes and able to give it the attention it requires.

> *"... ideas spend eternity swirling around us, searching for available and willing human partners. When an idea thinks it has found somebody who might be able to bring it into the world, the idea will pay you a visit. It will try to get your attention. Mostly, you will not notice. When it finally realizes that you're oblivious to its message, it will move on to someone else.*
>
> *But sometimes – rarely, but magnificently – there comes a day when you're open and relaxed enough to actually receive something. The idea, sensing your openness, will start to do its work on you. It will send the universal physical and emotional signals of inspiration (the chills up the arms, the hair standing up on the back of the neck, the nervous stomach, the buzzy thoughts of obsession). The idea will organize coincidences and portents to stumble across your path, to keep your interest keen.*
>
> *You will start to notice all sorts of signs pointing toward the idea. The idea will wake you in the middle of the night and distract you from everyday routine.*

The idea will not leave you alone until it has your fullest attention.

And then in a quiet moment, it will ask, "Do you want to work with me?"

If you say no, you're off the hook.

BUT if you do say yes to an idea, now it's showtime. Now you have officially entered into a contract with inspiration."
Elizabeth Gilbert, BIG MAGIC

When I discovered three 1940s Commonwealth Bank pass books and cash under the kitchen lino of my Milton Queenslander in 1996, I was absolutely the right person to find them. It just wasn't the right time to do anything about it so I must have emitted a big, fat "NO!" as I put them away for another time. David and I were knee-deep in renovations, poor as uni students and not only was the internet spanking new, we had no idea what to do with it. Luckily for me, the Big Magic that lived with the bank books was happy to remain dormant, inside a yellow envelope, deep within a wooden chest, for another 21 years.

On 20 August 2017, as I was digging around in my old wooden chest looking for high school memorabilia for my 30-year school reunion, I rediscovered the old money and bank books, safely tucked away in that yellow envelope.

Old Brisbane Album

I fought against social media for many years, in the same way I fought against digital cameras. I had my reasons but proved myself to be a fuddy-duddy in both instances. Once I got the hang of digital photography, I was hooked, and became its biggest advocate. Once I found the joys of Facebook, it was no different.

Social media has certain codes of conduct, and I had to learn the ropes from those who knew how to behave. In those early Facebook days, I was sharing funny memes and photos too much, as if I was the first person to have ever seen them.

It took a few choice words from my brother, Zan, to show me what to do, and more importantly, what not to do, to avoid people 'unfriending me'. Of course, I unfriended him immediately for being so rude to me! Sorry Zan, you were right.

A few years ago, I started seeing some lovely posts shared by a friend on Facebook about Brisbane from 'long ago', many years before my parents arrived in Australia in 1971. I have always counted myself as a true blue, dinky di Australian, with a strong connection to Brisbane, but my history doesn't travel back further than our arrival. My curiosity about early Brisbane has, therefore, always been piqued, and these black & white posts intrigued me even more.

I joined *Old Brisbane Album* as a dedicated fan when I saw some old photos of the 1974 floods. All of a sudden, I found myself transported back to being a three year old child, sitting high on the shoulders of my devastated father, wading through the streets of Newstead, watching his marine business, literally, float away.

Like nearly 30,000 others these days, I went on to spend many nostalgic hours trawling through other people's stories, memories and photographs.

Greg Davis, the co-founder of the *Old Facebook Albums* in Australia is an avid historian, and a keen and talented photographer, who has a way of making the very old look very beautiful. It's because of Greg and the *Old Brisbane Album* community that the events that are about to unfold actually happened.

Of course, the timing was also perfect. I had the opportunity, as a stay-at-home Mum, 'enjoying' a year or two away from paid employment. I absolutely had the energy, because one can only tidy up the house so many times during school hours. And I definitely had the experience, as a freelance writer.

My *Big Magic* idea was ripe for the picking, yet I could never have predicted what was about to unfold when I uploaded the photograph of my discovery onto Facebook. Knowing *Old Brisbane Album* was peopled by amateur historians, it was the first place I thought of sharing my find when I rediscovered the money and bank books I'd found Under the Lino.

My Original Post on Facebook
20 August 2017
Old Brisbane Album

"Found these 1940s Commonwealth Bank passbooks and four £5 notes under the lino in the kitchen of our Queenslander when we were renovating! Not sure what to do with it – probably frame them. Housewives squirrelling away money from their hubbies we suspect!"

The rest, as they say, is history...

Part 1

In the Beginning

2017 The Rediscovery

I didn't go to my 10-year high school reunion in 1997. It was too soon, too raw. It wasn't even a decade since my best friend, Clare, had died, and even fewer years since I'd last seen my first love – the one who'd broken my heart. I wasn't ready.

I'd heard stories of people at these early gatherings skiting about how much money they were earning, what car they were driving, where they'd travelled and where they were living. Given I was unmarried, knee-deep in a renovation on the worst house in Milton and surviving on baked beans and the fumes of No-More-Gaps, I certainly wasn't going to have much to add to the conversation of who's who and how much, so, hey, I just didn't go.

At the 20-year reunion in 2007, I was somewhere in the middle of the Atlantic Ocean, on an epic two-year sailing adventure aboard our boat, *Steamy Windows*... no roots, no job, no money, no keys but living the life of the truly free adventurer. We'd had a close call with terrorists in London a few years earlier and this was our way of meeting fear head on. I was as happy as a lark with David, now my husband and co-captain, by my side and unbeknownst to me at the time, our baby growing inside me. Ironically, I had hours of nautical anecdotes that would have been great to share at the reunion, but instead, I wrote them in the ship's log and e-mailed them to the nervous friends and family who were weathering the storms with us.

By 2017, however, life had settled somewhat and I decided it would be fun to go to the 30-year get-together. Comparing war-wounds, wrinkles and horror stories was a much more probable scenario facing us all. Very few people, I've learned, get to the upper reaches of their forties without having been knocked around enough to lose those edges of one-upmanship. Nobody at that age wants to win the war on who's been trampled the most, and with the hope of compassion and empathy, I felt much more confident about meeting with my school mates again. Being more certain about my place in the world I'd built around me certainly helped, as did all the advice I'd given my kids about bullying.

Having said that, I still made sure I had some close friends to hold hands with on the night. I met with Fiona, Rhonda, Vanessa and Flora a week before the reunion at Orleigh Park in West End for a picnic lunch. While discussing what we were all up to, one of the girls asked if I had any more books up my sleeve. I explained that I was waiting for the Universe to drop a project into my lap, for I was, at that moment, ready for something new. We gave each other some well-needed positive encouragement in preparation for the reunion, and agreed to meet for an ouzo at the Greek Club for some Aegean courage before the event, the following week.

As I drove home from the picnic over the William Jolly Bridge, I was feeling quite nostalgic and a little bit weepy. I decided to spend the rest of the afternoon delving into my wooden chest of memories, totally immersing myself in the '80s and collating some memorabilia to share at the reunion. I opened Pandora's Box with happy abandon, knowing I had a few hours to disappear into another time, while my kids watched a movie (or two!).

I sorted through letters from old friends, reading a few here and there, smiling and sometimes crying at the memories. I read old diary entries with a wry smile, pored through daggy song lists and listened to some old cassette tapes of Clare and me playing the flute together. The sound of Clare's laugh has never left my memory, but to hear her again, after so many years gone, was beautiful. Of course, there were heaps of old photos of school plays, parties, camping holidays and other shenanigans to trawl through, which took a lot of my time that afternoon.

When I finally reached the bottom of that wooden box, I pulled my 1987 Brisbane State High School yearbook from its depths. A bright yellow envelope fell heavily from the back of it, jingling like old war medals crunching together. I tipped out its contents, and when three bank books fell out with four £5 notes and a small arsenal of coins, a memory dawned fresh. It had been more than 20 years since I'd seen those historical items yet the sight, scent and feel of them barrelled me back into 1996 like it was only yesterday.

1996 David and Caylie buy their First Home

By the mid-1990s, Brisbane was starting to evolve away from that big ol' backwater country town image, following the success of Expo 88. The café scene had just kicked off after Lord Mayor Jim Soorley gave the nod for restaurants to put tables and chairs on the footpaths. Inner-city suburbs still had plenty of affordable housing, if you could stand to live in a dump and do it up yourself. It was the beginning of gentrification, and David and I only just made it into the own-your-own-home queue.

While the rest of the world was panicking about the Y2K bug, the young adults of Brisbane were worrying about how much the real estate market had blown out – even the worst houses on the busiest streets were too expensive for most first-home buyers.

It took David and I a year to raise the deposit for our first home. We lived in the cheapest rental house we could find in Ellena Street, Paddington, brushing our teeth in the bath (*who builds a house without a bathroom sink?*) and tolerating carpets that smelled like wet dog every time it rained. All because we had a goal we meant to achieve as soon as humanly possible. Luckily for us, smashed avocado on toast hadn't been invented yet, so we rarely went out, preferring instead to cook for ourselves, entertaining friends in our tiny kitchen, saving every penny we could.

One of David's old uni mates was a Banking and Loans Officer at the ANZ in Paddington, so that was our first port of call when we'd scraped together a 5% deposit. We both had solid jobs, David as an engineer, and me as a nurse, but we had no credit history. At only 24 years of age, we were seen as too risky for a bank loan. My mother generously offered to go as guarantor, but the old uni mate came through and scraped us over the line, jokingly asking for our first-born child as collateral. We did see his hand shake a little, though, as he signed the release of $140,000 for an old house we'd found on Gladstone Street! It had been advertised for auction to $140k plus buyers, the bank had inspected it and was more than satisfied that their money would be safe within those walls.

Now, David and I are no strangers to hard work. We had been raised by families who were builders and renovators, and we were both practical by nature, so when we initially inspected the Gladstone Street house, we saw a thousand different possibilities for improvement. It was on a 1000m² block in the heart of Paddington, with pressed metal ceilings and a bull-nosed, wrap-around verandah. It was any first-home buyer's dream, and at $140,000, we believed that house was meant for us.

Sadly, so did all the yuppies in Brisbane on that hot and humid December morning in 1996. Fresh from reading Nick Earls' *Zigzag Street,* they figured they could throw a few coats of pastel paint on this old worker's cottage and bag themselves an easy investment. They wore Gucci boots and Country Road chambray with popped collars to the auction, while we wore Blundstones and King Gees.

As we stood dripping under the poinciana tree, dodging the searing sunshine, our dreams faded as rapidly as the rate of the Auctioneer's gavel banging on the lectern. SOLD for $230,000 in less than three minutes.

We were totally dejected as we walked away from that house. Not only had we been duped by false advertising, we didn't have a backup plan. We should have thrown all those eggs in our Gladstone Street basket at the Real Estate Agency as we drove up to their front door to see what else was open for inspection. We'd put all our energy and future dreams into that house, and we didn't want to pay any more rent. We wanted to buy a house. That day!

We were pleased we didn't egg the agents' window that day... we'd have missed the only other open-for-inspection at that time, which fatefully led us to a property in Milton. 86 Heussler Terrace, Milton, to be exact.

We parked in front of the house under a bedraggled bottlebrush tree on the steep and busy terrace. The Open-for-Inspection sign was up, but we couldn't see Richard Ciobo, the agent and assumed he was walking other interested parties through the property. The midday sun was beating down on us as we stood on the drought-starved grass looking at the dilapidated shroud of a once-proud Federation Queenslander.

It looked as beaten and dejected as we had been leaving the auction only thirty minutes earlier.

The former-white wooden fence was held up by rotten palings and rusty chain wire. Even though the gate was open (in a permanent, rusted joints kind of way), we didn't feel welcome to enter the grounds. Several of the external window panes were missing, the timber walls were split and peeling and the heavily splintered front steps guarded the interior as if warning all visitors never to enter. Little did we realise what we were about to walk into.

As we stepped up to the gate, we noticed a well-dressed fellow trotting up the street from the butcher's shop near the corner of Baroona Road. He had a clipboard under his arm, and looked as if he might die at any moment in the suit he was wearing. Richard had been waiting under the only tree with shade for his first potential buyer, two houses away.

Thinking this was quite odd, we followed him into the house. After successfully bargaining with the rickety stairs for safe passage, we walked through the front door and were met full-frontal by a wall of hot, fetid, slimy air. No wonder he'd been waiting under a tree!

Here's a tip: when a Real Estate sign says, "Ripe for Renovation", take note. The house is going to smell really, really bad, and need a LOT of work.

It's a bit of Real Estate humour...

The House of Horrors

86 Huessler Terrace, Milton

There were several people in attendance during that first inspection on our house, none of them prospective buyers. They were the tenants and they did *not* want to leave. Not then, not ever. This was before the time of reality lifestyle shows that told vendors to have bread cooking in the oven, coffee bubbling merrily on the stove and fresh flowers everywhere, in order to sell a house.

This dwelling had animal faeces on the carpets, soiled mattresses on the floors and a drug den under the house complete with a broken sewerage pipe dripping onto the couch. There was a couple in the throes of passion on one of the aforementioned beds, and every window was closed, on a 36 degree day.

I walked through the house with my hand over my nose and mouth, because it smelled like rotting corpses, wincing at the rubbish on the kitchen floor, the dirty dishes piled on the benchtops and the dark stains on the ancient carpets. I wasn't even sure what colour the flooring in the kitchen was supposed to be.

Not wanting to touch anything, I told David I'd meet him in the back yard under the half-dead frangipani tree, next to the burned-out car bodies. I could not understand why he was walking around with stars in his eyes, and left him to deal with the rest alone.

As I climbed down the rickety concrete steps to the rubbish tip of a back yard, even the gulps of hot, sweltering, Brisbane summer air were a refreshing release from the stench and disease that had filled my lungs inside that house. I looked at the overgrown yard, the car wrecks and broken fences, and shook my head in wonder at the way some people chose to live.

David joined me a few minutes later, with the agent standing at a respectful distance away, as we had this discussion...

"Oh my God, Cayles! Can you believe this? What did you think?"

Oh good, I thought, *we're on the same page. He hates it too. We can go.*

"I know, right! It's the most feral, disgusting, pit of a house I've ever seen. How can people live like that? Let's get out of here before we catch something!"

"Whoah, hang on!" he exclaimed, putting his arm coercively around my shoulders. "You have to look beyond the filth, babe. To see the potential. It's a solid house, with gorgeous features underneath the gross veneer. The yuppies won't touch this one with a barge pole! Cayles, this is it!"

"Are you serious? There is NO WAY we are making an offer on this house. David, there were maggots on the kitchen floor. There was cat poo ingrained in the carpet. Those people were having sex! In fact, I have a few things I need to say to Richard."

I stormed over to our wilted estate agent, before David could stop me.

"Oi, what are you guys playing at? That is a disgusting attempt at getting a house ready for sale! First thing you need to do is to get rid of your tenants before buyers walk in. Second thing, get the house cleaned. Or burn it down and just sell the land. Oh, and remove the car bodies from the back yard!"

As Richard was apologising and agreeing with my rant, David was digging his nails into my arm, telling me through gritted teeth to shut-up. Calling back to Richard that we'd be in touch, he dragged me up the side of the house, and deposited me into our car.

It took David a week to forgive me for adding another twenty thousand dollars onto the house price by telling Richard how to improve his tactics. He also used this time to convince me to revisit the house for the next open for inspection. Of course, Richard had followed my advice, and by the following Saturday, the house had been opened up and aired, emptied of feral tenants and, hey presto! I could finally see the potential.

So, unfortunately, could half a dozen other people walking through the property at the same time, running their hands up the timber walls, picturing the finished product. Panic set in when we saw they were all wearing work boots, so David and I made an offer to Richard right then and there. Within an hour, we had a conditional contract in our hands and were the proud owners of the worst house in Milton.

When we visited our mate at the bank on Monday with the papers, we saw a lightning bolt of panic cross his face as he squeaked out, "What do you mean you bought a different house? I gave you a loan for Gladstone Street. Our guys inspected it. What's Heussler Terrace???"

The silence in that tiny office at the back of the bank was deafening to us all, as we realised that the money the bank had loaned to us was not for any old house. It was for a house that might actually be worth buying.

Luckily for us, the bank property assessor went out post-haste and gave us the thumbs up, "but not a penny more", said our mate, "EVER!"

We've never seen that friend again, and wonder if he was sent to work in the far western reaches of Queensland as a result, but hey, WE GOT THE HOUSE! Now all we had to do was make it habitable because there was no way I was going to sleep in it as it was.

My Parents Emigrate 1971

When my mother first met and fell in love with my father in the South of France in the late-1960s, she would never have guessed she'd be living in Brisbane in the worst house on the worst street of an industrial estate less than a decade later.

Mum was brought up in the North of England in a middle class environment, attending good schools and holidaying in the South of France. My father, the son of a successful businessman in India, was also well-educated and had never known poverty, until of course, he left his homeland to make his way in the world of white men.

When Mum and Dad met in that tiny seaside village, there was more romance than a Cary Grant movie. He was dressed in the navy and white uniform he wore working as a marine engineer on swanky Mediterranean yachts, and she was having a drink at a bar with her nursing friends from the local British-American hospital where they all worked.

I have visited Villefranche-sur-Mer, and as I wandered the streets, 25 years after my parents had met, I could feel them there, the Riviera sun touching their faces as they saw each other across that crowded café. My father was incredibly handsome (still is at 76), tall and slim with a movie-star smile. Mum was petite and very attractive – the sparks flew immediately.

Eighteen months later, they married against both families' wishes, without a penny in their pockets.

They settled in Malta, where they both worked and lived happily for a while, before deciding to move to India after I was born.

The 1971 Indo-Pakistani war broke out while they were there, and Mum demanded they move to a safe country immediately.

Interestingly, the war only last for 13 days, so if they'd held out for a little longer, I may well have been brought up in India! War changes so many lives, and in our case, possibly for the better.

Dad tells a story of giving Mum a map of the world, telling her to close her eyes and point. Wherever her hand landed, that would be where they'd move. Thankfully, she peeked a bit (according to Dad), and we ended up in Australia rather than some other war-torn country.

In 1971, my parents migrated to Australia, with the written support of my Uncle Neville and Aunt Gladys, who had already arrived from India a few years earlier. They settled on Breakfast Creek, in Newstead, with its fledgling boating industry, and carved a niche for themselves, despite living in the wake of the White Australia Policy.

If only they'd known that three years from then, the '74 floods would irrevocably change their lives.

Hemmant 1976

1198 Lytton Road, to be exact... my second Brisbane home. If you go there, even now, you'll wonder how anyone could have lived there, let alone raised a child, given its position in an area catering only to the Southside's tradesmen.

Living in the deep eastern industrial suburbs of Brisbane, in the ugliest of houses with no sewerage, my family did it pretty tough for a while there. We called it the *Land of a Thousand Smells*, with the mozzie-infested waters of Doboy Creek in our back yard, and the Murarrie Meatworks next door.

Mum worked as a night-duty nurse, and Dad as a boat builder, having moved to Hemmant after the '74 floods. Our first house was on Ross Street, Newstead, where the Harley Davidson premises are now, and Dad's boat building business was under the house and out the back, right on Breakfast Creek. Sadly, they lost everything in that flood – whatever didn't go under, literally went up shit creek.

It was a watershed time for my parents (forgive the pun) – I remember the arguments and the constant scrabbling around for money. My father's dreams of 'making it' in Australia, had ended up somewhere in Moreton Bay.

As my Mum remembers...

It was a stressful time, way back in the mid '70s. I was heavily pregnant, with a six-year-old daughter (Caylie), our once thriving business, Se7en Seas Marine, recently bankrupt after the '74 floods wiped our life on the banks of Breakfast Creek off the map. We had an urgency to find a place to live, without an asset or a penny to our name.

We were very grateful to a business acquaintance who pointed us in the direction of a small dwelling he knew about which could get us out of trouble in the short term. This little blue box of a house had been used as a place of storage for years and was probably ready to be condemned. We gratefully took on the task of making it habitable. We set to and cleaned it, painted the interior and generally got organised for our temporary stay – not quite temporary as we lived there for two interminable years!

However, I really am quite proud of the fact that we must have been one of the last homes to boast of a back yard dunny! Caylie was not so thrilled... she developed a tendency to judge people by the quality of their toilets after living with an outhouse for two years and I fear she has never recovered from the experience! (I haven't, thanks Mum!)

Back Yard Dunny, Brisbane C. 1950s
Photograph courtesy of Ross Palm

It was situated not far from the back door, constructed of hardwood with a corrugated iron roof. The unpainted timber was bleached like driftwood and the door didn't quite close, but hey, it was functional to say the least. There was a timber toilet seat situated above a little area which housed the can – no can in situ but there was a small collection of paper scraps hanging on a rusty nail... no need to use imagination here! Obviously it hadn't been used for some years but was quite sturdy and only needed a total clean out plus notification to the local council to be put on the list of services.

There were some strict rules for all who used this little room – always check under and around the toilet seat for spiders, keep a lookout for snakes which sometimes blocked one's retreat, and never, ever, go there in the dark without a torch!

I have a great deal of respect for the individuals who take on the job of looking after such things – it can't be an easy one, but there was much unemployment in those days. I quickly became acquainted with our dunny man... he was a cheerful and friendly fellow, tall and sturdy and he drove a truck which contained both full and empty containers. On a weekly basis he brought in two empty containers to replace the two full ones, plus an extra can full of sawdust.

He generally stopped for a welcome cup of coffee and a chat before returning to his route. I asked him once if he'd ever had a spill... "Oh yeah," he replied, sheepishly, "but only once!" and on that occasion he was forced to return home for a shower and change – it didn't happen again – he was very diligent and careful after that!

The dunny is such a huge part of Australia's iconic history and I really am quite proud to have had one to grace my home, although at the time, it was a far cry from the British middle-class life I'd grown up knowing!

Two years of that lifestyle, despite the amused, rose-coloured view we now hold of those times, was, sadly, too much for my little family, now a little bigger with the addition of my baby brother, Alexander.

Mum and Dad separated, and we finally left that little blue weatherboard box, with its one matching hydrangea bush, to move into a rambling old Queenslander at 105 Zillman Road, Hendra, only this time, there would only be three of us.

Hendra 1978

Despite the fact that the Milton house was in a dreadful state when we first walked into it in 1996, it didn't escape my attention that it was designed just like the house I grew up in – the Hendra house – a mirror image in fact. Not only did it have the same layout, it was also divided up into flats, created by my mother.

My Mum and Dad separated in 1978, which was just after Gough Whitlam's 1975 Family Law Act, introducing no fault divorce. My little brother, Zan, and I were two of the first in a new generation of kids whose parents divorced because they were unhappy together. No blame, nothing dodgy in the papers and no church leaders snapping at their heels. They cared about each other but they just didn't fit together anymore.

Dad helped us to move into the house in Hendra, which I took as a sign that my parents were patching things up. In my head, I pretended we were just moving house as a family, but the reality was somewhat different. It must have been very difficult for them, Dad especially, to go through the motions of moving house together, knowing a separation came at the end of it. There was a heaviness in the air for all of us as the axe hung over the family ties, ready to drop at any moment. That cut would set my mother free, send my father overseas in despair and turn my world upside down.

It was love at first sight for Mum and I with the Hendra house, though. After the little shack we'd been living in on Lytton Road deep in the heart of Hemmant's industrial estate, this four bedroom Federation style Queenslander was a mansion, perched in the middle of a double block of land, high on a Hendra hill. *Clayfield Borders*, our neighbours used to call it, because the Clayfield sign was outside their house.

My mum was no Hyacinth Bucket, however, and didn't care a whit for keeping up appearances.

We loved the trees, the huge yard, the massive bedrooms with the tall ceilings and the wraparound verandah. In the years to follow, we would adopt ducks, chooks and guinea pigs, dogs, cats and budgies. We'd grow chokos on the back fence, have a massive veggie garden and an 'A' frame cubby house, all materials sourced from the dump of course. Mum used to go to the Nudgee Refuse Centre with a full trailer and come back with a *different* full trailer. Between the dump and The Duka, on Nudgee Road, Mum certainly kept us well-furnished for very little expense.

Mum has always been a clever and practical woman who can turn a sow's ear into a silk purse at the drop of a hammer, a lick of a paint brush and the whir of a Singer. She wove us hammocks that she strung up between the huge trees in the front yard, which we used as a safe place to hide from Sir Frances Drake, our family duck, who had a taste for small children. She (yes, she... we got her sex wrong but the name stuck!) was known to grab hold of a tender piece of flesh and twist hard, causing unholy terror for all who made her acquaintance. The satisfied air that that bloody duck displayed as she waddled away from the carnage with her regal head in the air always made my mother smile as she examined the wounds and mopped up the tears.

Mum even sourced a second hand above-ground pool for $20, building a deck around it with reclaimed timber, so it felt like an in-ground pool. It gave us years of enjoyment despite giving Mum a headache for every hole we made in the liner!

There was so much space! The toilet was also a huge treat, as my first flusher, despite it being outside on the back deck. The Hemmant house had had a backyard dunny. And snakes. And mozzies from the mangroves behind the house.

There was no contest, except that this house didn't have my Dad. The day he said goodbye was the worst day in my eight-year-old life. He took me downstairs, away from the boxes and unpacking going on upstairs, where we could be alone. I refused to believe what was about to happen, even though I knew it deep inside. I jumped on my Malvern Star and started riding around maniacally in the red dirt under the house, weaving around the posts and ducking the lower rafters, making sure not to brain myself on the tin termite caps.

"Look at this, Daddy! Watch me, Daddy!"

"Pussycat, I have to talk to you."

"In a minute, Daddy, I just want to see how many times I can ride around without stopping."

I rode in desperation, hoping each circuit would take back the clock to a time when I couldn't sense the impending doom of change and loss.

Finally, my father lost his temper.

"Caylie! Enough of this. Come here, now!"

This inevitable moment must have been the hardest thing he'd ever had to do, and it's only now I'm a parent, that I can understand how much he would have psyched himself up to say goodbye to his firstborn child, the daughter of his heart. For many years, I only cried for myself. Now I cry for us both.

I dropped my bike at the sound of his anger, my heart hammering in my chest, not just from exertion. Tears began coursing down my cheeks, as I sat quietly beside him, arms wrapped around my knees, about to be introduced to the end of life as I knew it.

"I've written you a letter," he said, also crying. "It tells you lots of things that are too hard for me to say now."

He handed me a yellow envelope with a card and a folded piece of paper inside. The script, I knew, would be in his elegant cursive, full of love, regret and sadness. I thought I would never read that letter. I had never seen my father cry, and seeing him in that huge moment of grief was more painful than anything I'd ever experienced. That was the last time I saw my father for eight long years. Little did I know that I would read his letter hundreds of times in that time, hoping, wishing and mourning.

Being the first in a generation whose parents experienced divorce is a lonely, hugely difficult situation for a child. It doesn't detract from the current generation's pain or loss when their parents separate. The difference is that there is more empathy and compassion for those families NOW vs the stigma on our shoulders when my brother and I were children.

It wasn't easy for my Mum to break away from her marriage. She had to work hard to pay the rent and the bills, but she was determined to always be available for her children. She wanted to give us a life of peace and love, free from stress and arguments. She did some shift work as a midwife, and took on other random jobs like flower delivery and curtain sewing. We even delivered papers on the weekends to help her out, the fear of the rent being raised hanging over our heads, spurring us on – even a $5-a-week rise was devastating at the time, and Mum was visibly stressed each year when the lease was renewed.

The landlords once offered to sell my mother that huge house on Zillman Road for $39,000 in the early '80s. It kills me now to think of that missed opportunity, but as Mum rightly says, she was earning less than $100 a week, so not only was a deposit out of the question, the mortgage would have crippled her. Too proud to borrow from family or friends, she stuck her Geordie chin out, picked up a hammer and split the house up, creating separate living quarters for boarders.

Mum's ability to care for unloved and unwanted animals was recognised by the people who answered her ads. Over the next ten years, we had a variety of interesting, eclectic and just plain crazy people living in our house. Most were harmless, some were wonderful and others, well, let's just say that this time of our lives is a whole other book.

That huge house did provide a safe haven for many people and pets, however, with a non-judgemental, socially forgiving and pragmatic woman at the helm.

Our front door was never locked because people were coming and going all the time. Anyone planning to rob us would have had a hell of a time planning the event, because you just never knew the movements of all the residents in that place. Mum was also very trusting, her dogged belief that most people are inherently good getting her into trouble from time to time, but proving her right for the majority.

My mother gave us a fantastic childhood, with a heart full of love, good food on the table, and a roof over our heads. The people we lived with taught us many important lessons in life and in hindsight, it certainly wasn't dull with regular dramas and events to keep us all on our toes.

What stuck most in my gullet about those years was that it was always someone else's roof we had to live under. So when David and I moved in together in 1994, I was quite adamant that this rental malarkey was not for me, and that we must combine our income and save up for a house as soon as possible. No landlord would ever control my life again.

1996 The Initial Discovery

David and I were pretty excited to have the keys to the Milton house, despite knowing that the work ahead of us was going to be gargantuan!

Already dressed for hard labour, we came up the front stairs, and as David opened the front door, he looked down at me, with a worried frown, and said, "I hope you're not expecting me to carry you over the threshold?"

I think I actually snorted.

"Ha, you'd break your back and then I'd have to do all the bloody work by myself! Don't be ridiculous!"

And as we have with all things in our lives, we held hands and crossed the threshold together, as partners and as equals. It hasn't always been easy to maintain the equality status mind you. Despite David being thankful for the suffragette movement so he didn't put his back out that day, he still clung to a few outdated beliefs about men's and women's work. He tried to be a man of the '90s, but a pathetic attempt at ironing his work shirts one day had me grabbing the iron from him in disgust and he's not picked one up since. I will always maintain that our marriage has thrived as a result of the never-ending game of tug-o-war!

The first thing we did was to hire a skip. The previous owners had removed the car bodies, as per our stipulations, but the house had furniture, mattresses, cupboards and floor coverings that had to go.

It took us a couple of days, but we had a lot of fun ripping the guts out of this house. Loads of visitors came for a sticky beak on that first weekend, all of whom loved breaky noises as they joined us tossing things out of the back windows into the skip.

It didn't take long to overfill it, as you can see...

During Mum's first visit to the house that week, she warned us to take care when we were ripping up the flooring.

"People often hide things under old lino, and you might be lucky enough to find some old newspapers lining the wood," she prophesised.

As we pulled back the three layers of lino in the kitchen, stained and malodorous, we were disappointed that the newspapers we came across from the 1940s were unable to be salvaged. David explained that newspapers were used as a free way of lining the timber, to help seal the floor from draughts, as insulation, to protect the wood, to provide some cushioning and to make it easier to lift the old lino when it came time to replace it. Apparently, nobody in this house had ever replaced the worn-out layers – they just put a different one on top every thirty years or so, in keeping with the fashion of the era. The final layer was covered in yellow and brown mandala patterns, straight from the 1970s, with the layer closest to the floorboards a beautiful grey-blue, with a pink and white floral pattern, dating back to the early 1900s.

We were delighted to see that the rest of the house had beautiful wide, honey-coloured timber floorboards that would come up beautifully when polished. The kitchen timber was badly stained, however, and would have to be tiled.

The area where I found the money and bank books was next to the stove recess in the kitchen. When we moved the modern cooker, the lino underneath it wasn't attached at the wall, making it easy for me to peel back. It was there that I saw the documents.

I called David over, and we sat down on the floor to examine them all closely. We thought the four £5 notes were probably worth something to a collector, perhaps a couple of hundred bucks, but we weren't that desperate for money. We considered these to be a gift from the historical owners of our house, so we decided to frame them all when we finished the reno.

I tucked them away inside a yellow envelope and slipped it in the back of my 1987 school yearbook for safekeeping until we'd finished the renovation.

David and I spent the next three years working double-time – both of us putting on a suit each morning to head off to work, in order to earn the money to pay for our 'behind-the-scenes' activities. Every cent we brought in the door went straight back out to Finlayson's, Brett's Timber & Hardware and occasionally, when we were short on time, to Paddo Hardware, the most expensive shop for renovators in Brisbane!

After hours, we'd shed our image of the white collar worker, for our true-to-form DIY personas, and revel in getting dirty with real blood, sweat and tears. We continued to have friends around for dinner, cooking on a camping stove and serving meals on old timber doors laid across sawhorses. We started hanging out with other renovators, of which there were plenty in this area at the time. We would team up with the O'Briens and the O'Sullivans on weekends, sharing big jobs like building decks, painting walls or de-nailing fence palings. Our long-suffering families knew the only way to catch up with us was by donning their own work duds and making an appearance, paint brush and KFC in hand. Anyone wearing thongs would invariably stand on a nail (sorry Gordy!), but luckily for us, those were less litigious days and his tetanus shots were up to date.

We adopted Angus, a boisterous German shepherd (our first attempt at parenting), who barely tolerated us working such long hours, whining at us regularly to take him for a w... I still can't say the word out loud, despite the fact that he passed away many years ago. Even saying the letter 'w' would alert him to the fact that we were thinking about it. It got to the point where he would notice if our guilt-ridden eyes so much as looked over to his leash hanging on a nail in the wall.

Angus was our unconditional love for the whole renovation, and a pain in our butts! Hair balls getting stuck to the paint; wet nose in every corner, ready to be sawn off; running in front of the tractor while we levelled the back yard; and falling off the side of the rickety old concrete stairs behind the house because he was so eager to overtake us for a 'w'. He had to be coaxed up every set of stairs forever more.

We loved that bloody dog.

The Queenslander
by Magnus Eriksson

Queensland has a beautiful and truly vernacular architectural tradition. The term "Queenslander house" is used very broadly, but it can be defined most simply as a timber-framed building with timber walls and floors, which is high-set on stumps and capped by a corrugated iron roof. We can also add verandas to the criteria, which accentuate the light-weight, shady and inviting character of these homes. The style predominates in most of our older towns and inner suburbs built between the 1880s and 1930s, and throughout many rural areas.

If you've lived in such a house, you'll be familiar with the sensory experiences and peculiar rituals that it involves. Temperature fluctuations create a distinctly seasonal indoor climate and make the old frames shift and groan in a diurnal cycle. Century-old hoop pine floors have invisible minefields of creaky spots which parents with sleeping babies learn to navigate expertly.

You live amongst assortments of original and replaced windows and doors that more or less fit their apertures and let the breezes through whether they are welcome or not. You both love and fear that thunder of heavy rain on the iron roof, which reminds you of the hostile elements outside of your thin shell. If a neighbour runs down a hallway, the sympathetic resonance may be felt two doors down the street.

The first time you hear a possum on the roof, you might imagine that a deranged sumo wrestler is doing sprints on the veranda outside. These houses are alive and permeable, and each has its unique character and moods, shaped by more than a century of human occupation and the Queensland climate.

As for any architectural style, the Queensland house didn't evolve in isolation. Similar high-set dwellings can be found in the sugar plantations of the American West Indies, where they kept their occupants safe above floods and vermin. The plantation style was brought to Queensland with the emerging sugar industry and was quickly adopted as a preferred pattern for most residential housing in the 1880s.

Apart from separating the household from water and pests, it offered good ventilation, a large undercroft for laundry and sundry, the ability to build on steep slopes, and perhaps more importantly, the capacity to erect large amounts of housing, quickly, for a fast-growing population, using nothing but widely available and excellent Queensland timbers.

The preference for fire-prone timber drove the adoption of the "Undue Subdivision of Land Prevention Act" in 1885, which limited property sizes to 16 perches, about 400 m², and gave rise to the "big country town" layout of our cities and suburbs. The detached housing also resulted in a very gradual sequence of subdivision and diversified densification, sometimes spanning a century. Thus, our traditional architecture assumed a central role in Queensland's civic and physical fabric, and it defines our state more than anything else except perhaps the Queensland sun.

86 Heussler Terrace
Sketch by Sue Fernandes

Part 2

The Social Media Phenomenon

2017 Nostalgia

The first thing that struck me when I read the responses of people on Facebook regarding the picture I posted of the money and bank books was the nostalgia. Disturbing the dust on people's memories can be quite joyous, which of course, is why *Old Brisbane Album* and similar social media historical pages are so popular.

Many people remembered their old banking days when they saw the books. Most people over the age of 40 in Australia had a bank book as a younger person. The Commonwealth Bank had the monopoly on school banking (still does I believe) and I have strong recollections from the mid-'70s of receiving my navy blue-covered book back from the banking officer with a new balance in it after birthdays. Very exciting!

Some people were taken back to the smell and feel of the £5 notes, or 'old money' – just one photo was able to stir up many senses for them. The beautiful colouring, design and texture of the notes were preferred by some to the plastic versions of today, and I was able to sense many fond smiles under the words I was reading online.

Not everyone was happily nostalgic, however. Just the thought of a maths class on currency from the pre-1966 decimal conversion was enough to send a shiver of dread down many spines.

Chris *You can't go wrong with a few fivers under your lino. Yeah, and zacs and coppers and a guinea or two.*
Margaret *Yes Chris. A guinea wasn't slang though and I THINK it was £1/1/- but not sure. What a random amount... £1/1/- Seems strange now. Remember a zac well. So funny now. As for adding and subtracting pounds, shillings and pence... oh heck, glad that's gone* ☺
Chris *Yes, that's exactly what guineas were. Many items of clothing, shoes, white goods, other household furnishing and stock (cattle etc.) were quoted in guineas.*

Perfect notes worth $18,625
Imperfect notes $193
They're graded on their condition – very good, fine, very fine, extremely fine, about uncirculated, uncirculated

1940 £5 = 1 weeks wage
Average yearly wage for a female in 1940 was £146
Average yearly wage for a female in 2017 was around $80,000
Blocks of land were less than £100, inner-city family houses were £350

The Currency before the decimal system came in, on 14th February 1966 was in pounds, shillings and pence...
1 pound (£) = 20 shillings (s)
1 shilling (s) = 12 pence (d)
1 pound (£) = 240 pennies (d)
Threepence was known as a trey
Sixpence was known as a zac
Shillings were called deeners
2 shillings was a florin
1 pound was a quid
21 shillings (£1/1/-) was a guinea
There were no £20 notes, only the 10 shilling note, £1, £5, £10 notes in general circulation. The mint occasionally issued £50 and £100 notes and higher. There was a £1,000 note.
The Federation in 1901 gave the Commonwealth a constitutional power to issue coins, removing this power from the separate states. British coins continued in use until 1910 when Australian silver coins were introduced. Coins from that time had a portrait of a King Edward II on one side. Australian pennies and half pennies were introduced into circulation in 1911, and in 1931, gold sovereigns were no longer minted.

Groceries

	Bread	Milk	Sugar	Butter	Potatoes	Tea
1940.	5d.	7d.		19d.	12d.	30d
1950.	8d.	11d.	5d.	26d.	24d.	36d
1960.	18d.	18d.	10d.	57d.	47d.	77d

www.allcoinvalues.com

What did other people find?

Finding out what other people had tucked away inside their houses was also exciting for many of us... we are all inquisitive souls, and finding treasure has been part of our fantasy world since we were children reading Peter Pan or Treasure Island. The random nature of who finds what makes it more than a remote chance for any one of us to come across something of interest in our own lives.

Once people started sharing stories of things they'd found, we all had visions of people all over Queensland lifting up their flooring and looking through old drawers and cupboards!

Janelle *We've got a similar home and when we pulled the kitchen out, a big love letter from the '60s was written across about 10 VJs.*
Maggie *What about the guy who bought a can of paint from Vinnies and found $45,000 in cash inside it! Now that was a find!*
Storm *When my Dad passed away recently amongst his things were two of these old bank books. One belonging to him and the other to myself and my two brothers. Both had money in them.*
Margaret *I had an aunty who did just that. She hid it in a big light shade*
Paul *We found £5 notes recently in an old house as we got through the Reno. £300 total.*
Anita *This is sort of like the stuff I found when I renovated my cottage in Melbourne. No bank books or money though. I did meet a man who had been born and lived his childhood in my home. Told me a few stories. Was very interesting as I was only the 5th owner and his family the 3rd*
Narelle *I think people who lived through the depression found ways to hide money, they lost all faith in banks. I am sure a lot of old homes would have money hidden in them including members of mine however I was told about it before they died. Not a huge amount but enough for a rainy day. To wear all those clothes would have been so uncomfortable I would think.*

Jane *My Nana had 1, 2, 5 dollar notes stashed in so many books on her shelf... money for the milkman, bread man, poultry man. A habit that kept on even years after the last home delivery!*

Chrissy *I worked (briefly!) as a Real Estate salesperson in Toowoomba in the early 1990s and listed an old cottage where the entire placed had been unchanged for decades and ALL the old lino had newspapers from the 1920s underneath. Wasn't mine to take so I read a bit but sadly had to leave them there.*

Diana *Last time we could safely walk into my great Aunt's before they closed it (as it had become unsafe), my cousin asked if there was anything we would like to take, to do so. The look on her face when my husband and I start pulling up some lino because we had spotted old newspapers under it! She was even more confused that, besides some old books and a broken vase (that I think I broke on a family holiday), this was all we took.*

Donna *I have newspapers from between 1910-1912 from under my Aunt's lino years ago. It's pretty tattered but any chance I get I have a bit of a look.*

Caylie *So, picking up my daughter from her friend's house today a few blocks away on Baroona Road, when her mother, Katherine, asked what I was writing these days. I mentioned the Under the Lino Project and she and her husband, Cain,*

got very excited and brought out heaps of newspapers they'd framed that they found under THEIR lino! Date... August 7, 8 and 13th 1945... They also found a £1 note and some coins that they've had framed. #serendipity

Heather *I have the front page for Aug 16, 1945*

Diana *The newspapers we got from under my great aunt's lino are dated 1918, 1919, 1929 and 1936. I haven't decided still what to do with them. There are so many pieces of paper. It would be a wall full of frames. I have thought about donating them to the museum but I am having trouble parting with them.*

Pauline *Gees, all we found when we moved into our place, was a bag of marijuana in one of the cupboards. Maybe good for some people, but we don't smoke.*
Caylie *Pauline surprised they left that behind!!*
Pauline *Sure it wasn't intentional. Was in the cupboard over the fridge, right at the back, so not easily seen. Surprised the agent missed it too*

Megan pulled back the carpet in her Queenslander in Brisbane only to find letters and newspaper clippings that had been stored together for more than 60 years, dating back to 1942. So sad that this letter, written to a soldier, came back unopened.

During the Second World War, the Courier Mail used to have cut-out sections for people to send to their boys overseas inside letters, also found by Megan.

Merle *After the 1974 floods receded we went to clean up our old Auntie's house which had flood waters through, almost up to the ceiling and after throwing out a mattress, one Aunt came out, wanting to know what we did with the mattress as she apparently used to store her savings in it. Sadly, before she had realised it had gone, the council had picked it up and moved on to dump same. By you finding the bank books and money reminded me of the incident.*

Phill *Back in the 1960s friends of my parents were renovating their old house that was built in the early 1900s. They pulled up the lino, too, and found old newspaper articles that had been cut out and marked, so they got interested and decided to look through each room of the house carefully. In one room, on the bottom floor, under the lino which was not glued down, they found a trap door, so they got their torch out. They went down the ladder into a room about 7 metres long and about 5 to 6 metres wide, thinking that they might find something interesting. Well, they did but not quite what they were expecting! Inside the room was a whole pile of old cans, maybe around 80 to 100. All of them seemed to be about 2 kilograms in weight each. They opened one up and, well, there was this black powder in it. So they took a small sample to be examined. Turned out, the cans were full of black powder dating back to WWI. They informed the Army, who came out and gently and carefully removed all the cans and got rid of them. I guess they exploded them, somehow, but nothing else was found downstairs. They thought they'd best look into the ceiling to make sure there was nothing up there too. There were a lot of old letters dating back into the 1870s, so they started the search for relatives of the people mentioned in the letters. They tracked down relatives, and their grandparents had lived at that address in the early 1900s until after the 1930s when they moved. He was a demolition expert, hence the black powder. They met up and passed on the letters and they became good friends. They sold the house in the early 2000s to retire and downsize their property. The house was down near New Farm.*
Ian *If that black powder had ignited, which is not hard thing to do, it would have levelled the house and probably a couple around it! Many early Queenslanders had secret cupboards etc. I had one in Bundaberg which had a secret cupboard which was accessed by sliding up a section of VJ wall above a picture rail. It had a rope and pulley device as well to allow access from another adjoining room. The cavity was about the size of a large wardrobe. Nope... nothing in it!*

Phil *Back in the 1980s, my Dad pulled up the carpet and lino in my sister's bedroom at the house we had lived in since 1969. Underneath was a whole lot of complete Woman's Days, Women's Weeklies and newspapers from 1958. One of the newspapers contained an advertisement for a new War Service Home subdivision in Sydney's North Ryde and incredibly the house in the ad's photo was the home of my sister's boyfriend (now her husband), which he had grown up in and who she had met only a couple of years before. It's amazing that a photo of his house had been under my sister's feet for around 12 years before she met him. My jaw hit the floor when we recognised the house lol*
Caylie *I can imagine it did! Darcy Maddock has a similarly spooky story...*
Darcy *Back in 1973, Lyn and I had been married four years and the "lino" in my mother-in-law's bathroom needed renewing. Lyn's father had laid it in a bathroom reno in 1954 not long before he passed away. There were newspapers under the lino and as I lifted the lino, this was the first page that came into sight. This is my father winning the Qld Cup on Big Spree, November 1954. I would have my 11th birthday a couple of days after the race. We have 7 very large scrapbooks of Dad's career from 1936 to 1969. Full of clippings and photos. Just so strange that this particular article had lain there for 19 years...*

Caylie *It was placed there well before you met your wife too!*
Darcy *Yep I met Lyn early 1969 and married her in December of the same year. Her uncle, who lived with them, was a keen race-goer. Sadly we never looked under the lino in his room but every drawer we opened after he passed away had money under the drawer paper linings. I took an old case off the top of his wardrobe and paper in the old currency fell all around me – it was all in bits from insects. I forget how much exactly, but we were able to get enough together with numbers that the bank exchanged them. Then I moved some old wooden Venetians under the house and more glass bottles with tightly wrapped notes inside came to light. As he also did the garden, heaven knows what might have been under the bushes.*
Caylie *Such a load of money to hide away and never be realised by him! Shame, but good the bank honoured it. Insects! Shocker! Plastic money is way better!*
Darcy *Things that have occurred with both our families. Now "In the Clock" may sound funny but Lyn's grandfather's pocket watch was in a largish mantle clock that was given to a cousin by my mother-in-law. She had forgotten and the cousin has never mentioned it. We are talking over 28 years ago but Lyn wonders if it is still there undiscovered. "In the Clock" applies in my family also – tall, beautiful, weight-driven grandfather hall clock. After Mum passed on, we found the deeds and the will in the bottom of the weight well. "In the Book", also Mum. Three and a half walls of shelves filled with books on art, racing, photography and some history. Every time we pick one up, we give it a good shake and a quick flip through. Photos and letters are often the result.*

2017 The Missing Headstone

One of the early highlights of the Under the Lino (UTL) project was the Forbes Strachan headstone discovery and subsequent match-making of his extended family.

When we first moved in to No. 86 in 1996, Stan Dowdle was our uphill neighbour. Stan's parents had owned 'Aberdeen' since he was a young boy, 70-odd years earlier, and upon their deaths, Stan and his brother had stayed on in the house. There'd been a whisper of a girlfriend at some point in Stan's life, but he'd never managed to pin down a woman in marriage; a confirmed bachelor who cared for his disabled brother until his death. He'd told us the story of the one girl he'd brought home to meet his mother, but upon her immediate disapproval, he'd never brought another woman home again.

Stan used to be the Milko for New Farm, and was the fittest 80 year old we'd ever seen. Before he took over his father's milk run, they'd kept the dray horses and cart behind the house in the back yard. New Farm might have been a small footprint for deliveries, but the number of apartments made it a hefty job for the pair, having to run up so many stairs – it was easy to see why he was so fit, even into his 90s. One of the bedrooms in his house was even filled to the brim with all of the milk receipts for every delivery he and his father had ever made.

Stan used to service his two Kingswoods (the milk Ute with a cold box on the back and his personal-use station wagon) every few months on old timber ramps in the backyard, despite only driving 20kms a week to the golf course for a few games.

He also spent many hours a week raking up the 'bloody leaves' from under the hundred-year-old mango tree in his backyard.

Stan enjoyed such a strict routine that he was visibly shaken when we invited him to dinner at our house for the first time.

"Well, what sort of food would you be cookin'?" he said, peering at us above his bifocals. "None of that spicy stuff I can smell comin' from your place, I hope. I can't be eatin' spicy foods. On Wednesdays, I always eat corned beef and potatoes, carrots and beans."

So I made Stan his favourite Wednesday meal, with the added extra of parsley sauce – not even slightly spicy – to make a point that he was eating 'out' and true to form, he still complained that the meal would play havoc with his 'system', bless him!

We were very sad to say goodbye to Stan when we moved overseas in 2000, knowing we probably wouldn't see him again. He'd been a good neighbour, and it bugs me no end that we didn't spend more time talking with him about his life, and what he might have known about this house and its inhabitants. He'd have been a font of knowledge, but our disinterest in the history at the time is the cross that we now have to bear.

Stan Dowdle died in 2006, leaving his house and belongings to his sister and her children, who soon sold the property to Mark and Louise, who have been our neighbours since we moved back to Brisbane in 2008.

As with our place, Aberdeen was built in 1912 by Master Builder, Alfred Richer, who matched its structure to No. 86. It needed a full renovation to suit its new family of six, despite being immaculately kept in its original state. Both Mark and Louise are practical and creative people, so they threw themselves into the renovation with much gusto and have done a beautiful job together. They even turned that old mango tree into stunning hardwood stairs and benchtops. Sadly for them, however, we planted a poinciana in our backyard that now half hangs over their pool. Even though we all love its brilliant summer blossoms, David and I still hear, "Bloody leaves!" floating over the fence on a regular basis! Stan would smile.

One evening, Mark and Louise came over for dinner. It was early days in the UTL Project, and we were keen to talk to them about what we'd discovered relating to the money, the bank books and our house. We brought out the documents, and spent a good half hour discussing what had come to pass since the first post had gone up on Facebook.

We also showed them some of the other bits and pieces we'd found during renovations – old glass bottles and metal odds'n'ends.

Suddenly, Mark jumped up out of his chair and said, "I'm just popping home. We found something, too, that I want to show you. Maybe you could get your Facebook crowd to help us find out more about it."

He returned a few minutes later with a rectangular slab of marble, about as long as a forearm and a third as wide. On it was the inscription, 'Forbes Strachan 1833-1919'. Mark had dug it up out of the dirt underneath his house while he was clearing it out for restumping. After much oohing and aahing, I took a few photographs and posted them on *Old Brisbane Album*, just as I had with my own discovery...

Caylie to *Old Brisbane Album* 24 September 2017

For fear of starting another mystery... my next door neighbours from Heussler Terrace, Milton, just showed us what they found under their house – the twin of our Under the Lino house – an old headstone maybe? Any suggestions?

Forbes Strachan 1833–1919

Thanks to some amazing sleuthing, some timely media exposure and some intense work by Darcy Maddock from the Friends of Toowong Cemetery, the Forbes Strachan headstone not only located its owner in an unmarked grave at Toowong Cemetery, but found relatives who'd never met each other as well! The Brisbane Times article by Rachel Clun, and a radio segment on ABC Radio National with Rebecca Levingston had reached delighted family members, some of whom attended the reinstatement of their relative's headstone.

The full story of Forbes Strachan can be found on the webpage: http://www.underthelino.com.au/forbes-strachan/

Lino

It's a very Aussie word, **lino**. We say it with a nasal twang up here in Queensland, but I'm not sure you can say Lino in a posh accent. I imagine our southern neighbours all say, Lin*ooo*leum, to avoid sounding like we do!

I've been surrounded by Lino my whole life – in the Hendra house I can remember the lime green pattern in our bathroom, and the ugly orange and brown mandalas on our kitchen floor. We also had a lot of sea grass matting, that wonderful receptacle for dust, the smell of which I remember keenly when changing our guinea pigs' hay.

Our Milton house had several layers on lino (and vinyl), just plonked one on top of the other every time the house needed a refurb. I kick myself now that we didn't keep any of it, but David reminds me that not only was it probably lined with asbestos, it was absolutely feral, and we just wanted to get every last thing out of that house so we could live in it.

There are a few photos of the flooring in the kitchen and I'm pictured here sweeping up the last of the lounge room remnants. The kitchen floor was as ugly as the one in my childhood kitchen but the remnants here were quite pretty.

The History of Linoleum

Linoleum, also called **Lino**, is a floor covering made from materials such as solidified linseed oil (linoxyn), pine rosin, ground cork dust, wood flour, and mineral fillers such as calcium carbonate, most commonly on a burlap or canvas backing. Pigments are often added to the materials to create the desired colour.

Frederick Walton was the English manufacturer who invented Linoleum in 1860. When he was only 21 years old, Walton forgot to properly seal the linseed oil that he was using as paint thinner, and a skin of rubbery linoxyn, or solidified linseed oil, formed across the top. Walton was a well-educated man so, knowing that the India rubber was expensive and hard to get a hold of, he suddenly saw the potential in this new material as a replacement for it.

Unfortunately, it takes too long for linseed oil to oxidize to the point where it might be of any use, so Walton had to work to find ways to speed up the process by introducing other chemicals and heat. In 1860, Walton patented the first linoleum manufacturing method, despite the fact that the material still lacked durability, and took too much time to create.

Eventually, after three years of trial and error, Walton found a new linoleum-making method, and patented this process in 1863, naming the new product 'Linoleum,' a combination of the Latin words linum (flax) and oleum (oil).

In 1887, Sir Michael Nairn, an established floor covering manufacturer in Scotland, opened the American Nairn Linoleum Company in New Jersey. Seeing the success that Nairn was having with his product, Walton decided to sue him for trademark infringement for the use of the word 'linoleum,' which Walton had invented. Walton had not actually patented the name (only the process), so the courts ruled against him, determining that the term 'linoleum' was so prevalent as to be generic. Barely two decades after its invention, Linoleum was the first product ever, whose name became a generic term.

Wikipedia: Linoleum

What should I do with all that money?

The big question hanging in the air when I posted the picture of the bank books and money was...

What would you do if you found old money and bank books under the flooring of your hundred year old house, dating back more than 70 years?

At first, several people thought I should frame them, which was always my original thought back in 1996. These people saw the documents as belonging to the house, and believed they should be kept as an historical conversation piece.

Some people sent me links to web pages that explained exactly what you should do if you find a large amount of money, from a legal point of view.

Others believed the money should be handed to the authorities, who might track down the heirs, or that the bank books and money should be returned to the bank if no heirs were found.

Tony *If you cannot locate heirs to this money I'd hand it in to Police. They will hold it for a mandatory period where upon if no one comes forward it will be returned to you. Unfortunately, under Queensland Criminal Code, you are technically liable to charging for, 'Stealing by Finding.' If it was me I'd run it past them. Whilst the notes are not legal tender, they are still valuable to collectors and someone could come forward to claim them.*

Historical preservation was also high on the list of priorities...

Benita *I highly recommend scanning the documents and submitting them to NLA for record purposes. Not so much of the persons to which the documents belong, but for history of Australian way of life etc. Or a Brisbane Historical association may accept it as a donation for it to be shared with the public. Either way it would be great to see them preserved.*

Some even thought I'd be able to collect a large amount of money from the CBA for myself, and one chap even wanted to buy them all from me!

But the majority believed I should investigate the history of this house, track down any direct descendants and relatives of the original owners and return it all to the rightful heirs for remembrance, knowing that they could be a priceless memento for family members.

Jennifer *Yes, frame them it's the house history and it's important. Be nice to find the owners.*
Brenda *Caylie, as you've bought the house, would it be possible for you to view the title deeds? The rules have changed over the years and I believe even providing copies isn't done anymore unless requested but you should be able to get some information from the Titles Office or whatever it's called now?*

Around the Houses

Now, if I had been any sort of historian, I would have sat quietly for a few hours and worked out a plan for looking into the history of this house and the people who used to live here. I might have done a Google search and come across Magnus Eriksson's *House Histories* website, and started from there with his amazing set of 'how to' instructions; or perhaps read the Brisbane City Council history web page and started there. I may even have paid for a subscription to Ancestry.com.

But I'm not an historian. I HATED history as a child, having had the world's most boring history teacher, whose voice I can still conjure up to put me to sleep at night. I couldn't have even told you what the study of genealogy was before this project... I still have to spell check that word every time I write it!

I am a huge advocate for the idea that asking for help is a strength and not a weakness. I'm not always good at it, and I don't always walk the talk, I admit, but this was one case where I knew there were others out there who knew a lot more than I did and might be willing to help.

When I decided to throw that photograph of the money and bank books to the four winds and see what blew my way, I had no idea that a cyclone of assistance would come back at me! The Under the Lino research has also been somewhat serpentine, often tangled and absolutely fascinating. This project has led us a fine chase, into new and exciting areas of Brisbane's history.

In the writing world, we refer to plotters and pantsers – people who carefully plot out how their story is going to unfold, and those who scribble by the seat of their pants. Both will come to an ending, just in a different way. Plotters wince at pantsers, completely baffled by the seemingly unorganised way they manage their words and time; and pantsers roll their eyes at plotters, believing that being so organised must mess with their creative flow.

I run most of my life by the seat of my pants, wishing to the Universe that I was more organised and planned. True to form, I get there in the end, and despite a fair measure of stress, I live a rich, complicated yet fulfilling life. This book is my way of organising over a million words written to date about this subject.

The Right Girl for the Job

I've always loved people. My first memories of meeting strangers go back to the early 1970s, as a three year old imp, sitting on the front fence of my house in Newstead. Another home spookily like our Milton and Hendra Queenslanders.

Anyone who walked past was greeted with, "Hello! My name's Caylie Anne Fernandes. What's yours?"

They all returned my greetings and I like to think they walked away from that child, smiling.

One day, a man approached me, and asked if I could come down to the boat ramp with him at the end of the street to help him with something. I willingly agreed, and when we got there, he asked me to get into his car, so I did (Mum is cringing as she reads this).

That lovely man promised me twenty cents if I would put my foot on the brake to stop his car rolling into Breakfast Creek while he unloaded his tinny. Mum and Dad didn't even notice I was gone, and I thank the Universe regularly for only putting good people in my path on those latch-key childhood days.

I see the good in most people, and love to share their stories. Everyone has a great story to tell, and my time as a counsellor at Lifeline taught me how to be a good listener. A born chatter-box, it was important for me to learn that it was not all about me. Yes, I can spin a good yarn, but one's own stories get boring after a few tellings, and other people's tales are much more fascinating. Hearing them lets me know that I'm not alone, that many people have shared experiences but that every story is unique.

From the moment I posted the photograph on *Old Brisbane Album*, I have had a relationship with the people who responded. It was a mystery that needed to be solved and in the course of 24 hours, a project team was formed. People who had never met were sharing ideas and opinions. There was no shouting. No tantrums. We couldn't see anyone storming out of the room, or sulking in the corner if their voice wasn't heard.

My husband wasn't so sure – David is not a big fan of social media, and worries about the crazy element of society who lurks in the shadows of the internet. The thing is, the only people who became part of this movement were people with a common interest. Old Brisbane. Historic Brisbane. Back when we were all children, regardless of what era we'd come from, our childhood memories were being dusted off and allowed to shine proudly, and not so proudly, in some instances!

The people who signed up to the Under the Lino (UTL) Facebook page are some of the most interesting people I have never met! They're older, wiser and have awesome stories that they love to share – most of them relevant to whatever we're discussing at the time.

When I started to communicate with the UTL Team on Facebook, it was a whole new relationship experience. We were all talking, sharing and listening from the comfort of our own homes, with absolutely no face to face interaction.

I had learned from experience how important it is to engage with your social media audience – otherwise, every potential conversation dries up. All of the articles I have written invite opinions and shared experiences. If someone identified emotionally with one of my stories, pouring their heart out in response, I had to reply. Not only would it be rude not to, it would be inhumane.

It hasn't been perfect, mind you. There have been challenging conversations and opinions aired that weren't shared easily by others. Topics such as homosexuality, religion, paedophilia and Freemasons have all been discussed with varying levels of compassion. For the most part, people who challenged ideas have done so assertively, yet kindly. The responses have always been apologetic and explained, after which people have been able to move on with the business at hand.

Having a goal really helped with this process. We have always known the questions we wanted answers to, despite the convoluted path we take to get to them!

My dear friend and accountability partner, Cherri, writes delicious children's stories that convince me that this world is peopled with angels. She has also followed this project from the very beginning, so I met with her for a cheeky dessert one night when I became concerned about the way I should write this book – should it be a fictionalised account where I use what I know and fill in the blanks with what I've guessed, or should I keep it dry and factual.

Cherri explained about the three levels of evidence in research…

---

1. Level 1 High level evidence: These are facts that can be validated by other sources or documentation (e.g. statistical data).
2. Level 2 Anecdotal evidence: Information gleaned from first-hand accounts of people who have known and interacted with the person or event
3. Level 3 evidence: Community and popular opinion derived from facts, figures, anecdotes, rumours and beliefs – the human hypotheses.

So, opinions, when it comes to historical research, come way down the bottom of the list of reputable evidence. Facts are what we were aiming for, i.e. that which can be validated with supported documentation. Anecdotal evidence from people who were there when it happened was always the most interesting, followed by opinion and deduction, all of which provoked thought and discussion.

We have all had the opportunity to hypothesise during this journey, and even though people have disputed some theories, very few have been shot down in flames. Maybe just a few singed egos, mine included. For the most part, all it's taken was a few gentle reminders to refocus our attention on kindness, compassion and enjoyment of the journey.

Valerie Strauss (*The Washington Post*, 20 December 2017) says that the top characteristics of success at one of the world's largest social media corporations are all soft skills: being a good coach; communicating and listening well; possessing insights into others (including others different values and points of view); having empathy toward and being supportive of one's colleagues; being a good critical thinker and problem solver; and being able to make connections across complex ideas.

The Under the Lino Team displays all of the above characteristics, and for that reason, we have been able to achieve amazing results throughout the entire project. The main questions we wanted answers to were these:

1. Who were the owners of the money and bank books?
2. Are there any descendants or living heirs?
3. Why did they hide their documents in a secret place?
4. Why did they have so much money in difficult times?

The most obvious place to start the investigation was the Commonwealth Bank.

Part 3

The Commonwealth Bank

The Bank Books

Here's what we knew from the outset... There were three bank books from three different Commonwealth Bank branches, with three names and two addresses. They had had over £2,000 in balances. I also found four £5 notes and some pre-decimal coins.

Commonwealth Bank Book 1
Owners: Arthur William Joseph Webster and Mrs Eleanor Webster
Address: 86 Heussler Terrace, Milton
Branch: King George Square, Brisbane City
Account details: Opened March 1, 1945 with £100. Last transaction July 31, 1951. Final balance: £500/10/-

Commonwealth Bank Book 2
Owner: Mrs Eleanor Webster
Address: 86 Heussler Terrace, Milton
Branch: George Street, Brisbane
Account details: Opened October 18, 1948 with £510 carried forward. Last transaction July 31, 1951. Final balance: £469/8/5

Commonwealth Bank Book 3
Owner: Mrs Muriel White
Address: Bristol Street, West End
Branch: South Brisbane
Account details: Opened October 1955 with a starting balance of £425. Monthly deposits between £12 and £35. Last transaction was a £27 deposit. No withdrawals ever. Final balance £1,013 in July 1958.

For starters, there was a solid acknowledgement that we were looking at a lot of money for those times. The notes, as collectors' items were worth around $1,000, but as currency back in the day, the cash alone constituted a month's wages for a blue collar worker. The notes, apparently, are also still legal tender, and a bank would have to exchange them.

The bank balances were significant too...

Lee *Given the average annual wage for 1940 for a female was £146 – that is a lot of money. The bank balances are equivalent to $143,000 in today's money...*
Chris *Our term ticket to travel to school on the train was £1/13/4. It was a cardboard ticket in a plastic sleeve which we tied on our school bags. Every term was a different colour. It went up a few years later to £1/17/9. We were scandalised.*
Barry *Those £5 notes featured a design that was last minted in 1939, so that confirms the 1940's connection*
Grace B *When I started work in 1962, I was earning £6/week*
Greg *As an accounting clerk, I was earning £2/10 when I started work in 1965 but this is 20 years before then. That was a LOT of money!!*
Skubi *The accrued interest on these would be huge!*
Kevin *Those bank books were a great visible lesson of how you were managing your worth. And, no passwords needed.*
Jackie *I called the oldest person I know, my 92 year old Granny (Joan) to tell us what the general cost of living was in the '40s and '50s... e.g. how much money would Eleanor have needed to run a household? "Wages were around £5/week. A good wage was £7. Families were frugal. And saving money was important. My Grandma's Dad was a war veteran, and he was given a war service home that they paid off, like rent. Once it was all paid they owned the home. In Granny's family the wife took the wages from her husband and paid the bills and did the groceries. Groceries, baked goods and ice would be delivered to the home and the family had a cow for their dairy."*
Debbie *Just to keep this amount of £450 in perspective... my parents bought a three bedroom weatherboard home at Gordon Park in the '50s for £550!*

Darcy *My parents bought a house in Hendra in 1941 for £395*
Cheryl *My parents bought a house in Everton Park for £300 in 1952*
Lyn *In 2015, Muriel's £1013 from 1958 would have been $29,433. Eleanor's £469 from 1951 would have been $19,012 and the £500 works out at $20,269. £5 translated to $145 in 2015. That was a lot of money in anyone's books.*

By now, we'd worked out exactly how much money we were talking about, for any family from the 1940s and '50s. What we had to do next was to find out if the money was still available, and whether there was anyone around today who could claim it.

The Commonwealth Bank might still have a record of the accounts, and if the money was still in them, then it would go to their legal heirs. The major hurdle I would have to face was the fact that I was not a relative, and confidentiality would be adhered to.

Unclaimed moneys from disused accounts would have been absorbed back into consolidated revenue with the Commonwealth Government, but could be made available if heirs came forward.

Julie *That money goes to the Australian Securities and Investments Commission (ASIC) after seven years to free up the bank's responsibility. Then the true owner can claim whenever they wish.*

I started the search by visiting the local Milton and Toowong branches of the CBA, which resulted in a lot of personal interest in my discovery but not a lot of helpful information. The tellers I spoke to were of the opinion that relatives would have tracked down that money by now, especially for the joint account, and any unclaimed money would have gone to ASIC.

Phone calls to the Brisbane and Sydney CBA Head Offices came up with nothing, and contact with the CBA Archives only resulted in a postal delivery of some 1950 advertising paraphernalia sent to appease my curiosity. It didn't.

Some members of the UTL Team are current or ex-employees of the CBA and they were the most helpful with ideas and detective work surrounding the bank books, within the bounds of privacy. As far as we know, any money that was left in those accounts, not found by living relatives, was swallowed up by the Commonwealth government. They doubted the old paper records would have been uploaded as computer records.

It was at this point where we needed to look more closely at the people who owned the money and accounts. We had to establish whether these people were tenants at the Heussler Terrace and West End addresses.

In the 1950s, people usually knew their bank managers and tellers well, and mostly did their banking in their local area. Cheryl looked at the different teller initials, and Hamish wondered if we could track down employees who would have worked in the branch and may have had good customer relations with Muriel and Eleanor.

Lyn *All three accounts were at different banks. Arthur would have known about the joint one but not necessarily the other two. I would have thought that you would use the same branch most times.*
Kym *OK... I wonder does this mean that there was no "central register" or whatever you'd call it for Commonwealth accounts then? If they were investigating someone they'd have to get each branch to check their records.*
Shane *I was talking a person last weekend about the CommBank and he said when he started there in the 70s all the accounts were written in a ledger. I would think that applied when these bank books were done and given the bank was government owned these ledgers should still exist in some archives somewhere.*
Sharon *When I worked at the Commonwealth Bank in the mid-'80s, I found the records for my school banking account. It had been more than 7 years.*
Janelle *When I worked at the Commonwealth Bank at Toombul in 1975, we still had the big old ledger books.*

Everything hand written in but from memory that was totals for the day, not separate transactions.

Martine *Yes all transactions recorded in huge general ledgers and we calculated interest by hand. You could only deposit and withdraw at the branch your account was held.*

Jane *Caylie, do you think an appeal through this page and/or maybe the Brisbane pages might yield an ex-staffer or someone who could at least give us some general information about banking in the "olden" days?*

Caylie *We've had a few CBA staff offer some info which I am collating and quite a few people on this page either worked there or know someone who did. I'm keen for a person on the inside to talk to, but I'll have to just manage with the snippets I have.*

Shane *If as people have said before re-writing everything in ledgers, somewhere those ledgers exist because at the time it was a government organisation and somewhere in their archives they still exist. It's just getting someone to find them. Also the people are dead and as far as we know there are no existing relatives to any one*

Allison *Not so sure the ledgers still exist. They didn't when I joined CommBank in 1981. Microfiche was the new technology back then. Don't forget we are talking about accounts that were inactive or unclaimed long (decades) before that. Even finding a retired staffer alive is a very long shot if you want to go back that far.*

Glen (from CBA Archives) *The Commonwealth Bank of Australia opened in 1912, in two separate parts... the Savings Bank for citizens, and the General Bank for businesses. In order to open an account, you would require some form of identification, such as a birth certificate, and present it to the teller. Any money in those accounts would have been put in consolidated revenue after 7 years of inactivity, having accrued interest over that time.*

So, I contacted the Retired Officers Association at the CBA and this is what I got in return...

"Good Morning. I have referred your email to both the President and Vice President of Qld Retired Officers Assn and we are not willing to be involved based on Privacy and Confidentiality concerns. The President has recommended you contact the State Administration of the bank in Queensland at 180 Ann Street or the Banks Media Dept. in Sydney. Copy has been sent Administration. Regards LM, Secretary".

His response officially closed all avenues into CBA for assistance. It was such a shame nobody wanted to talk to me about this project from anywhere within the bank, past or present. I have contacted absolutely everyone I could think of to ask some general questions as well, and we continue to be disappointed by the (lack of) response relating to our general banking queries. The personal confidentiality issues were understandable.

The only thing left to do was to turn to the greater community, and see if anyone knew people who'd once worked at the Commonwealth Bank. While we waited to hear from CBA staffers, other people were starting to investigate who the owners of the bank books were.

Part 4

Arthur
and
Eleanor Webster

Arthur William Joseph Webster

Arthur Webster was the owner of this house from 1914 to 1976, as per the house's historical title deeds. He was relatively easy to track down through online searches (Trove, Ancestry.com) and the State Archives. Electoral roll records were located, for various years between 1900 and 1990, which also gave us his job description. Lyn started building a family tree for the Websters, which dates all the way back to the mid-1800s, with information gleaned from the discussions.

When we found traces of Arthur online, we thought he'd worked for Queensland Fire Services, after an electoral roll search put his occupation as Fireman in 1914.

Nicole *Morgan won the Thallon medal in 1928 and 29, this was awarded to the children of railway men. So Arthur may have been a fireman on the trains! The Telegraph, Brisbane. Tuesday 5th February 1929, Page 16.*
Felice *Arthur was a Train Driver*
Lyn *Arthur was a Fireman (on the train) and then a Train Driver. A Fireman on a train was the bloke who shovelled coal into the fire.*
Steve Webster *In the days of steam, railway Firemen didn't put out fires, indeed, they invariably fed them.*

Arthur's Queensland Rail Years

Arthur Webster started work for Queensland Rail (QR) in 1906 (aged 16), when he began his apprenticeship on the trains as an Engine Cleaner. His father, John Webster, was the Station Master at Corinda, and Arthur was his only child to continue the family line into the railways. He worked his way through the ranks to become a Fireman, on the steam engine locomotives, before finally reaching the position of Locomotive Engineman, or Driver.

My first point of contact for QR was one of the UTL members, Janelle, who not only works for QR currently, but her 88-year-old father, Norm, is an ex-QR driver (1947-1992).

Janelle *I work for Queensland Rail now. Dad knew Arthur Webster. Very small world we live in. Here's the photo of Dad with my older brothers.*

Janelle's friend, Gillie, who worked closely with Arthur, gave us an exclusive peek into what life working with Arthur 'Jumbo' Webster was like, despite being gravely ill.

From what Janelle was able to ascertain, Gillie didn't have too many good things to say about Arthur. He confirmed that his nickname was Jumbo and he was an unsavoury fellow. He recounted a story about a time when QR staff had to pay to travel on the train... *One day, two ticket inspectors caught Arthur without a ticket and gave him a fine. Arthur complained about them and the Inspectors got an even bigger fine.*

Arthur treated all he worked with dreadfully, called everyone Jimmy, didn't socialise with anybody at work, would go straight home at the end of his shifts and was universally disliked. When asked if Arthur might have been involved in any illegal pursuits that might explain the large deposits, Gillie said, "No, he wouldn't have done anything illegal." Gillie knew he had a son, but didn't know anything else about his family. When asked if he thought Arthur's wife might have been hiding the bank books and money from him, Gillie replied that she wouldn't have been game if Jumbo treated her like he treated everyone else at work.

My next port of call was Greg Hallam, an amazing historian and archivist at QR, who was very helpful when I contacted him to discuss the acquisition of Arthur's service records. Greg has written extensively about the history of QR, and I was very fortunate that he gave me quality time and information to help me investigate Arthur's working life.

Greg sent me a swathe of valuable information about the railways from the 1920s to the 1960s – photographs, stories and some wonderful contacts, as well as explanations about the hierarchy on the trains: from Porter Lad to Locomotive Cleaner to Fireman to Engineer and Guard to Driver and Inspector.

C17 723 Mayne Locomotive Sheds Photograph courtesy of Queensland Rail Archives

Greg shared stories about the strong union culture within the railways with the Labor influences and the pecking order. We discussed payday – each worker had a cash tin with their number on it, and their weekly wages would be paid into the box. Each payday, the wives would wait outside the gates to collect the majority of the wages before it ended up at the pub, despite the strong temperance movement within QR.

Railway women held the families together, with their husbands away for long stretches, on difficult shifts. They were tough and brutal roles, and despite many amazing fellows working in the industry, some were not so well-regarded. The Engine Drivers were self-regarded as the aristocrats and the big guns of QR, with some loathed by those who worked beneath them.

Arthur Webster, for example. He was a hard-bitten Driver, who was said to be very tough on his Firemen and difficult to work with, often beating his juniors if they didn't do their jobs properly.

I told Greg that I was surprised anyone still remembered Arthur Webster, singled out from one of many men from so long ago! How was that possible?

"Oh," he said, "Jumbo's infamous reputation was very well known and many of the older staff will have had a tale or two to share about him. In fact, you should get in touch with Noel Condon, who was a Locomotive Driver and later, an Inspector, for QR while Arthur was working. He's 88 years old, bright and active, with a fantastic memory for people and events."

"If anyone would know anything about Jumbo Webster and life at QR during the 1950s, it would be Noel."

Greg Hallam then passed me onto Brian 'Sully' O'Sullivan, a Heritage Driver for QR, who reinforced Greg's stories about Arthur, describing him as a hard man and, although he never worked with him directly, Jumbo Webster's terrible reputation was well-known. Brian said Jumbo was the sort of bloke who'd make a pot of tea, pour himself a cup and tip the rest out so his Fireman didn't get any!

Brian also told me to speak with Noel Condon, who, in his retirement, ran the Enoggera Memorial Hall and Historical Society. He confirmed that Noel joined QR in 1949 as an Engine Cleaner and worked his way up to Inspector. Noel's father, Jack, was a Driver before him, and he also knew Arthur well. Brian assured me that Noel had several stories to share about Arthur, so I made it my priority to contact him at the earliest available opportunity.

Greg also suggested I call Rob Shiels from the QR Museum in Ipswich, who invited me to come there to see some of the history up close – the payday tins, for example. He also has notebooks that were recently donated by the son of an Engine Driver, called Harry May, from Arthur's time, which paint some fascinating pictures of the working life, savings plans and recording habits of railmen in the 1940s.

I had a wonderful day's outing to the Ipswich Rail Museum, where I met with David Hampton, the Head Curator, who showed me Harry May's notebooks and taught me how to handle precious documents correctly with white gloves and mats. I spent hours perusing the notebooks, reading rail journals and old maps in the Ipswich Workshops Rail Museum Library, wishing I had more time to read everything they had.

Jim *I have a copy of my grandfather's employment record with Qld Rail in Cairns (ca. 1913). From memory it was quite easy to obtain and there was a small fee involved. It might be worthwhile contacting QR's Records Management and Storage Services to see if they can supply the information you're after.*

I did apply for Arthur's work history through QR Records Management, which unfortunately didn't give me any more clues about the man, being only a copy of a pay slip. Given the number of people who have worked for QR over the years, I was very surprised that they were able to draw me such a vivid picture of this man from 100 years ago. Being infamous in Brisbane seems to last forever in people's memories.

Meeting Noel Condon

My next port of call was to meet Noel Condon, who had worked for QR for 46 years. Not only would Noel be able to shed some light on the era and the working life at QR, he had also worked closely with Arthur Webster and was one of the only living people who could tell me stories about this man.

After a long conversation on the telephone, introducing myself and the Under the Lino Project, Noel was intrigued enough by my discovery to invite me to come to his home. I wasn't surprised to find myself standing outside a typical post-war Brisbane house, kept in tip-top condition, surrounded by garden beds that were looking a little lonely.

Noel was mowing the lawn when I arrived, and as I sat on the concrete step waiting for him to put the mower away, I had one of my black and white moments, which happens a lot these days! I slowly morphed Noel's garden into 1960's faded chromatic – choko and passionfruit vines curling through the chain wire fence, pawpaw trees growing from seeds haphazardly dropped by well-fed fruit bats, beautifully tended roses in the concrete garden beds and an incinerator, gently chuffing smoke from the day's cuttings.

In my reverie, Noel's wife had just finished taking in the washing from the Hill's Hoist before the flannel sheets got smoky, and was preparing scones and tea in the kitchen while Noel showered after his morning in the yard. I visualised him walking into their Formica-decked kitchen in his smart navy blue uniform, complete with pocket watch, ready for his afternoon shift on the trains. Never one to be late, I saw him snatch up a warm scone smothered in passionfruit butter.

He followed that with a swig of hot, milky tea before sneaking a kiss from his wife and heading off to work.

NB: How wrong and sexist was I? Noel was actually the family kitchen whiz, whose scone recipe made mouths all over Brisbane's northern suburbs water at the thought!

Noel and his wife had obviously been avid gardeners at one time, but he confirmed that the gardens were a little too much for him these days, scoffing when I offered to bring along some roses to plant in an empty bed. "No time for that!" he said, which, by all accounts, was true of the man. Noel never indulged in afternoon naps, because, he said, "There's too much to do!"

Noel Condon was known as a great bloke by all who worked with him. He was indeed a wonderful man to make acquaintance with. At 88 years of age, he was bright-eyed, fit and healthy, still taking care of himself well, with a memory like an elephant. Noel had lived alone since his wife passed away 13 years ago but maintained a close relationship with his children and grandchildren. The walls and bookshelves of his home were heavy with family memories, railways photographs, community awards, and books.

While the tea brewed, I started asking Noel questions. Lots of questions. I wanted to know everything and I wasn't disappointed.

Noel James Condon was born in 1930 and started working for Queensland Railways (QR) in 1949, after he'd finished his plumbing apprenticeship. Noel absolutely loved working for QR, as his father before him had. I commented to Noel that there's often a lot of family history in the railways, wondering if any of his kids had followed him into the railways. "No, my son broke the run!" he said, with a wry smile.

By this point in my conversation with Noel, I had gained a new respect for the railway workers of yesteryear, and was fast turning into a train tragic. I was also keen to hear more about Noel's relationship with Arthur Webster, so I brought out the bank books and notes to do a little show and tell.

Noel *had* known Arthur Webster, having worked as his Fireman for a time. He also knew Arthur lived in the second street behind the XXXX Brewery, on Heussler Terrace. "I never went out there because people rarely went to visit him at that time. He had a phone and a brand new Morris car that he never used," he recalled.

I explained that Arthur was the nephew of David Webster of the famous Webster's Biscuits family and Noel was fascinated to know that Arthur was actually related to them. "Jumbo used to gloat that the Websters were his cousins, and that he used to go over there and get his bread for half price!"

It was such a surprise for me to know that Noel had been so close to Arthur in proximity – they'd worked together for the last six years of Jumbo's time on the trains from 1949-1955, and Noel said he often saw Arthur on the trains well after his retirement, while Noel was working as a Guard and Inspector.

When Noel first came on the job, Queensland Rail only had one tank engine working but they eventually got six blue tank engines.

"There were two crews to each engine, one in the morning and one in the afternoon. They had a good thing working – finishing early enough each evening to catch the tram home, and they came in on the first tram in the morning. A lot of blokes didn't have cars, and had to walk to work, which was why many of 'em lived so local to the Roma Street Depot."

Noel went on to explain that, "Originally the train depot for Brisbane was in Roma Street, until the Sunday after the Brisbane Exhibition in 1927, when they shifted the depot to Mayne. What that meant was all the blokes who lived in Red Hill and Paddington now had to walk so much further to get to work. Jumbo had his Morris car, but never took it to work (probably because the lads would have let his tyres down!). He caught the tram or train into work from Milton.

Some QR workers would walk from Toowong to Mayne. When they kicked Arthur out of working the tank engine crew of 12, he then had to walk from Milton to Mayne. He would be wearing a full-length, dark leather coat walkin' along the road, trampin' along, tampering with the odds of gettin' run over in the dark."

Arthur Webster was involved in at least two tragedies, one the UTL researchers found on Trove, and the other inquest was found by UTL researcher, Lyn, at the State Archives. The first incident involved Arthur's engine running over his Fireman, killing him in 1937, and the other, in 1950, was when Arthur was driving the train that hit and killed an elderly man at Northgate/Geebung. He'd walked over a level crossing, not hearing the oncoming train because he was deaf.

The inquests deemed them both accidents, and I asked Noel if he knew anything about them...

Townsville Daily Bulletin, Thursday 4 November 1937, p8 Trove

FIREMAN'S DEATH.

Ipswich Fatality.

IPSWICH, November 3. Leslie Woodgate, aged 37, a fireman, was killed when he was crushed between a locomotive and a coal chute at North Ipswich railway yards.

"The first one was before my time, but I saw Jumbo's accident in 1950 at Northgate. His Fireman, Pat Cronan, was with him and it was an open level crossing that this bloke went around and crossed in front of the train. I was a Cleaner on the engine at the time. The engine had come in and run over the fellow – very difficult to clean up the waste afterwards – they were using kerosene to get it off after he'd smashed his head open."

Arthur became a Fireman in 1909, and was probably a Driver by the time of WWI in 1914. BDM records state he was a Driver by 1918. They usually had to wait until they were 21 before they could be a driver, and Arthur would have turned 24 by then. We were able to ascertain from his work records, that in 1912, just before Arthur 'Jumbo' Webster moved into this house, he was working as a Fireman, Class 2, having already committed three years to service as a Cleaner. He was yet to become a Driver.

"Arthur would try and catch you out, if you were his Fireman. Every locomotive has two injectors. These force the water against the pressure into the boiler. The tanks would grow green moss that would sometimes come into the injectors and block them. When they started for the day, the Fireman would have to clean both injectors. Most would only clean one but not two, because the injector on the other side doesn't get much use. That one is only used for when you're sprinkling all the hot ash underneath the engine with water to stop the sleepers catching fire."

"Arthur would watch closely to see if they'd cleaned both of them. He'd wait until they were just about to leave and knock the block off anyone who hadn't. I always came in early to clean down the screens and both injectors. If he'd come along and just seen you cleaning the injector that feeds the boiler, he'd say, *Have you done the other injector, boy? You'll put a quid in the treasury if you don't!* meaning you'd get a QR fine from the department if you were reported by Jumbo. They had an appeals court and the maximum fine was £5. All sorts of things they'd fine you for; not coming to work, for example."

Because Arthur wasn't kind to his co-workers, they took opportunities for anonymous payback when they could, like taking out the horse hair in his leather seat to make it as uncomfortable for him as possible!

"I was in the boardroom when this happened one time, and down came Jumbo. Alwyn Dunlop was the Fireman at the time. *Oh,* he said, *someone's cut the back out of me seat.* Alwyn said, *Oh that's a terrible thing, Arthur,* smirking and laughing behind his back."

Noel, being a sociable, affable fellow, went out of his way to try and get along with Jumbo.

"I just had to. He was a tall and broad man, a big man. Some blokes didn't make the effort and they fought with him, coming off second best. But it wasn't easy to keep the effort up... Arthur used to tell me to turn the fire on whenever I went to talk to him, just to annoy me."

"Towards the end of his career, Jumbo and his crew had a head-on crash. Old Jumbo finished up there and never worked after that. It wasn't a severe accident, but he hurt his back."

"Old Jumbo would get off the trains in the middle section (after he'd retired) and walk away leaving the door swinging open, singing out, *It's not my job, boy!* to the poor guard who had to run down the length of the train to close it. He did it to me a few times when I was driving. I had a young Fireman working with me who I'd sometimes let drive the train out of the station, while I would fire for him. Jumbo would leave the door open and I'd be the chap who'd have to run down the platform to close it!"

We finished our discussion about Arthur that day, wondering whether he was a complicated man or a man with simple needs and a bad temper. Noel suggested he was a rough and tough character who had no sense of culture at all. Despite having a son who was very well-educated and working in the bank, Arthur worked hard in the railways and did nothing much else. He was tight with his earnings and never spent money on anything extra but Noel confirmed that Jumbo wasn't a gambler, and couldn't imagine him doing anything other than working.

Jack *Hi Caylie, Might also be worth asking on the* Qld Gov't Railways Days Gone By *Facebook page. There could be someone on there who might have worked with him before his retirement. There a lot of ex-railway workers on the page with a vast knowledge of the last 70 years. Hope this helps! There are some great railway workers on the page with some great stories.*

Thanks to sharing Noel Condon's story on that particular Facebook page, I was contacted by an elderly colleague of Noel's, who also had a big story to tell about Arthur.

Bernie Kiernan *In 1950, I was a 19 year old working for Queensland Rail, in Alpha (I wrote the book about the Bogantungan Crash).*

I worked as Arthur Webster's Fireman three times. He was universally despised from Mount Isa to Coolangatta, by all who knew him at QR. He once kicked a Station Master in the head while I was firing for him, because he made the mistake of calling him 'Jumbo'.

Nobody ever called him Jumbo to his face. He was known to threaten people with iron bars for doing it.

He was a vile man to work with and any venom the man had was all directed towards work. He only ran passenger trains towards the end of his career and mellowed after his retirement. He wasn't a particularly astute or clever man, he just plodded along, doing his job. He would have been useless outside of the railways, with nobody ever wanting to employ him because of his attitude.

I remember coming to Arthur's house, near the brewery in the early 1950s – it had an outhouse in the back yard and a cast iron clothes boiler downstairs. His father bought him that house.

His son, Morgan, was a real gentleman, always very well dressed and very religious. He did all the shopping and cooking, taking care of his parents. He shopped at Pratt's Grocers, next to the Iceworks on Given Terrace.

Morgan would take his parents out for a drive every Sunday, usually up to Scarborough and Redcliffe. It was the only outing they had each week.

I used to live with my Aunty on Mayneview Street, but the house was demolished to pave the way for factories and workshops.

I was working with a senior driver called George Hickling, who knew Arthur Webster very well. He told me that Arthur had been given money by his father some years earlier, to buy shares in the XXXX Brewery. Instead of buying the shares in his father's name, Arthur bought them in his own, and hung on to them. Nobody in Arthur's extended family knew anything about the shares after his old man passed away in 1933.

Arthur later sold the shares, and bought a Ford Prefect with some of the money, pocketing the rest.

This piece of information relating to XXXX shares is an important piece of the puzzle, but we only heard about it after a lot of research had already been done. Keep it in the back of your mind as we move forward with the investigations.

Janelle *Amazes me that so many railway men still around, remember Arthur. Although, working for the railway, I can confirm that they still love to talk about interesting characters. He definitely had a reputation and it wasn't a good one.*
Dolly *My father's family history is full of railwaymen. My great-great-grandfather (a fettler with Qld Rail) was run over and killed by a train in Maryborough Qld in the early 1900s. My father was an assistant station master and also a Freemason.*
Janelle *I've seen Dad's work record and he got fined £1 for taking a train early one day and another time his crew were seen having lunch in a pub in a break but in work hours. They weren't fined that time because even though someone saw them in the pub, and obviously dobbed them in, they didn't actually see them drinking alcohol. This was in the days of steam trains so it was pretty thirsty work...*
Cheryl *Hi Janelle, I was wondering if your Dad knows or remembers how the Engine Drivers and crew would have received their wages during the war when they were away from home for long periods taking the troop trains to North Qld. I have read that the armed services would pay directly to the wife if the husband nominated her as next of kin. I imagine that the State Government may have done something similar for their employees. It would have been very difficult for the wife and children if only the husband had access. My late father-in-law, Noel, was an Engine Driver or Fireman, taking the troops to NQ during the war but he was single and a young man at the time. He joined the army but when they learnt what his trade was they discharged him and sent him back to QR as this was deemed an essential service and he was not permitted to join up.*
Jim *QR were very helpful in giving me copies of my grandfather's employment records from Cairns in 1914-1917. Can't remember who I contacted but it was very straightforward. Amazing that they keep all that info so just ask.*

Lou *I just remembered that my grandfather worked for the railway in Toowoomba. I never knew him as he had passed away before I was born but the few things my late Mum said about him lead me to believe he was probably a lot like Arthur!*
Grace *So exciting, our adventure continues. It is amazing how information entwines with our lives. My great-grandfather worked for the railways painting the bridge at Albion station late 1890s or early 1900s, and died in 1908 as result of a tragedy there. He lived in Paddington, close to Milton. Everyone knew everyone in the area in those days, although he would have been much older than Arthur.*
Ian *Apart from coming from Milton, I also came from a Railway family. I don't know if it still exists (be surprised if it doesn't) but the Queensland Railway Institute had a huge membership of its social club etc. They had a separate building near Central Station for many years. They may be able to help.*
Gay *My grandfather's name was Edward Staunton Denman and he worked as a Shunter at Roma Street rail yards. He was involved in an accident where he was crushed between two trains, (which happened quite a lot I believe) and passed away 12 months later in hospital in 1929.*

My Connection to Queensland Rail and Arthur Webster...

As we dug deeper and deeper, Sharon, one of the Facebook members, said, "Caylie, with all of the coincidences we've discovered, wouldn't it be funny if you were related to the Websters!" to which I quickly replied, "Ha! That would be funny, given that it's not even remotely possible! I'm of Anglo-Indian descent and only arrived in the country in 1971."

The thing is, I'd forgotten I was married to a Jeffery who has a strong connection to Brisbane's past.

My mother-in-law, Kay, was one of my soul-sisters. From the day I met her, grubby from gardening with one shorts leg hiked up higher than the other, I knew she was a kindred spirit. I'd only been dating David for a little while, and I didn't know too much about his family, so as we drove up the long driveway towards 'The Rectory', I closed my eyes and shook my head, with that sinking feeling that I'd fallen for a rich kid. I walked past the Mercedes Benz with a shudder of doom, wondering what sort of people they would be, knowing David had been privately schooled.

So, you can only imagine my delight at meeting my sweaty, mud-encrusted future mother-in-law with her foot in the basin of the bidet.

"It's the only way to wash your feet properly," she said, as I started giggling. "It sometimes doubles as the dog's bowl. We never use it for what it's really for!"

The Rectory was a millstone around the Jeffery family's neck, since they'd moved it from St Andrew's Church grounds in South Brisbane, a decade earlier. The house movers, akin to the Dean Brothers, had literally chain sawed the Old Rectory into four pieces, before manhandling them onto wide-load vehicles to do the midnight run along Logan Rd all the way to their 10-acre block in Eight Mile Plains.

Non-stop renovations were to follow, with never-ending yard work and countless rooms to keep clean! By the time I arrived on the scene, however, they'd done a beautiful restoration job.

Kay then filled it with heirlooms from the Redcliffe and Toogoolawah branches of the family.

When I met David's father, Bob, a self-employed Business Accountant, it was more formal and infinitely scarier for me. Fortunately, I saw the twinkle in his eyes when I said I'd gone to Brisbane State High School, and that I'd remembered this house when it had been part of the church over the road. Turned out, he'd been the school captain of State High in 1961, and I was immediately accepted into the family as an 'old girl'. David hardly got a look in after that and I know they'd have disowned him if he hadn't married me!

Kay and Bob had been together since they met in high school, having lived not far from one another in Fairfield as youths. Kay was Bob's biggest supporter, on the Rugby field, at awards ceremonies and throughout his career. They'd travelled extensively and worked hard renovating and bringing up three children.

So, when Kay was diagnosed with pancreatic cancer in 2007, Bob's world came crashing down around him. The day we called them from the middle of the Atlantic Ocean to share the news that we were going to have a baby, Bob had to tell us that Kay was going to die. The statistics were ghastly; the doctors had given her a year at most.

Suffice to say, we came back to Australia to share our children with Kay, and she attributed her love for her three grandchildren as the reason she lived for two years longer than they'd predicted.

We'd only been home for a couple of months when the Universe decided to add a little fuel to the cancer fire. David was diagnosed with a brain tumour. We had Will, about to turn one, and I was pregnant with Kitty, when David went under the knife. I'd stopped listening to the neurosurgeon after he's said that David could die during the operation, and it took me a few years to realise that he hadn't. It was a massive emotional output for me to care for a baby, a sick man and a pregnancy, but I had Kay with me that year, to lean on when I thought I couldn't manage another day.

Exactly a year after his first surgery, David was diagnosed with a second tumour, and we had to go through it all over again. Only this time, Kay was in palliative care at the Wesley and I had two babies. On his last visit to see her, Kay asked David if he was hiding anything from her, that she felt something was wrong. Of course, he denied everything, and they spent a lovely evening together talking and sharing stories. She was never told about the second tumour. A week later, I drove David to St Andrew's Hospital for his second brain surgery. During his operation, his mother, and my soul-sister, passed away.

When David woke up in recovery, I was holding his hand, making all sorts of silent promises to the Universe and to Kay.

He looked at me and asked, "Has Mum died?"

Tears followed my silent shock.

"Yes, my love, she has. How did you know?" I asked him incredulously.

"I don't know," he replied. "I just knew."

We had lost a dear, wonderful woman from our lives that day. She'd been there for us when we needed her most, even though she was suffering herself. She'd loved our babies as if they'd been her own, and she continued to support her own family all the way to the end, even planning her own funeral.

It took us all of eight years to finally clean out her clothes, her documents and her physical presence. We knew it had to be done, but out of respect for my father-in-law, we didn't push too hard. He had to be ready.

In September 2017, he called his children to help him clean out his house, so he could move. Move on.

Working from home usually gives me the ability to take time off to attend to family matters, and I was knee deep in the first month of Under the Lino research when I went over to help Bob. I was desperate to talk to him about everything we'd discovered especially given that he was born in 1943, grew up in Fairfield right near Hughie Lunn, and has such vivid memories of the '50s. I was sure he'd be able to give me loads of historical references, while we sorted through Kay's belongings.

What I didn't realise was how emotional it was going to be for us both to see all of Kay's things again after eight years.

Photographs, diary entries, funeral notes... The children loved trying on her tattered fur hats, reading her moth-eaten books and drinking tea from her grandmother's china. Watching them gave me a terrific sense of melancholy that Kay could not be here to enjoy them, and that they no longer had any memory of her. Bob wanted to keep a lot more of her things than he needed to, and we had to be mindful not to be too brutal when giving her things to Vinnies. It was a bittersweet time, not to be shared with my Lino project. Or so I thought.

As I was sorting through Kay's desk, I found a navy blue notebook with a train embossed on the front cover. It said Queensland Gov't Railways. The Facebook group had recently discovered that Arthur Webster had worked as a Train Driver.

When I thrust the notebook accusingly under my father-in-law's chin, asking him why he had it, Bob replied, "Oh, that notebook must have belonged to my maternal grandfather Jimmy. He worked as a Fireman on the old coal fired trains at QR until he died. Shovelled coal all his life. Because of his lung disease, acquired during the Great War, he was never well and died at 47. That would have been a standard issue notebook for all QR employees."

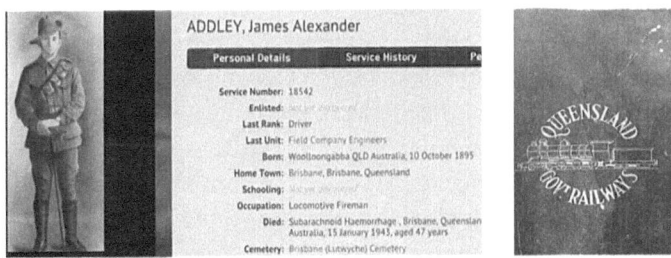

James (Jimmy) Alexander Addley died in 1943 from the long term effects of his being gassed in the trenches in France in 1917

I have never found a direct link between Arthur and Jimmy, but I still imagine them working together on the trains as Driver and Fireman.

Little would either of them have imagined that 100 years from the day he was gassed in WW1, Jimmy's great-grandchild and his wife would be living in Arthur 'Jumbo' Webster's house.

A few months into 2018, I received a very sad message from Janelle, to tell me that Gillie, who'd helped us with stories about Arthur, had passed away just before Christmas. Such a sad time for all who knew him, and I wish I'd had the chance to meet Gillie.

Rowland Gault Gilford Williams 'Gillie' 1925–2017

A short while before this book was completed, I was also told of the passing of my new friend, Noel Condon, the delightful octogenarian who helped me learn so much more about Queensland Rail (QR) and Arthur Webster, from days gone by.

All I could think about after I heard the news of his death was, *Thank goodness I met him before he was just a legend from the past*. Holding his hand, sitting opposite him in his kitchen laughing with him, sharing scones, tea and stories was an unforgettable experience. One I'd have missed if I'd waited another couple of months.

Noel taught me to strike while the iron is hot, to not put off until tomorrow what could be done today and that men, too, can make great scones! I never did give him a copy of the newspaper article, or the story I wrote about him, but was told by his dear friend, Merle, that he had read my words with the help of his friend Lorna. That made me feel happier, but I wish I'd seen him again.

Noel James Condon 1930–2018

Noel's funeral was a very dignified affair. One of the UTL members, Nicki, joined me there to pay our respects to Noel, his family and his colleagues, on behalf of our online community. We were delighted to meet several of Noel's old mates, including Brian, Bernie and Greg, and really enjoyed hearing stories about him from those who gave eulogies. The guard of honour was particularly poignant, as the railway elders all held old railway lamps to send off this lovely, well-respected man.

I would like to dedicate these pages to the men and women of Queensland Rail, who have done so much to help us on this project. Janelle and her father, Norm Duncan; Janelle's dear friend, Rowland 'Gillie' Williams; Greg Hallam; Rob Sheils; David Hampton; Brian 'Sully' O'Sullivan; Bernie Kiernan; and Noel Condon.

Arthur William Joseph Webster... The Whole Man

I wonder what you're thinking about Arthur Webster now? Do you see him as Jumbo the Tyrant, an abusive man at work who probably beat up his wife at home? Many people did. Most things I have read, heard and discovered about Arthur Webster paint him as unsavoury, unhappy, angry, abusive and miserable. It's very easy for me to sit here, in a room where Arthur sat over a hundred years ago, and judge him based on the information I've gleaned about his work life.

But our lives are so much more than work.

When I was a nurse, I was so compassionate, working my tail off to help those in need, with authenticity and love. When I came home, I expected my family to be able to take care of themselves, and if you ask them, they'd snort at the thought of me being caring! They'd quote me as saying, "If you're not bleeding out of your eyeballs, don't come near me about it."

Builders often live in unfinished houses and educators don't always walk the talk they give their students. I recently listened to Trent Dalton, a journalist at *The Australian*, tell a story about the first man he'd ever loved as a child. This man was a hardened criminal, but as the partner of Trent's mother, he cared for her sons like they were his own, protecting them against the evils of his profession. He was able to love his family deeply despite the crimes he committed 'at work'.

Different hats for different places. Arthur may have worn a calmer, more relaxed attitude at home, compared to the fighting cock behaviour he exhibited on the trains. Of course, he may well have been a difficult man to live with but he may not have always been like that. If we consider what life he's come from, we might be able to understand the man's behaviour a little more. To really know Arthur Webster, it's very important to look back at his history and see where he's come from.

When I started to meet extended members of Arthur and Eleanor's respective families, I began to see them as real people, who had a real place in this world, in *my* world. What if Arthur had once been a nice guy?

Eleanor Webster (née Murphy)

One of the journalists I spoke with early in the project asked me what my relationship with Eleanor was. At this stage, I wasn't emotionally invested in these people yet. I was having some fun, on a sort of reverse treasure hunt, and hadn't actually thought much about who the Websters were to me.

Now, after a year of living and breathing everything Webster and Murphy, I have developed a great deal of empathy towards Eleanor, as a mother and as a woman, but to be honest, I don't know her any better now than I did back then. I haven't even seen a picture of her! From her death certificate, I know she was small-statured and I know her extended family called her Aunty Nellie.

It's sad that I don't know Eleanor better and this is where history has let me down. One can't take photos of personalities, so when stories and relationships die as the generations pass by, some of the quieter members of society get forgotten. I can paint a picture around her, but I will never know if she was tough as nails, or meek and mild.

We can make some assumptions about Eleanor from the behaviour she showed with the banking, and of course, the hiding of the money, but that's about all. We may never know what her motivations were. Her husband, Arthur, may be remembered for his infamy as the squeaky wheel on Queensland trains, but this story, right now, pivots all around Eleanor, the quiet Webster achiever.

1914 Arthur and Eleanor buy their First Home

On 29 July 1914, Australia's Governor-General, Sir Ronald Munro Ferguson, was told by the British Government to "adopt precautionary phase" for war, the "names of powers to be communicated later if necessary".

Germany declared war on Russia two days later and proceeded to invade Belgium, who had declared neutrality.

The following day, the Governor-General of Australia proclaimed "the danger of war" and called upon the enlistment of the Citizen Military Forces (now known as the Army Reserve).

On 4 August 1914, less than three weeks after Arthur and Eleanor had welcomed their first child, Morgan, into their family, Great Britain declared war on Germany.

Australia relayed a message to the British Government on that same day saying they would offer up 20 000 men. The reply that came two days later accepted this offer, and asked for the troops to be sent to them as soon as humanly possible.

The recruitment drive that followed in Australia was massive, with propaganda messages at every turn. Songs were sung, and flags were flown, posters papered the streets, shouting words like, "YOUR COUNTRY NEEDS YOU!" and "AUSTRALIANS ARISE!"

The pressure on the young men of Australia was extreme and the appeals were extensive, calling on them to join up, to fight for freedom and peace. Those who stayed would have to prove their worth as essential servicemen, or be treated as cowards.

The shame involved with being a man of serving age who was at home while his fellow countrymen were dying on battlefields was enormous.

Most who chose not to volunteer did so for practical reasons. They had a family to provide for. They had a business to run. Their community depended on them.

Chris Sheedy, Canberra Times, 13 November 2014

Arthur had two reasons not go to war. He was a Locomotive Driver for Queensland Railways, and he was a new father, with family responsibilities. He had a choice, as conscription was not in play at this time – he could stay and provide essential service on the home front, or he could go and fight abroad. Either way, he would save face, and be contributing to the war effort, but to stay at home meant he would remain with his wife and newborn child.

The number of men enlisting for active service at the outbreak of the First World War was high. However, by late 1915, as casualties rose and enlistments fell, the AIF faced a shortage of men. The railway industry was a vital but often unrecognised part of the action, with impact on operations both on the home front and in combat zones (on both "sides" of the conflict). From troop trains to Australian Light Railway Operating Companies on the Western Front, or indentured prisoner of war labour to recruitment trains that travelled across the country, equipped to enlist and dispatch, the rail work on the home front was ever present.

The contribution of railway workers went beyond active service as soldiers and seconded technicians and labourers. Workshops throughout the British Empire maintained production and servicing of rail networks, supplying troops, horses, goods, medical facilities, munitions and equipment, as well as transporting nurses and those wounded for Australia's war effort at home and overseas.

There were hardships and challenges, as well as hope and camaraderie, experienced on the railways both on the battlefront and the home front. Great resourcefulness was applied to adapting technologies to suit a range of purposes.

Teacher Guide, Railways 1914–1918 Exhibition

Eleanor's initial relief and visions of maintaining a normal life with Arthur staying home would have been shattered. QR workers spent more and more time at work during the war years, often doing double shifts, and even with baby Morgan, Eleanor was probably kept busy with her own community efforts. She may well have joined the ranks of women in voluntary organisations contributing to the war effort.

Not only did these women provide comfort for sick and wounded soldiers, they sent troops on the frontline morale-boosting gifts and clothes. The Red Cross Society, for example, began work almost immediately upon the declaration of war, starting knitting circles, teaching handcrafts to convalescing soldiers, mending hospital pyjamas and baking food for military hospitals, both here and overseas.

Rosalie and Milton Patriot Fete 1915
Photograph courtesy of the State Library of Queensland

According to the Australian War Memorial website, the *Order of the White Feather* was founded in Britain in August 1914 as part of a strategy to encourage women to pressure their family and friends into enlisting. White feathers were given to young, fit men who did not volunteer for service.

Arthur continued as a Queensland Rail locomotive driver throughout WWI, potentially experiencing troubles from locals for remaining at home, despite working hard in Brisbane maintaining the transport system. He may never have shared any of this with Eleanor, however, but from all accounts, Arthur Webster got tougher as he got older. Perhaps coming home to his family relieved him of the pressures of the war years, and despite the dark clouds that overshadowed their lives, Nellie and Morgan were Arthur's silver lining.

The idiotic practice of indiscriminately distributing white feathers appears to afford a peculiar pleasure to some people who have impudently taken on themselves the role of judging who should enlist for active service.

If, through an unfortunate lack of brains, this appears to them an effective means of aiding the recruiting movement, they might at least make inquiries as to whether their victims had not already offered to fight for King and country.

Hamilton Spectator, 2 August 1915, p. 4 Trove

As the war years rolled on, Morgan would have spent much more time in his mother's industrious company than with his bluff and bluster father, who would have been exhausted from his work, with little time to spare for his family.

*

In 1917, when it seemed as if the war would never end, Eleanor was blessed with another pregnancy. So many young men who'd enlisted from Queensland Rail had died, and several of their neighbours from Heussler Terrace had lost their sons.

The Hartshorns and the Parkers had lost their boys, and young Fred Lucas had been wounded twice, the second time causing him such shocking facial damage, that he would always need to eat and drink using a straw. The Websters had witnessed so much loss by this time, the news of a baby on the way would have been a shining beacon at the end of a very long, dark and horrifying tunnel.

It was more than apt, then, that Colin Webster was born on Valentine's Day, 1918, a reflection of the love they all needed, and a reminder that joy was still possible, even in the midst of war.

2018 Finding Colin Webster

I love cemeteries as much as I love libraries. For me it's like walking into a room full of books where most of the words have been washed away by time. Each headstone represents a life with more stories than anyone could ever hear, yet so many of those stories have never been heard, having gone to the grave with their owner.

Many years ago, I visited a tiny chapel in a village just outside of Bath, in England, and spent some quiet time wandering through the graveyard with my mother-in-law, Kay, also a lover of history and stories. We met one another in the middle with the same question... *Why were there so many graves here with the same date of death, outside of the war years?*

Between us, we counted more than twenty-five, mostly children, and besides feeling terribly sad that so many had died from a village simultaneously, our curiosity was piqued.

A short time later, we asked some questions at the local pub which gave us the answer we sought. It had been a plane crash, with the village basketball team and several adults escorting them, on board. A terrible tragedy that these villagers had barely recovered from, two generations later.

On the first day of research, some of the members of the UTL Team had discovered that Arthur and Eleanor Webster were buried at the Toowong Cemetery, which is just at the end of my street. I pass the extensive grounds several times a day and have spent many an interested hour walking through the stones, wondering about those who lay beneath them.

It was already becoming important for me to connect with these people. After only 48 hours, we knew so much about them, and I felt myself being drawn into a significant journey of discovery, but I couldn't get a feel for who they were. I needed more.

As we left the house on that cold late-August morning, the children and I grabbed our umbrellas. The rain was falling steadily – perfect weather to take the children to Toowong Cemetery to go grave hunting. It felt very exciting to know that Arthur and Eleanor were there, the closest I had been to them yet. We took the long route from the western entrance so I could build up the suspense, taking the opportunity for some supplementary education as we drove around the uneven streets and lanes.

We parked at the front entrance, and met with Wendy at the little City Council office, in order to get directions – this woman is a true gem... she has been known to direct people, on the telephone, step by step, gravestone by gravestone, until they find what they're looking for. On this day, however, once we had the approximate location of the Websters' grave site, off we went on a treasure hunt by ourselves. The rain had stopped to allow us easy trespass, lending just the right atmosphere for our endeavours, with dark grey skies and water dropping off branches landing noisily on the dead leaves all around us.

When we finally found their headstone, it was a sombre moment. Not only did it make Arthur and Eleanor real to me, it gave us some unexpected news. My children always get very sad when they see babies and children on headstones, and this was no exception.

Arthur and Eleanor were not alone in their grave. There was a baby buried in there with them. As I sat there pondering this new information, I suddenly understood what could have happened to set this family's path askew.

1918 Colin Webster

Colin Webster passed away two weeks short of Christmas, 1918, aged 9 months and three weeks. Doctor Kelly would note cause of death as Gastroenteritis, Colitis, Acidosis and Coma.

Colin Webster's Death Certificate 1918, Office of BDM

*

One doesn't need to be a counsellor or a social worker to understand the massive impact the loss of a baby has on a family. Colin was not even 10 months old when he died, full of the joys of life a baby exhibits at that precious time – smiling, giggling, laughing, starting to talk and learning to crawl.

Colin's brother, Morgan, was four years old and no doubt loved his baby brother deeply.

I can easily picture the panic that Eleanor must have gone through when she was unable to manage Colin's illness. The constant boiling of sheets and nappies in the copper downstairs, the washing line strung across the back yard, always hanging heavy and low. The sleepless nights with a baby screaming in pain would have been enough to drive them all to distraction.

What had she done when she found him unresponsive in his bed? Was Arthur with her, running to the Paddington ice-works for blocks of ice to cool his fevered body down? Or did he go to work, leaving Eleanor alone to manage a sick baby and a four-year-old child? Morgan might have been bundled off to the Dowdles next door when the doctor came, and after Colin died, perhaps neither Morgan nor his father were given the opportunity to see the baby before he was buried.

It has been said by many people in history that 'back in those days, people lost many babies, and just got on with it'. In large families, several babies and young children might die, and their names would carry forward to the next child of the same sex. With few options for contraception, it often wasn't long before a grieving mother was pregnant again, with little or no time to grieve for the baby she'd lost.

There are no records of Eleanor having any further pregnancies, and the one thing I always hate hearing about history is, *It was the way of things back then – people just got back in the saddle and moved on with their lives.*

I don't believe that for one red hot second. Grief and loss can be hidden deeply when life gets in the way of the feelings one experiences after such a traumatic event. How many hours did women used to spend crying in solitude for their lost children – behind closed doors, in pantry cupboards, in bathrooms, beside their beds and on the kitchen floor? How many men would have no idea how to manage their feelings, heading off to work to drown their grief in hard labour, and later, at the pub? How much domestic violence has manifested from untapped wells of grief and personal suffering?

As a nurse and counsellor, I have worked with grieving parents for many years through the Royal Women's Hospital, *Sands Queensland* (Miscarriage, Stillbirth and Newborn Death support) and *The Compassionate Friends*, who support families after a child dies.

I have been a willing witness to the huge pain and loss that families feel when they lose a child. I have watched my amazing mother, Sue Fernandes, a midwife and baby artist, draw hundreds of portraits of stillborn babies while working for Sands over the last 30 years. She let me read the letters of countless parents who drew comfort from her pictures because they had nothing else to remember the face of their lost child.

When a child dies, families begin a long journey along the tortuous and never-ending path of bereavement. They will experience different and shattering kinds of feelings, at any one time... disbelief, sadness, deep anguish, loneliness, fear, jealousy, anger, regret. Often, those feelings of grief are so intense, that parents do not understand what is happening to them or to their partner and other children.

It's no secret that many marriages fall apart after the death of a child. You're the same people, but at the same time, you're really not. Everyone changes throughout the course of a marriage, but it's rarely so sudden and complete. So you have to get to know each other again in one of the most harrowing circumstances imaginable.

No two people grieve the same, even when they're grieving the same loss. One partner might be very vocal about how he or she is feeling, while the other is quiet. One might express grief in "traditional" ways (crying, etc.), while the other does things his or her partner finds odd.

You're also rarely grieving on the same "cycles," so to speak. Sometimes you resent your partner for bringing you down when you're having a good day. Sometimes, you feel guilty for bringing your partner down.

Heather Spohr, The Hard Truth about Staying Married after Losing a Child, Huffington Post 23 July 2014

Just a fleeting thought of ever losing my own children is enough to make me weep, so to stand in front of this family grave and imagine what they went through in 1918, towards the end of the Great War when the world had already lost so much, was humbling and sorrowful.

I desperately wanted to reach out to Eleanor and Arthur, to tell them I understood some of what they'd been through and it was at that moment that I fully invested in this family's story.

I drew my children in close for a hug, cleared a few weeds and errant pebbles, and took some photographs to share with the group.

14 February 2018 It just occurred to me that Colin Webster would have turned 100 years old today. I sat with those thoughts for a few minutes, closed my eyes and slowly disappeared back in time...

Reverie... Milton, 1918
(this is the fiction bit)

Australia had a population of less than five million people in 1914, at the beginning of World War I. One in ten of Australia's population enlisted. By the end of the war, over 60 000 of those had been killed, and over 170 000 were wounded, gassed or captured – just under half of the men who went to war. The other half were left with the massive psychological wounds of warfare.

And then there were those who had stayed at home, to work in the essential services, or who'd been deemed unfit for active duty. Their suffering was of a different type, and many of these men were unable to avoid their feelings of shame and grief. Add their own personal losses of family, friends and neighbours into that scenario, and it's easy to see what a huge impact this world event had on the people of our country, and of course, the western world.

So much death, so much to grieve, and then in the midst of watching their community fall apart, Arthur, Eleanor and Morgan lost Colin.

How could Eleanor cry on the shoulder of a neighbour who'd just lost her only son in battle? How could she weep in the arms of her best friend, whose husband had returned from the war in a wheelchair, unable to give her the child she'd always dreamed of? "Consider yourself lucky you have Morgan"... "You can always have another baby"... "You have no right to complain"...

She spent many hours on her knees in the little chapel of the Holy Spirit next to the Bishopsbourne behind her house, tears rolling down her face as she asked Him why? She had lost such a big part of herself the day Colin was taken from her and she had no idea how to get it back. She should have taken him to the doctor sooner. She should have done more. It was all her fault. Nobody understood, few people listened and the one person she should have been talking to about her sadness was in a world of hurt, too.

How could Arthur share his pain and suffering with his colleagues at work? The ones who might have left him that white feather?

He was angry. He was angry with himself, first and foremost, believing he could have saved his son if he'd found a doctor sooner. He hadn't been as worried about the baby as Eleanor, and had gone to work, ignoring her request to get the doctor earlier that day.

Arthur wrongly believed that Eleanor blamed him too, so in his shame, he kept his distance. He shut himself off from his wife and from Morgan. Without Eleanor's love and support to guide him, Arthur took out his pain and anger on the rest of his world, physically at work, and emotionally at home.

Morgan knew to leave his mother alone when she was inside the stone chapel. He knew she would be there for a long time, talking to Colin and to God. He played outside on the rock walls, counting pebbles and stacking stones, talking to his little brother, too. Morgan explained to Colin, glancing up to the clouds from time to time, that he was sorry for praying to God to make the crying stop on the last night he saw him. When he had woken up the following morning, Colin was gone.

Morgan hadn't meant for God to take his baby brother away forever.

He believed it was his fault that Colin wasn't there anymore, and that he was the sole cause for his parents' misery. His mother reminded him of one of his wooden toys – she worked the same, keeping house and making sure good meals were on the table, but she'd lost the spark that kept the home fires burning.

The only time Eleanor hugged Morgan was when she would crawl into his bed in the small hours of the morning, when she thought he was asleep. Holding him like a teddy bear, his mother would cry quietly into his pillow, until she had no tears left. Morgan was always awake when she did this, but lay there still as a rock, more frightened and alone than he had ever been in his life because he knew she wasn't holding him. His mother was holding Colin.

Whatever love Morgan had felt from his father had gone with his little brother. He watched Arthur go to work for longer and longer shifts, taking as many extras as he could. He would fall into bed at the end of his 14 hours days, sleep dreamlessly and do it all over again the following day. He barely even acknowledged Morgan.

Eleanor never ran Arthur another bath, never washed the stress of the day from his shoulders and never looked him deeply in the eyes again.

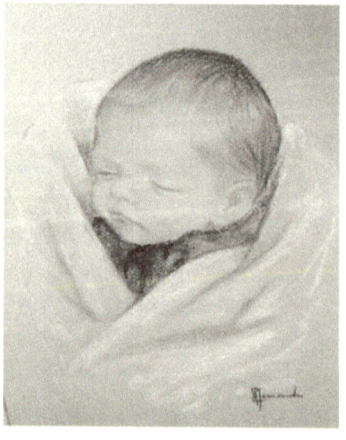

I dedicate this chapter to the families of lost children, to the people who love and support them, and to the community organisations like Sands and Compassionate Friends, who continue to walk beside those who grieve, always there to help us remember our angels.

Morgan Webster

When I discovered Morgan Webster's name on Arthur and Eleanor's gravestone on my visit to Toowong Cemetery, it was a light-bulb moment. It was only a few days into the investigation, and we hadn't come across Morgan's name yet.

Morgan was the heir we'd been looking for.

Using a variety of investigative methods, we were able to build up a picture of this man, in our efforts to discover whether he had any family still living, and why the money may have been hidden under the lino.

I interviewed neighbours who still remember Morgan, and met relatives who'd had a relationship with him. The UTL Community traced archival records back to his school, which answered some questions for us, and discovered newspaper articles from the 1940s, using Trove, which gave us more clues about this man – in our pursuit of answers.

Elderly railwaymen, who used to work with Morgan's father, Arthur, were able to give me some hints about Morgan's family life, and finally, because of the Courier Mail article about the Under the Lino Project, the Morrow family tracked me down to tell me what Morgan was like to live with because they'd moved in with Arthur and his son after Eleanor died in 1960.

Some people have questioned why the necessity to delve into the life of Morgan Webster, and we have always been able to justify it as 'investigative history' because we were looking for heirs, as well as trying to solve mysteries about hidden money. Information we have gleaned has opened up more about this man's life than we expected, and as a result, we have had to learn how to walk very carefully in the valley of public discussion.

You'll see what I mean in a minute...

Soon after the end of WWI, Morgan started his formal education at Milton State School. My own children attended the same school, and when I went to speak to the Year 6 students about the Under the Lino Project, they were delighted to know that Morgan had attended the school, walked the hallways and played on the oval just as they did. They loved the old black and white pictures I'd sourced, showing that not a lot had changed… children still played ball games and did Phys. Ed.

Milton State School, 1951 Queensland State Archives

All accounts from this time suggest that Morgan was an extremely clever person. He used to play with an abacus as a child, and had a propensity for numbers like nobody else. Morgan attendance at Brisbane Grammar in his senior school years was a mystery to us for a little while. How could the son of a railwayman and a house wife, with an income of just over £5 a week, be able to attend a prestigious Brisbane boys' school?

Maureen summed up why this was so important in our investigations when questioned by another member…

Maureen *It's interesting – Morgan's dad was an Engine Driver yet there was the money to send the son to Grammar…*
Bob *That savings bank account may be the answer.*
Maureen *I suppose he could have got a scholarship.*

A photograph in the newspaper, discovered by several members using Trove, supported Maureen's prediction…

THALLON MEDALLISTS

CHILDREN OF RAILWAYMEN.

THE FOUR WINNERS.

The Thallon gold medals, which help to preserve the memory of a former Commissioner for Railways, are awarded to the sons and daughters of Queensland railway employees who made the best passes in the Junior University Examination for 1928. Pictures and particulars of the winners appear below.

MASTER M. WEBSTER.
Master Morgan Webster is the son of Mr. Arthur Webster, engine driver, Brisbane, and was a pupil at the Milton State State school. He gained a State school scholarship at the age of 11 years, and at the recent Junior Public Examination secured a very creditable pass. He is a pupil of the Brisbane Boys Grammar School.

Brisbane Courier Saturday 4 May 1929, page 20
The Week, Brisbane, Friday 10 May 1929, page 9

The Thallon Medal

In 1908, the Commissioner for Railways, James Forsyth Thallon, established a fund which introduced the Thallon Medal for outstanding results to the student with the highest marks in the annual first aid examinations. Following his death in 1911, the fund was used to provide a further two gold medals annually. From 1912 to 1962, one medal was awarded to the son and one to the daughter of a Queensland Railway employee who achieved the highest results in the State Scholarship Examination. The Thallon Medal is still awarded today and is considered to be one of the most sought-after and prestigious medals a Queensland Railway employee can receive.
Memoirs of the Queensland Museum

James Forsyth Thallon 1847–1911
Commissioner for Railways 1902–1911

An odd coincidence had me contacting the archivist at Brisbane Grammar School – at this early stage of the investigation, I wasn't really aware that schools had archivists, so needed a little prompting from the Universe to get me looking in the right direction.

I was visiting my local printer Martin, at *Brisbane Digital Imaging* in Milton, to get some work copied. I was admiring the new layout of his workshop, and commented on some large framed pictures of black and white school photos leaning against a wall.

Martin explained that he'd had a lot of work coming in from schools for restoration, which started a chat about the Under the Lino Project. I'd just discovered that Morgan Webster had been both a Milton State School and a Brisbane Grammar student.

I saw Martin look at me strangely while I prattled on, and then he leaned over to a pile of black and white photographs within arm's reach. He smiled as he showed me an order form pinned to the plastic bag which contained them.

It said, *Vivien Harris, Brisbane Grammar Archivist.*

Well, knock me over with a feather! Apparently, she was due to collect these old photographs that he'd restored and if I'd been able to hang around I may have met her that morning. As it was, all I needed was her name and number, and off I went – serendipity had struck again, pointing me in the right direction.

As has been the way of this project, whenever I open my mouth to tell people about the Under the Lino story, they will undoubtedly have something worthwhile to offer that takes us closer to the answers we seek.

I contacted Vivien and explained about the project, and within a few days, she'd sent me information about Morgan. So, now we have the answer to the question, *How could the Websters have afforded to send Morgan to Brisbane Grammar?*

All roads this far point to the fact that Morgan was a very intelligent and diligent young man, who worked hard at his studies and was afforded scholarships to both the Brisbane Grammar School and the University of Queensland, where he commenced a Bachelor of Commerce in 1931, qualifying as an accountant.

NAME: MORGAN WEBSTER

Source: *Brisbane Grammar School General Register*, Vol 2, p. 267
Date of entry: 3rd Quarter 1926
Previous school: Milton State School [state scholarship]
Age: 16 July 1914 [born]
Parent's name and address: A.W.J. Webster, Heussler Terrace, Milton
Date of leaving: December 1930
Career in School: Passed Queensland Junior Public Exam 1928
Awarded Thallon Medal 1928
Passed Queensland Senior Public Exam 1930
"Able and industrious"
On leaving School Went to work in the Commonwealth Bank

Brisbane Grammar School Magazine, June 1930, p. 33
Winners of Scholarships (Open, Social Service, B.G.S.) to the University of Queensland.
Top left: M. Webster (A.J. Mason Scholarship)

And he continued studying well into his 40s... An account from Noel Condon, who used to work with Arthur on the trains, suggested his father was not happy with Morgan's chosen profession and career.

"Arthur had no friends, but he talked to me about his son. He said to me, *He's over 40 and he's still studying, boy! He's still studying!*"

Morgan joined what is now the Commonwealth Banking Corporation on 12 January 1931, and after serving in several parts of Queensland before 1944, he spent the majority of his career at the CBA in Queen Street, retiring on 12 July 1979, shortly after his father's death.

*

Morgan's Marriage

Trove records show that Morgan, aged 25, married a woman called Gladys Rachel May Hack, from 10 Annie Street, Torwood. Their wedding was on 25 August 1939 at St Albans, in Auchenflower.

AUCHENFLOWER CEREMONY

Webster—Hack

ST. ALBAN'S Church of England, Auchenflower, was decorated with white and pink lilies and sweet peas on August 25 for the marriage of Miss Gladys Rachel May Hack (only daughter of Mrs. W. G. Hack and the late Mr. W. G. Hack, Auchenflower) and Mr. Morgan Webster, Cairns (only son of Mr. and Mrs. A. Webster, Milton)

The Courier Mail 30 August 1939 p 2

Keep in mind that at this stage, we were still looking for heirs. This was exciting for the group to find this information, because usually, people started having a family after they married.

What happened next came as a shock and surprise to us all.

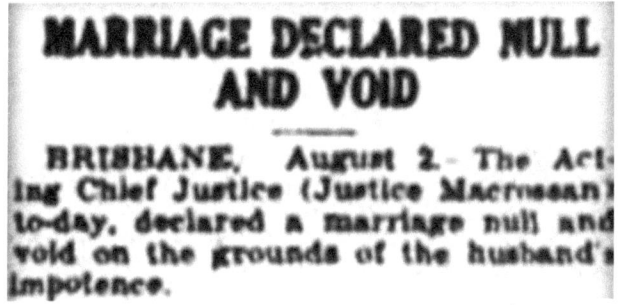

Townsville Daily Bulletin 03 August 1944 p 1

Noel Condon also remembered that Arthur's son had been written about in the Sunday Truth one weekend. Even after 60 years, Noel still recalled the article about Morgan's unfortunate marriage and his inability to consummate.

"In order for people to get a divorce back then," Noel recalled, "they had to prove that their spouse was having an affair. So private detectives used to force themselves in to people's houses on a Saturday evening, while the chap usually leapt out the back window pulling up his trousers. Then the next morning the paper would write it all up."

In this case, Gladys Webster (née Hack) had asked for an annulment – her plea was non-consummation. According to Noel's memory of conversations with Arthur, Morgan had been born with a physical deformity that precluded him from having a sexual relationship. It came out in the newspaper evidence – Morgan had no function at all, and was unable to consummate his marriage or have children.

The effect that this information had on the group was similar for most of us. Firstly, it was so sad to see information such as this splashed across the newspapers of the day. Having one's personal life on display on social media, by choice, is nothing compared to airing personal stories such as this for the whole world to see.

Harry *It was the old Matrimonial Causes Act, civil proceedings brought before the Supreme Court. By the mid-20th Century, it was achieved by consensual and 'outrageous' evidence, confessions of 'misconduct'.*

But by then it was well-known that a bored couple, lacking real grounds, would privately agree and arrange for some willing friend to act-out the role of 'co-respondent' (when nothing had happened at all!). I know someone who persuaded a work colleague to sign a co-respondent affidavit 'admitting' to 'fabricated misconduct' to enable the dissolution, and even the Court would know it was baloney. Or conversely, a ground was 'non-fulfilment'.

> ### The Matrimonial Causes Act 1959
>
> *The Act provided 14 grounds for the grant of a decree of dissolution of marriage ('divorce'), including adultery, desertion, cruelty, habitual drunkenness, imprisonment and insanity. To succeed on one of these grounds, a spouse had to prove marital fault. In reality, obtaining proof often necessitated hiring a solicitor and/or a private detective to collect evidence to support the claim (e.g. statements from witnesses, photographs and hotel receipts). Such processes usually involved great expense, making it difficult for the less wealthy to access them. The media reported the salacious and intimate details of some cases (e.g. those involving celebrities), thereby adding an element of public humiliation to the system. The system was designed to permit genuinely injured spouses to end their marriages, but it was also intended to protect the institution of marriage by not permitting bored or disillusioned spouses to divorce at will (e.g. the law did not permit couples to consent to a divorce).*
>
> **Australian Parliamentary Library**

Jay *Bringing that change to matrimonial law was one thing the Whitlam gov't did that improved the lives of many families. The lies that had to be created to enable willing couples to part ways...*

> ### *The Family Law Act 1975*
>
> *Enacted in 1975 by the Australian government, this change was led by then Prime Minister Gough Whitlam. One of the main innovations was the introduction of no-fault divorce. Couples no longer needed to show grounds for divorce, but instead, just that their relationship had suffered an irreconcilable breakdown.*
>
> **Wikipedia**

Secondly, we may have solved the question of surviving heirs...

Vivianne *That was the way they did divorces in those days – you knew if you wanted to file for divorce then all the muck would be raked up and put in the papers – the fact that people still filed meant they were determined to get out of the marriage.*
Kym *Pretty lurid for 1944 and as others have said how sad it had to be broadcast for all to hear just so she could end the marriage.*
Emma *My grandparents' divorce was prominent in the papers because it was linked to an assault and extortion... fascinating to read because of the style of the writing but must have been quite embarrassing*
Marisa *By stating that the husband was impotent, they were able to declare the marriage 'null and void' i.e. never valid, therefore avoiding divorce. As awful as this accusation is, it's actually beneficial for both parties if they wished to remarry in the Catholic Church (assuming this was the case with them in the first place)*

Group members spent quite some time looking for Gladys's son after hearing that she'd remarried. They checked electoral rolls for current addresses and letters of a general nature were posted but we didn't hear anything back from anyone.

In the interests of privacy, I decided to leave that part of the investigation alone. Suffice to say that six years after the annulment of her marriage to Morgan Webster, Gladys Hack remarried and gave birth to a son in 1952. It's enough that we have them on the family tree, and given the rest of the information we have about Morgan, there was really no need to investigate this part any further. It doesn't add to the story at all, and we're all happy to know that Gladys was able to have a second chance at having a family.

Morgan seemed to have disappeared from their marriage in 1942 before Gladys applied for annulment in 1944. Electoral roll records show that Morgan moved in with Arthur and Eleanor after his marriage dissolved.

According to family reports, Morgan took care of his parents, doing all the shopping, cooking and driving. He continued to live in this house after his mother passed away in 1958, and then, after his father died in 1976.

The Dangers of Researching Other People's Stories

Because of this project, I have developed a new appreciation for the difficulties experienced by biographers and journalists. They spend countless hours researching their subjects, trying to get the facts straight, as well as providing an interesting read for their audience. It's all fine and well to write a completely factual story about John and Jane Doe who lived a wonderful life and never really did anything. The only people who would actually love that tale would be John and Jane.

We all like to hear interesting stories that showcase people who have gone above and beyond, or below and behind, in the case of the more macabre tales. My children's favourite show on *ABC iView* last year was *Horrible Histories*. No longer are children bored with monotone recounts of explorers, wars and monarchs.

Now, with the use of technology, they can become witnesses to the clash of cultures and atrocities that followed exploration.

They can experience the dangerous exploits of Ned Kelly, watching in rapt horror as the blood sprays out from every bullet hole in his armour onto the camera lens. They can see the heads being chopped off all of Henry the VIII's wives and hear them thud as they hit the floor. The gorier the better. Their imaginations explode and their nerve endings spark with the truth and reality of what happened in the past.

As we enter modern history, the events are no less horrific, but we have a duty of care when reporting them. Our UTL group has been very careful to remain non-judgemental about information we have revealed, but occasionally, personal experiences, opinions and beliefs have been challenged. It's been the responsibility of every member of the team to remind each other from time to time about the gravity of discussing other people's lives.

The tacky newspapers of the day were called the Tattler and the Truth, and they were responsible for naming and shaming people and events. Reporters would hear a tip, or be paid off to catch someone out, doing midnight raids for a juicy story. Many of those articles are still available online, so gone is the adage, "Today's news is lining tomorrow's rubbish bins." All news in this country, thanks to the internet and social media, is available for anyone to dredge up, at any time.

Thankfully, articles about non-consummation aren't printed in the paper anymore, but we still had access to this information and shared it far and wide. It reached further than we intended…

John *Let's stick as close to the facts as possible and not jump to unsupported conclusions. Stuff that is put out on the internet gets a life of its own. Morgan will have family that are still alive and some of the supposition borders on defamation.*

Morgan is obviously not alive to be concerned by this, nor does he have any direct descendants, but I was still reminded by a family member that he would be horrified to have his personal life discussed by strangers in this forum.

After the Courier Mail article about this project came out in the paper, I received a message from a family member called Jennifer...

I am related to Morgan Webster via my late mother. Morgan visited us in the family home, quite often bringing a box of chocolates for my mother. He was a very proper little man, always dressed in a neat suit, and very genuinely religious. He would be mortified to have his sexuality discussed. My mother told me a slightly different version, but she was fond of Morgan and may have erred on the side of kindness!
Jennifer

I was truly shaken at first when I read this message. It was a startling reminder that we were telling someone else's story, and should tread carefully. While I wanted everyone in the world to read that article, Jennifer made a good point. Morgan wouldn't have.

Feeling quite sick about the thought of offending one of Morgan's relatives, I knew I had to make it right with her as soon as possible. I responded very carefully, after a lot of thought.

Dear Jennifer,
Thank you for getting in touch with me regarding the Websters. I am very happy to make contact with you and would love to talk more about Morgan. It is always difficult with a community research project when information arises that might impact negatively on a person.

I remember when we first discovered the newspaper articles about Morgan's marriage annulment – we are a decent group of people who are just looking for answers and we walked pretty carefully around this topic, not knowing the full story, even to this day.

Your point is well made about Morgan being mortified about people discussing his sexuality. I can't imagine what it was like for him to have it published in the papers while he was alive.

His father's colleagues all knew about it at work and it was a common way for them to tease Arthur I have been told, behind his back though.

I want to assure you that in writing the book, I am taking particular care when discussing facts, reminding readers to keep an open mind and kind heart towards these people we didn't meet but feel we know.

I am writing this story with full respect to the memory of this branch of your family, and I appreciate you getting in touch. I'd be interested to hear what your mother had to say about Morgan, to be held in confidence unless you give me permission to write about it. I want to give Morgan his due as a kind hearted man.

Kind regards, Caylie Jeffery

To which she replied...

Dear Caylie

Thank you for your considerate e-mail. I am happy to communicate further with you, though I do not know a great deal about Morgan's parents, except my mother called her Aunty Nellie, and I believe she and Morgan were very close.

I have no knowledge of his father except what I have read. I have contacted my siblings to gain any extra information that may help you. My younger sister remembers visiting Morgan's house.

Regards, Jennifer

Other family members who had read the article in the Courier Mail were delighted with the piece Leanne Edmistone wrote. They reassured me that they were not in the least offended about mentioning Morgan's sexual history in the papers of today.

Those articles from long ago were available at that time for everybody to look at and we are completely entitled to discuss it now, in terms of historical reference.

Even still, it was a good lesson, and has made me extremely cautious and mindful, as you'll see later when I share the experience of researching the Milton murders...

Eleanor's Death

Extensive research found that Eleanor Webster died of heart failure on 24 August 1958, at an address in Wilston. She was 72 years old. The post-mortem showed that Eleanor was a small woman with a slim build. She'd been to the GP the day before complaining of chest pain. On the day of her death, she sat down in a chair at the house she was visiting, had a heart attack and died.

When Lyn told us that Eleanor had died at 47 Montpelier Street, we looked at people who'd lived in that house at the time, with a view to perhaps finding some living relatives. They might know more about the Websters' habits and behaviours, and why Eleanor might have been hiding money. Perhaps they could help us fill in some back story.

Electoral Roll records showed that the O'Donnell family lived at that address in 1958...

>John Vincent O'Donnell (1889–1970)
>Ellen Imelia O'Donnell (née Haren) (1895–1989)
>And their children
>Josephine O'Donnell (1921–2007)
>Veronica Ellen O'Donnell (1926–2006)
>Married Robert Anderson 1953
>[Children Trish and Helen]
>Bernard John O'Donnell (1928–2015) was an officer and
>Dental Surgeon in the Royal Australian Navy
>Married Narelle Knight Wyer 1953

We all wanted to know what the connection was between the families, so we compared dates of birth, where they grew up, what schools they'd attended, where they'd worked and lived as adults, and what they did in their retirement years.

John Vincent O'Donnell was retired at the time, but had worked all his life (by the look of it) in the Post and Telegraph Office, ending up as a Postmaster. He was born in Brisbane. His wife, Ellen, was born somewhere in Queensland according to her birth registration.

They married in 1918, at Herberton, presumably in Ellen's home town. They probably met while John was working in the Post and Telegraph Office – between Gatton in 1915 and Georgetown, where he lived with Ellen in 1919. Before this, he was in Cairns and surrounds for several years. Ellen's father, Patrick Haren, who died in July 1897, is buried at the McLeod Street Cemetery in Cairns. John and Ellen could even have met in Cairns.

MARRIAGE.

O'DONNELL — HAREN.—On the 31st August, 1918, at St. Patrick's Church, Herberton, by the Rev. Father Downey, John Vincent, second eldest son of Mr. and Mrs. J. O'Donnell, Herberton, to Ellen Emelda (Nellie), youngest daughter of Mrs. E. Haren, Mareeba.

The Northern Herald Thursday 19 September 1918 Trove

It appears that the O'Donnells were just friends of the Websters, although we don't know *how* they knew each other.

Cheryl *I found what looks like other extended family members living in the Milton, Auchenflower and Toowong areas, with children who possibly went to Milton SS. Maybe Morgan knew them from Cairns and it is possible that Arthur could have met them if he drove troop trains to Cairns when Morgan lived there. I feel that there was a connection with them and St Albans, Auchenflower, and St Albans, The Grange, which was around the corner from Montpelier St.*

There was some evidence that before the O'Donnell family bought their house, it was owned by the Hornibrook family, which was interesting for a little while – I mean, we all have fond memories of the famous wobbly Hornibrook Highway Bridge over to Redcliffe – but it was a red herring to our process because we needed the people who were living in the house when Eleanor died, in 1958.

Michelle *The Haren family seem to have included railway workers, so perhaps a connection there?*
Kerry *Some Post Offices were agents for the Commonwealth Bank, insomuch as you could withdraw limited funds. My parents did this if we were visiting a country town. Just food for thought. The post office employee could do the bank transactions. I was wondering if they could have met across the counter.*
Diana *They still are Commonwealth Bank agents in some small towns Kerry. In the small town we lived in until four years ago, there was no Commonwealth bank so any banking was done through post office.*

John O'Donnell, top left
Photograph Courtesy of National Archives of Australia

Ellen O'Donnell's brother, John Haren, worked for Queensland Rail from 1911-1940 in Cairns, so it may be that John was a friend of Morgan's via Arthur's QR connections.

Catherine *I remember going to Milton State School with a girl called Ann Haren in 1950 (Year 3), who might be related to Ellen Haren. It is possible that's how Eleanor knew the O'Donnells – through Ellen Haren, who may have lived in the area... Ann was a new girl to the school when Catherine met her and quite exotic – possibly a niece or nephew relation to Ellen's side of the family?*

We chose to leave the thread of research alone at this point because it was taking us further and further away from the goal. It is possible that the O'Donnell's grandchildren might still be alive, and know something about Eleanor's death... They may have photographs of their grandparents with Arthur or Eleanor Webster, or overheard discussions about Eleanor's death at their grandparents' home in Wilston in 1958.

Maybe one of them is reading this right now, and is about to call me...

*

Cheryl, a very active member of the UTL Team, with an eye for detail, has been an incredible asset to this project, often noticing things that have slipped past the rest of us.

Cheryl *No wonder Eleanor had chest pains. I was looking at her family events and deaths... I took this from a tree on Ancestry.com*
Death of sister, Agnes, on 25 August 1954 (the 4th anniversary of her death was the day after Eleanor's death)
Death of brother, Frederick, on 2 May 1958 (less than four months before Eleanor's death)
Death of brother, Frank, on 4 August 1958 (three weeks before Eleanor's death) and...
OMG Eleanor died on Arthur's birthday!

It would have been easy to miss all of these significant dates, without a visual timeline. Dates like this provided so much more information, as well as giving many of us a sense of compassion for the Webster-Murphy family.

This information also suggested that Eleanor not only had a family history of heart disease (her own mother died very young), but that she had been experiencing a high amount of family stress in the years and months preceding her own death, losing three siblings in a very short space of time.

Because it was Arthur's birthday, it was highly likely that Arthur and Morgan were present at the time of Eleanor's death, and as it was a Sunday evening, it was unlikely they'd have been on public transport. We had considered that Eleanor may have caught a tram to the address from Milton, and walked up the steep hill to the house, which could have been the tipping point for her heart attack – the result of some excellent sleuthing from the team. However, we know that Morgan did all the driving in the family, because even though Arthur owned a car, he didn't drive.

Lou *No cardiology clinics like now. Family history of heart disease? Probably didn't even know that was what it was. Just suck on Quickeze and have a Bex and have a lie down! And we know now that women's heart attack symptoms are often more subtle than the crushing chest pain. Poor Eleanor.*
Kym *Even if they knew what the problem was, no CABG surgery or similar back then (or statins) to give you a second chance*

We can only imagine how stressful it would have been for Eleanor's family and friends to witness her passing.

Betty Shanks

During the search for information about Eleanor Webster, Lyn discovered that Eleanor had died in 1958 on Montpelier St, Wilston. Many, many people over the age of 60 in Queensland know the significance of Montpelier Street, Wilston, and it all revolves around a woman called Betty Shanks.

Nathan *A bit off topic but the O'Donnell's must have lived across the road from Betty Shanks, the poor girl who was murdered in 1952. She lived at number 52. If you look at her case, lots of witnesses were interviewed. It's possible and probably a very long shot that you may dig up some names that may still be alive and could've known the O'Donnell's to some extent.*
Kathy *Montpelier Road Wilston was the street of Betty Shanks who was brutally murdered in 1952. Poor young woman was walking home from tram terminus.*
Cheryl *Betty was murdered cnr Thomas & Carberry Sts.*
Pauline *Diagonally across the road from 47 Montpelier St is no, 54. This was the home of Betty Shanks. Not sure if you know the case, but it's one of Brisbane's early murders (1952), and still unsolved. Interestingly Frank Bischoff, who we mentioned the other night was involved in the investigation.*

Unsolved Murder of Betty Shanks, 60th Anniversary 15 Sep 2012
by Myles Sinnamon, Project Coordinator
State Library of Queensland Blog
(Printed with permission)

Betty Thomson Shanks. Murdered on 19 September 1952 at The Grange. September marks the 60th anniversary of Queensland's oldest cold case, the murder of Betty Shanks. It's a crime that shocked Queenslanders to the core due to the brutality of the murder and the apparent lack of motive.

Queensland Police are still offering a reward of $50,000 for any new information which leads to the arrest and conviction of the killer. However with the passing of each year it appears likely the case will remain unsolved.

On the evening of 19 September 1952, Betty Shanks was travelling home to the Brisbane suburb of Wilston after attending a night lecture at the State Commercial High School. Betty was 23 years old, a University of Queensland graduate and a Commonwealth public servant with the Department of Interior. Betty had grown up in the neighbourhood and still lived with her parents.

Betty was last seen alive at 9:32 pm departing a tram at the Days Road Tram Terminus. It was only a short walk from the terminus at The Grange to home on Montpelier Street, Wilston, walking via Thomas Street.

Sometime before 10pm screams were heard by several residents. Many believed it was teenagers misbehaving in the nearby Wilston State School grounds. An off-duty policeman, Alex Stewart, heard the screams, but after looking out his window and seeing nothing he returned to bed.

According to newspaper accounts Betty's father David had stayed up when she did not return home. At 1:30am her parents reported her missing to the local police.

The next morning at 5:39am Alex Stewart went outside to collect his newspaper when he discovered the body of Betty Shanks in his neighbour's front garden. This was on the corner of Thomas and Carberry Street, only 150 metres from the tram terminus. Stewart immediately notified the CIB and 15 detectives rushed to the scene.

The scene was an especially grizzly one. Betty had been savagely kicked, beaten and then strangled. Although her underwear had been removed there was no evidence of sexual assault. Police speculated that the killer may have been disturbed when Alex Stewart switched on his light. It appeared that theft was not the motive as her jewellery and handbag were not taken, although the contents of her handbag were scattered all over the yard.

Betty's parents both spoke to the media in the days following her murder. David Shanks told reporters, "little did I know such a shocking thing had happened to Betty on a street she had known ever since she was a toddler".

In an interview with the Sunday Truth newspaper on 21 September 1952, Betty's mother spoke fondly of her daughter: "She was all every mother could wish for, in a daughter. We were a real team. Everything we did we did together...I know of no enemies of Betty's. She was the type of girl everybody loved. My husband will be lost without her. They were particular pals."

Police team investigating the murder of Betty Shanks Brisbane, September 1952. Detective Inspector Frank Bischof confers with investigators at the scene of the crime. Detectives Bauer and Mahoney consult their notes

Concern in the community intensified after the murder due to its brutal nature, the lack of motive and the fear the killer would strike again. People were locking their doors and windows. Newspapers were dubbing the killer as a "sexual maniac" which only heighten the fear. School teachers at the nearby Wilston State School made sure children kept to the opposite side of the road to where the body was found. There was also alarm among the residents of Wilston and The Grange that the killer was a local. CIB Inspector Donovan said there was no cause for panic but advised girls not to stay out late unattended.

Over the years there has been plenty of speculation about this vicious crime, including possible suspects and a number of false confessions. However despite this, no one has ever been arrested.

Last photograph of Betty Shanks before her murder, taken at the wedding of a cousin

In 2006 former Telegraph journalist Ken Blanch (the first journalist at the crime scene) published a book on the case entitled "Who Killed Betty Shanks? Brisbane's Greatest Murder-Mystery". Blanch theorizes that the murder of Betty Shanks was a case of mistaken identity and that the intended target was a doctor's receptionist who regularly travelled home on the same tram. On the evening of the murder the receptionist had caught an earlier tram than usual.

Newspaper articles published at the time of the murder in The Courier Mail newspaper can be found on Trove Newspapers. Further articles can be found in The Telegraph and Sunday Truth newspapers which are available at the State Library of Queensland on microfilm.

If you have any information which may assist police with this case please phone Crimestoppers on 1800 333 000 or visit the Queensland Police website.

For the record, there is no evidence or suggestion that the Websters knew Betty Shanks. Arthur and Eleanor were most likely visiting the O'Donnell family on Arthur's 66th birthday.

Let's get back to it then!

Splitting Houses into Flats

When David and I moved into the house in 1996, it had been divided up into two separate living spaces. We didn't know when this had occurred. We thought Morgan may have lived in a separate flat to his parents, so it was possibly built in the 1940s.

86 Heussler Terrace 1960s

The discovery of other tenants living at our house in the early 1960s arrived on the back of a Courier Mail article about the UTL Project called, "What Lies Beneath" written by Leanne Edmistone, which appeared on 26 May 26 2018.

That same evening, I received an e-mail from a man called John Morrow...

Evening Caylie,
I read the article in today's QWeekend. I just felt compelled to drop you a line. What a complete surprise and thrill for me to discover what you had discovered and read about the place. Made the hairs stand up on the back of my neck.

My parents, David and Anne Morrow, moved into the flat on the western side of your house a couple of years after they emigrated from Northern Ireland in 1959 as £10 Poms. I was born in 1960 and my next sister down was born in 1962. We lived there for a few years until my father was transferred to Bundaberg.

I have vague memories of old Jimmy (Arthur) carting me about Brisbane City as a small child. He treated me like a grandson.

My father and I attended Arthur's funeral in 1976 and met with Morgan again. My folks had kept in touch with him over the years periodically. We were living in Toowoomba at the time.

I commenced university at UQ in 1977, stayed at Emmanuel College for 12 months, ran out of cash, as you do.

My folks approached Morgan and asked if I could move into the old flat. My mother and I tidied it up and it did take a few days. Morgan even arranged for new vinyl to be laid in the flat so there was definitely no hidden gems on that side of the house. I used to sleep in the room on the corner, not the main bedroom. I stayed about 6 months and then moved in with some mates down the road in Auchenflower.

Morgan would take the bus into work each day at the Commonwealth Bank and he drove into church on Sunday morning. He had a white EH manual sedan, rode the clutch like you wouldn't believe and drove with his wheels about 20cm on his side of the centre line. He was a scary driver.

Anyway, my Dad is still alive, he is 81, lives at Ormiston but is staying with my younger sister recuperating from knee replacement surgery. The sister who was a baby at the time we lived at Heussler Terrace lives in Brisbane also.

I have spoken to the old man this evening about the article. I am sure he would be quite interested in having a yarn to you about the antics that went on in your home between Jimmy (Arthur) and Morgan. Apparently they argued fiercely.

We always reckoned that Morgan probably left the lot to the church. My father talks of them having some sort of connection with the Webster biscuit makers before our time. Maybe that was a story too.

Kindest Regards
John Morrow

Of course, I called John immediately and had a wonderful conversation with him, sharing what I knew and listening to his stories. He didn't have a lot to do with Morgan, who kept to himself. He remembers that he was a small-statured man, who was always dressed in a suit. He would come home from work each evening on the bus from the city, and eat a light meal, before settling himself next to the radio for the evening.

Morgan loved the serials – he would spend his relaxation time listening to crime programs, such as *Inspector West*, and a program from the pioneering days called *Dad and Dave*.

After the programs finished each night, Morgan would retire to bed, and the next day would start all over again, with his morning routine followed by a long work day at the bank.

Interestingly, Morgan never caught the train.

John and his baby sister, Suzanne, with their mother Anne, early 1960s, sitting in the same spot as David and I, with Will and his baby sister, Kitty, on her first day home, fifty years later.

John's father, David Morrow, turned out to be a delightful octogenarian with a gentle Northern Irish brogue. He was very welcoming, as were his daughters, Caroline and Suzanne and his son-in-law, Robert, as we sat together on their back deck in the cool afternoon shadows, sharing stories of the Websters like we'd been friends for years. It was just a shame that John wasn't able to join us.

David Morrow *In 1959, my wife, Anne, and I migrated to Australia from Northern Ireland, as £10 Poms. When we answered Arthur and Morgan's accommodation ad in the local paper, we were only a small family of three, with our young baby, John. Eleanor had only died a year earlier, and the Webster men eagerly welcomed us into their home, despite never mentioning Eleanor to us in conversation.*

Neither Morgan nor Arthur were handy in any way so they would have had the flat built by tradesmen at some point, but I'm not sure if it was newly completed or had been like this for many years already.

We lived in the north-western section of the house, with the afternoon sun breathing fire all along the verandah into their kitchen and dining room every summer.

The back yard had a big chook shed, a large veggie patch and green grass in front of that, closer to the house. There was a choko vine on the back fence and a passionfruit vine on the western fence. The laundry was under the back of the house, as was the garage, and our toilet.

We paid £6 a month in rent and lived in the house for nearly three years while I worked at Goodna Mental Hospital as a male nurse, and Anne stayed at home with John.

Arthur really took to Anne, calling her 'Missus' and treating her like his daughter. He also loved John, a toddler at the time, like a grandson.

Arthur was a big man who was heavy set and well over six feet tall. Once, he took the top of his head off on the chook shed out the back and Anne had to patch him up!

David & John Morrow c. 1960   **David Jeffery c. 1997**

Now, Arthur had more than the legal number of chooks, and was always in terror of the Council inspectors. People could only have a maximum of 11 chickens at the time and Arthur had many more than that! He'd have had to pay for a license if he'd been caught but he had an arrangement with the neighbour a few doors up, that we called, 'The Rat', because he was a rub-his-hands-together kind of fellow. 'The Rat' would bring his dog cart down the back to take some of the chooks up to his house whenever the inspector was coming.

Arthur used to sell the eggs locally each week, taking young John with him when he went. He'd been told to dig a pit in the back yard in order to dispose of all the chook poo, but one day, young John fell into the pit up to his armpits. Arthur found him and pulled him out, calling up to Anne, "Missus! Jimmy's fallen into the chook poo! You'll have to come and sort him out." After which she came down and hosed off John! Arthur called everyone Jimmy, so little John used to call him Jimmy, too.

*

As David was telling me about Arthur's relationship with little Johnny, all I could think about was Morgan, and how he was feeling when he watched his father with this young lad. Did he stand there at the back window, with a cup of tea in hand, musing about his own youth, when Arthur had withdrawn his affection after Colin's death? Did he ever wish his mother had let him play outside more often, get dirty with the other kids and not have to wash his hands all the time? Did he ever wish he'd been the kind of son his father had once wanted? Did he ever come to the realisation that his father loved him but could never show it?

*

One day, David continued, *young John walked away while the tap was running in our kitchen sink – he'd been trying to be a good boy by doing the washing up for his Mum! Morgan came home, and while he was parking his car, saw water gushing through the ceiling from upstairs into the garage… he thought the pipes had burst!*

Despite these little episodes, both Arthur and Morgan were very kind and helpful to our family. Every Saturday morning, Morgan would do the shopping and on Sundays, they would visit relatives, some of whom were pineapple farmers in Beerwah. They'd always come back with a big box of pineapples for us all.

Morgan was a terrible driver and would drive down the western side, spending half an hour reversing the car in the garage under the house. When Anne was about to give birth to our daughter, Caroline, in 1962, Morgan drove us all to hospital, Arthur as well. He drove a Vauxhall Velox at the time and drove so slowly and badly, we were sure Anne was going to give birth in the car!

Morgan was an interesting and intellectual conversationalist, as well as being a dapper gentleman, who always wore a suit and tie. He never joined the armed forces in WWII, despite being of an age to – I'm sceptical about him passing the physical examination, to be honest. Morgan was a very slight man, and could never have become a soldier.

Arthur and Morgan had a difficult relationship, though, and fought a lot – Morgan would nearly be in tears each time. He was brilliant, however, and excelled at accounting, with a good job at the Commonwealth Bank on Ann Street. Morgan was also extremely religious, but never preached to any of us. He was very involved in the Anglican Catholic Church.

I transferred to Bundaberg in 1963 after sitting the public service examination, and moved my family there. We kept in touch with Morgan and Arthur over the years, though, and attended Arthur's funeral in 1976, which was a big, high church affair with the Anglican Church.

Arthur and Morgan had tried other tenants in the flat after we left, but they never worked out. In 1978, two years after Arthur's death, Morgan took John in again, charging him no rent while he was at Uni. John spent his life playing U18's Rugby and drinking with the lads at the Regatta, and admits to being a bit of a layabout at the time!

86 Heussler Terrace 1980s

An interview with my neighbour, Di, also confirmed that Morgan had other people living in the house with him during the '80s, which is when we found out about Pat and her son, Warren.

Di *I remember Morgan as a loner and a quiet fellow, who kept to himself. I never really warmed to him, although we were friendly across the back fence, which was covered in a grapevine then. He used to drop the grapes over to me that grew on his side. It was hard to make small talk with him.*

We were all quiet, older people in this neighbourhood – very working class area back then. We all knew each other on the bus, but Morgan drove to work. He wore suits every day – we never saw him in casual clothes, even on weekends. He was very involved in the church, and had a clergyman visit him at the house every week. He originally attended church behind us, at the Old Bishopsbourne [now St Francis' Theological College], but when they split (I think it was Anglican/Catholic), Morgan moved to the breakaway church, which was possibly in Alderley. Morgan's life revolved around work, home and the church. He drove a white Holden.

While we knew him, the house was divided into two flats. Pat and her two sons (Wayne and Warren) lived with Morgan, as housemates. I was the florist for Warren's wedding – he should be alive.

After Morgan died in 1989, Pat and Warren moved out, and the people from the church came to clean out the house and get it on the market to sell.

Of course, this information had us all scrambling to track down Warren. Many people in the group seemed to know who Warren was, oddly, and I had several members offer to help find him for me.

Just 10 days after the research began, we heard from Warren directly, which was very exciting!

AUG 30 2017
Warren *Hi. A friend has told me that you may be looking for me for some reason?*

A lot of messages, some emails, a phone call and a visit later, and we had a lot more information with which to work.

Warren is a lovely man, a couple of years older than me, with a strong memory of his time living at this house with his Mum in the '80s.

Pat originally lived in Prince Street, Paddington, with her two sons, Wayne and Warren, until 1983, having left an abusive marriage several years earlier. Wayne suffered from a heart disorder and required care at home. Pat also took in her mother, Agnes 'Miriam' Fallon (née Hegerty), who originally hailed from Ipswich, after she developed dementia. Warren was at school locally, and helped take care of his grandmother and brother.

They were difficult times for the family, and in 1982, when Wayne died of a heart attack, aged only 23 years old, life got a lot tougher.

When their landlord, who lived next door, lost his wife to cancer, he suffered from a mental breakdown. Having previously been very close to Pat and her family, he came over one day and turned all their hot water taps on while they were out. The hot water bill nearly broke Pat, who was working three jobs at the time, so, not being able to live under those conditions, Pat turned to Morgan Webster, her mother's cousin, for help. He, being a generous and kind soul, invited them to live with him.

Miriam lived with them in Heussler Terrace until she became too unwell with dementia. She was moved in to a nursing home at the Gold Coast, where she soon passed away. Miriam had been the lynchpin between Pat, Warren and Morgan, being Pat's mother and Morgan's cousin. Warren spent his teenage years fending for himself, as his mother grieved for her first son and worked hard to support them.

Pat worked for Austcare, above the CBA branch where Morgan worked on the corner of Edward and Queen Street. She also worked for IBM in the SGIO building and took in ironing, before she got a role as an electoral secretary for Pat Comben in Stafford and Lutwyche.

She went on to work for Peter Beattie and Paul Brady at Qld Police, sharing many 'interesting' 1980s' police stories at the dinner table.

Warren and Pat didn't have a lot to do with Morgan. He used to go visiting on Sundays, and didn't drive much. He had a white HR 'three on the tree', and he was a terrible, terrible parker! The whole family recalls how long it used to take him to park when he visited their houses. It used to take him half an hour to park the car in the garage of his own house!

Warren described Morgan as a very factual man, who'd rarely had a deep conversation with him. He was reserved, very private and had no visitors to the house apart from a clergyman from time to time.

Warren continued to live with Morgan and his mother until he turned 21 – he had his 21st birthday party at the house, with a pig on a spit in the back yard.

While he was visiting me that day, our neighbour came over to meet Warren, having not seen him for many years. They shared memories of Milton in the '80s, describing it as a working class neighbourhood, in the era of Joh Bjelke-Petersen and police corruption.

Warren had worked at the Terrace Butchers a few houses down on the corner of Baroona Road. It had a smokehouse out the back and was, at that time, owned by George and Ronnie. George was fond of a brew or two and would have his first beer at 10am, cut meat drunk all day, and have more after work. He'd even take a six-pack to drink in the car on the way home to Springwood (!!).

The butchers provided the meat trays to raffle at the Police Club in North Quay. Warren would cycle the trays into town, and would always get invited in for a beer. All the police would be there having a beer or three before work, blowing into the bag for their friends before they went on duty.

He recalled that *Epic Cycles* on the corner used to be a petrol station owned by a man called Lance Hill; *Paddington Antiques* used to be a picture theatre; Lang Park and the *Paddo Tavern* were rough as guts; the owner of *Silvio's Pizza* used to go to school with him and we all fondly recalled our exploits at *Café Neon*, aka, *Café Win-On*!

Morgan had always led Pat and Warren to believe that he would take care of them in the event of his death, but did not include them as beneficiaries. Warren was surprised Morgan had so much money to give away, but then, again, he'd led a frugal life.

Pat died of cancer on December 29, 2003, soon after moving in with Warren and his family at the Sunshine Coast having had a fall. Warren's grandparents Agnes Miriam Fallon and Vincent William Fallon are both buried in Toowong Cemetery.

The End of an Era
86 Heussler Terrace, 1989

On Sunday, 17 December 1989, Morgan was on his way to church when he had a 'turn' in his car. He pulled over on Samford Road to call an ambulance from a phone box, but died on the side of the road before they arrived, having suffered from heart failure at the age of 75.

Morgan's funeral was held three days after his death at the Church of the Resurrection Anglican Catholic Church at 19 Chapel Street, Nundah. He was then laid to rest at Pinaroo Cemetery, nowhere near his immediate family's grave, which sits high on a hill in Toowong Cemetery.

Morgan's Beneficiaries

Morgan had made a will before he died, which made it easier for those left behind. Franki, a lawyer in the UTL Team, helped us with the legalese behind wills...

Franki *When you die with a will, and have property to deal with, then your executor needs to apply to the court for Probate. Morgan's documents relate to the probate application, as opposed to Eleanor's husband, Arthur, who had to apply for Letters of Administration as Eleanor died without a will (intestate).*

A couple of things to note:-
1. *Morgan still lived at Heussler Terrace property at the time of his death,*
2. *His last will was made on 10 October 1988 (just over a year before his death)*
3. *He was 75 when he died of heart failure on 17 Dec 1989.*
4. *He appointed Christabel Tomlinson to administer his estate.*
5. *The will is very straight-forward.*
6. *Only two family beneficiaries were named in his will (Christabel Tomlinson and Edwin Murphy). They were each bequeathed money from his estate.*
7. *The remainder of his estate was given to the Synod of the Anglican Catholic Church in Australia (Queensland) Inc.*
8. *There is no information relating to what his estate comprised (as this is not required for probate applications); however, it is likely to have been the property.*
9. *The rest of the documentation relates to formal court procedure required when applying for Probate.*
10. *The property was sold in August 1990 for $144,000*

Of course, this seemed to have closed the door on the chance of finding any direct heirs to Arthur and Eleanor's money. We had the names of two beneficiaries, though, so we decided to investigate the extended Webster and Murphy families to see if there was anybody alive today who might be able to help us.

Part 5

The History of the Webster Family

The History of the Webster Family

The UTL group did a lot of research into Arthur Webster's extended family, before we found a couple of living relatives who set us straight about a few things. Perhaps if we'd put a call out earlier, however, we wouldn't have had so much fun trying to find the answers ourselves!

The very first relative we met was Steve Webster. His name had come up a few times on the Trove searches, and also on the Ancestry.com pages, and we wondered what his relationship to the Heussler Terrace Websters might be. A few of the UTL Team also knew Steve, so we found it easy to track him down. He had already seen the original post on OBA, though, so wasn't surprised when we contacted him.

I thoroughly enjoyed talking with Steve while I was investigating the history of his extended family. He has one of those wonderful radio voices and a strong interest in Brisbane history – we could have talked for hours!

Steve Webster *I am Stephen Victor, a direct descendant of John and Margaret through their son David and his wife Clara Amy (née Porter), his son Albert Victor (Bert) and wife Dorothy (née Dorethe Mathilde Kirsten Jensen), his son Albert Keith (Keith) and wife Valerie Colton (née Stevens).*

As it turns out, Arthur William Joseph Webster (1890–1976), was a grandson of my great, great-grandfather John Webster who migrated to Moreton Bay in 1857, so he's my 1st cousin twice removed. John Jnr was my great-grandfather David's brother. Arthur was one of two of his boys who joined Qld Rail. It was my understanding that the home at Corinda went to John Jnr's daughters, none of whom married.

Steve has continued to be really helpful throughout the investigation, sharing family tree information, photographs and stories about the Websters. His great-grandfather, David Webster (Arthur's paternal Uncle), has also played a significant role in the iconic history of Brisbane, as you'll soon read.

The second family member we came across was Ross Webster, who arrived on the scene from two different directions. One was via a newspaper article about the project and the other, through Darcy Maddock, a member of the UTL Team who is also the president of the Friends of Toowong Cemetery. Darcy had met Ross at the Toowong Historical Group's monthly meeting, when he'd given a talk about the Webster family.

Ross and Morgan shared great-grandparents (John and Margaret Webster). Ross was generous enough to share the complete Webster family history, providing me with several documents, including one called The Westhaven Story written by Louis Carter, who owned a house called Westhaven, that had previously been owned by the Webster family. Ross was also able to provide me the following about his family, written in 1982 by Mervyn James Webster, of the third generation.

Roberta (Bobbie) Edes, another Webster descendant, also provided some of the following information, having studied the genealogy of her family for many years.

What you're about to read is especially notable since it predates the internet and home computers – knowing how difficult it has been for hundreds of us to do this work *with* the help of technology, one can only imagine how time-consuming their research would have been without it. I have reworded many parts of it and printed the Webster family tree at the front of the book, for easy reference.

The Webster Family

There are a number of different families called 'Webster' in Brisbane, e.g. the family of Joseph Webster who settled in Craigslea Estate (West Chermside) after whom Webster Road, Chermside is named; and the family of W. Webster whose name appears on the monument at the corner of Queen and Eagle Streets, Brisbane, which was erected by the Corporation of Brisbane in 1879.

The Websters we sought originated in the south-east part of Fifeshire, Scotland, particularly in the area surrounding the town of Crail.

The First Generation: John and Margaret Webster (Arthur's Paternal Grandparents)

John Webster was born in Crail on 16 Jun 1833, the eldest of six children of David Webster and Euphemia Webster (née Brown).

At 21, John was working as a farm servant in Cabbagehall in Kingsmuir when he married Margaret Ramsay, aged 25 on 6 April 1855, in her home village and their first son, Daniel, was born on Jan 30, 1856.

Margaret Webster (née Ramsay) was born on 28 Apr 1830 the daughter of George Ramsay (a fisherman) and Janet Ramsay (née Peattie) both of whom had also been born in Nethergate, Crail.

Crail is a royal borough, sea-port, and parish, in the district of St. Andrew's, county of Fife. It lies 10 miles from St. Andrew's, and 40 miles from Edinburgh, the most easterly town on the northern shore of the Firth of Forth. In the 1830s, Crail and surrounds had a population of 1737 inhabitants. Nethergate is within the fishing village of Crail and still maintains its original looks, according to Bobbie Edes, who stayed there in 2008, where she wandered down to the stone-built harbour shielding the local fishing boats for centuries.

The family's presence in Brisbane dates back to 14 Aug 1857 on which day John and Margaret Webster arrived in Brisbane on the sailing ship "Mary (of) Pleasants" when it was still part of the colony of New South Wales. They arrived as bonded settlers (assisted immigrants)...

Scots in Australia

The links between Scotland and Australia stretch back to the first British expedition of the Endeavour in 1770, under the command of Lieutenant James Cook, who was himself the son of a Scottish ploughman. Three of the first six Governors of NSW, John Hunter, Lachlan Macquarie and Thomas Brisbane, were Scots.

The majority of Scots arriving in the early colonial period were convicts, making up 5% of the convict population. Although Scottish convicts had a poor reputation, most were convicted of minor property offences and represented a broad cross-section of Scotland's working classes. As such, they brought a range of useful skills to the colonies.

Prior to 1830, most Scottish immigrants were farmers and landholders who chose to emigrate willingly due to the Scottish economic recessions of the 1820s.

By 1830, 11% of the colonies' total population were Scots, which increased by the middle of the century to 25,000, or 20-25% of the total population. During the 1830s, a growing number of Scots from the poorer working classes joined the diaspora.

Immigrants, including skilled builders, tradesmen, engineers, tool-makers and printers, settled in the commercial and industrial cities, Sydney, Adelaide, Hobart and Melbourne.

As the migration of skilled workers (including bricklayers, carpenters, joiners, and stonemasons) continued, they settled in the colonies of Victoria, New South Wales, South Australia and Tasmania. Much settlement followed the Highland Potato Famine, Highland Clearances and the Lowland Clearances of the mid-19th century.

Their preponderance in pastoral industries on the Australian frontier, and in various colonial administrative roles, meant that Scottish migrants were involved in the colonisation of Indigenous Australians throughout the colonial period, including in the dispossession of Indigenous land, the creation of discriminatory administration regimes, and in killings and massacres.

The Australian Gold Rush of the 1850s provided a further impetus for Scottish migration: in the 1850s, 90,000 Scots emigrated, far higher than other British or Irish populations at the time. Literacy rates of the Scottish immigrants ran at 90-95%. Throughout the 19th century, Scots invested heavily in the industries of the Australian colonies.

Wikipedia: Scottish Australians

On 26 April 1857, John and Margaret Webster boarded the ship, *Mary Pleasants*, in Liverpool, with their first son, Daniel. The reason for their emigration is not known, but they were amongst those who arrived as free settlers, leaving their homeland at a time of drought and poverty, in the hope of a better life.

Mary Pleasants was registered at Liverpool on 3 April 1857, with a deadweight of 768 tons. She left on what appears to have been her maiden voyage on 26 April 1857, under the command of Thomas Slawson with a crew of 36. After calling at Point de Galle (Ceylon) and Akyab (Burma), she arrived in Moreton Bay on 14 August 1857.

The voyage log survives, with entries in it including the following:

> *Tuesday May 26, 1857. Lat. $3°\ 39'$ N. Long. $20°\ 21'$ W.*
> *We do hereby certify that at 3.15 p.m., Daniel Webster infant son of John and Margaret Webster, passengers, departed this life aged 15 months. At 7.30 p.m. committed the body to the deep same date.*
> *Signed Thomas Slawson, Master, Richard Corfe, 1st Officer, William McDougall, 2nd Officer.*

Imagine if you will, for a few seconds, what it was like for John and Margaret to leave their home country behind them – everything they'd ever known: their families, their farms and their culture – to face a new life, months away, in a frontier colony rife with hazardous conditions, unfamiliar terrain and terrifying native inhabitants. I picture the little family boarding the ship, with dreams of prosperity and a home where they could raise their beautiful son and future children with freedom and opportunity, hidden deep within their fears and concerns.

After four weeks at sea, they lost their beloved son, Daniel – an experience that would have devastated the young couple and put a black mark across all of the future aspirations.

At the time John and Margaret Webster arrived, Brisbane was described as *an unattractive settlement. Queen Street was irregular in shape, rutty, uneven and so narrow in most places that two drays or carts could not pass at the same time.*

At night it was not safe to venture out without a lantern, as there were so many holes and gullies, and in wet weather the street was a bog. Creek Street was a tidal creek, and the favourite swimming place for school boys. Over the creek in Queen Street was a log bridge. Most of Brisbane's business activity centred around the upper end of Queen Street and along William Street to the Commissariat Building. The top of Queen Street was flanked by the old military barracks on the east and on the west by an old lumber yard. The old convict hospital was on the site of the Supreme Court. Across George Street, Mr. Wynn kept cows and supplied the town with milk. On the site of the present City Hall was a large lagoon called the Horse Pond and people used to shoot ducks there.

The hilltop around the windmill was still scrub but farther along the ridge (towards Petrie's Bight), Spring Hill, had been parcelled out in one acre blocks. Below them were tightly packed clusters of spec-built houses. (Source unknown)

John and Margaret, shortly after arrival in the Moreton Bay settlement, went to live on Tarampa Station as bonded immigrants. Tarampa was a pastoral holding of 24,000 acres in the West Moreton district, taken up by J.F. MacDougall in 1848. This land, upon which Gatton Agricultural College now stands, was called McDougall's Run.

The Websters soon welcomed their second son, George, who was born on 4 January 1858, but sadly, he died a week after his first birthday. Their first surviving child, John Jnr, was born on 25 May 1859, a mere four months after the death of George. (NB This John is Arthur's father).

John and Margaret were blessed with four more children in Ipswich after John Jnr – George, 1861; David, 1864; Thomas, 1865; and Jessie, 1868. Tragically, their last child, and only girl, died after only five days.

Again, I ask you to think about the tragedy that had come to this family with the loss of three babies in ten years...

The practice of giving a child the same name (George) as one who had died, had been followed by John's parents who'd had a son David (born 1839) and another son David (born 1845).

The movements of the family within the West Moreton district are unclear, though it seems likely that they spent a significant part of the 1860s in or near Ipswich.

In 1872, Calvert State School, number 12 on the list of schools of the Queensland Education Department, opened in a slab hut and David and his brothers started school. John Jr was twelve years old, George ten, David eight and Thomas six.

By 1874, John Sr was listed in the Post Office Directory as "Farmer Grandchester". The farm was actually at Western Creek (now known as Calvert) about two miles on the Grandchester side of Calvert Railway Station.

Philip Webster (a grandson of John and Margaret and one of Arthur's cousins) has written the following about John Sr...

My grandfather was an expert bushman and fencer. It remains a puzzle how a ploughman from Scotland could come to this country and, in a short space of time, become expert in many of the skills which were needed in this new country.

My father often spoke of fencing with my grandfather on Tarampa Station and in the Ipswich-Rosewood areas. The fences were split posts and rails. The posts, rather solid, had two mortices which, after boring with an augur, were chopped out with a mortising axe. The rails were not so solid, split also and trimmed at the ends to enter the mortices. There were two rails to each panel.

Payment was made by the rod (5.5 yards or 5.03 metres) which consisted of two panels of fence.

When travelling in the Amberley area, I have often noticed old examples of post and rail fences and wondered if they may have been erected by my grandfather and father because such fences have a long life.

While in Grandchester, the family became associated with the Rosewood Scrub (now Lanefield) branch of the Ipswich Baptist Church. In 1866, John purchased 18 acres of land for £18 in 1866 in the Parish of Yeerongpilly in Brisbane whilst working as a farmer near Laidley.

In 1884, John and Margaret moved to South Brisbane, settling in Walton Street. John worked with his son, David, in his bakery business which was established on a property bounded by Boggo (now Annerley) Road, Walton Street and Nelson Street.

When they relocated, they transferred their Church membership to South Brisbane (Vulture Street) Baptist Church, beginning an association that their family continued for more than sixty-five years.

Margaret died at her home on May 3, 1893, and was buried in the South Brisbane cemetery.

On 17 April 1896, John remarried Janet (Jeannie) Christie, a widow.

John died at his home on 3 November 1901, aged 67 and was also buried in South Brisbane cemetery. Jeannie died on 12 June 1908, aged 77. She was survived by one daughter about whom nothing is known.

*

The Second Generation
(Arthur's father and Siblings)

George Webster (Arthur's Uncle)

George was born on 5 July 1861, at Woodend Pocket, Ipswich. He worked for a time, after leaving school, on his father's farm at Western Creek and then, for a short period, for a carpenter in Toowoomba.

In 1882 (aged 20), George found work as a Lad Porter at Roma Street goods shed, working ten hours per day for 25 shillings ($2.50) per week.

He was soon promoted to Head Platform Porter and then, in 1885, George was transferred to Nundah for six months to learn stationmaster's duties.

After passing the examination, he became a relieving porter, for three years, working in Pengarry, Oakey, Miles and Dulacca (Western Line), Harristown and Dalveen (Southern Line) and Nundah.

In 1886, George married Christina Elder. A strong co-incidence was that George's father, John Sr, who'd left Crail in 1857, had worked as a ploughman on the farm next to Christina's father's farm. He'd been a blacksmith there until his departure for Queensland in 1884. George and Christina leased land from the Crown in the Grandchester area, working it at weekends and other available times.

In 1888, George was promoted to Station Master at Logan Village. The railway reached Beaudesert in 1888 but the Logan Village-Canungra branch was not built until 1915. He remained there for eight months and then resigned from the Railways Department and went to work for his brother, David, riding first on the baker's cart and later, working in the bakehouse.

In December 1889, however, he re-joined the Railways Department at 5/6 (55 cents) per day and on January 1, 1890, George opened the station at Yandina when the line was extended from Landsborough. Subsequently, he served at Morningside/Coorparoo (1892), Nudgee (1893), Walloon (1894–1899), Park Road (1899), Palmwoods (1899–1902), Nambour (1902–1908) and Strathpine (1908–1910).

In the bedroom of the Station Master's house at Nambour was a single wire telephone connected with Kenilworth cattle station. This was used to transmit information on Mary River Heights at Kenilworth so word could be sent to Gympie and Maryborough about possible flooding. Sometimes, on Sunday afternoons, one of the sons of the station owner would play the violin and George's wife, Christina, would listen in on the phone in the bedroom at Nambour.

George resigned from the Railways in May, 1911, and bought eight acres of rain forest near Nambour, which he cleared for small crop growing, orcharding and grazing. He died in Nambour on 30 June 1948.

David Webster (Arthur's Uncle)

David Webster was born in Ipswich on 29 January 1864. He spent his early life in the Grandchester area going to school at Calvert and then went to Toowoomba to learn the baking trade with Webb Brothers.

When he was 19, he came to Brisbane and commenced business with Norman McLeod as Webster and McLeod. Subsequently, he took over the McLeod interests.

By 1885 (aged 21), David was listed as a sole trader in the Boggo Road Bakery on the corner of Nelson Street and Boggo (now Annerley) Road.

In 1886, David married Clara Amy Porter at the South Brisbane Baptist Church. They had six sons and two daughters. In the beginning, they lived on the bakery premises but, as they prospered, they moved to Dutton Park.

David Webster & Sons, and Webster's Bakeries

These two companies trace their origin to the bread bakery founded in 1885 at the Boggo Road site occupied until the 1960s. After this time, both businesses passed from the family to George Weston & Sons (Australia) Ltd.

It is said that, at the beginning, David delivered his own bread in a basket. In the early days of their marriage, his wife, Clara, helped him in the business which he expanded to include a chain of cafes (including one called the Shingle Inn), and catering, cakes and biscuits departments.

As the business prospered and diversified into cakes and biscuits, bread making was moved from Annerley Road to a new bakery established on the corner of Gladstone Road and Grantham Street. David and his growing family moved to Beulah on the corner of Gladstone Road and Lochaber Street and later to Folkstone, two blocks south on Gladstone Road between Denbigh and Malden Streets.

James (Jim), the eldest son, managed Websters Bakeries Proprietary Limited (the bread factory) and lived in Beulah after David and Clara moved to Folkstone. Albert (Bert) and Dorothy, who managed the cake and biscuit bakery, lived next door on the corner of Gladstone and Malden St.

Thus each of the facilities and the homes of the managers were all within walking distance of each other.

David Webster (left) with workers, 1927
Courtesy of John Oxley Library

While David's business prospered despite the depression, drought and flood, he and Clara suffered personal loss, in that a baby daughter, Millie, died before her first birthday from complications of whooping cough. Three of their adult sons, Bombardier Roy Mervyn (killed in action in France) 1918, John Francis (Frank) 1922, and Cyril Claude 1934, also predeceased them.

David's business grew partly as a direct result of his use of the most modern machinery then known. David imported most of this machinery from America and initially had difficulty with his employees as they were concerned for their future. It would appear that very little has changed in that respect.

David also diversified his business by opening tearooms and cafes with several in Queen Street at 79, 81 (Imperial Café), 142, 200 (Central Café), 270 (Post Office Café) and 368. Others were located at George St, Brunswick St, Ann St, Stanley St, and Wynnum South.

97 Queen Street Tearooms,
Courtesy of John Oxley Library

The most recent ones are Haddon Hall in Queen St; and Yorktown and Shingle Inn in Edward St.

The Shingle Inn was built on Edward Street in 1936, with a view to it becoming an elegant, English-style teahouse and restaurant, known for its high quality products and stylish decor.

David also branched out into catering and hosted several large and significant events including regal and vice-regal visits to Queensland. David was a committed Christian and he and Clara taught Sunday School for many years as well as David serving as President of The Queensland Baptist Union. He was also well known in business circles with Who's Who listing him as the inaugural President of West End Arctic Ice and sister company, Townsville Arctic Ice, forerunners of Peter's Ice Cream.

David and Clara Webster 1936, 50th wedding anniversary
Webster family photograph

David died at home in 1937 and Clara in 1951. After his death, the businesses continued to be run by his three remaining sons, James (Jim – bread), Albert (Bert – cakes and biscuits) and Wilfred (cafes and catering, then after Bert's death in 1953, the whole business).

By the mid-1960s, the business was sold to George Weston Foods and two of David's grandsons, Bert's son Keith and Frank's son Noel, remained with the new owners. In fact, two of David's great-grandsons, Noel's son, Peter and Keith's son, Stephen (Steve Webster) also worked there for a time.

Both the Shingle Inn and Yorktown were purchased by Noel and Barbara Bellchambers in 1975. In 2003, the Shingle Inn was recreated in Brisbane City Hall, where it continues to operate in full style today.

The above family history is entirely attributable to one of David and Clara's grandsons, Mervyn James Webster, Cyril Webster's son. All photographs have been supplied by Steve Webster from the Webster family archives, Ancestry.com and the John Oxley Library.

Sundays with our Grandparents, David and Clara Webster
by David Colin Webster

"Sunday with our grandparents began for us in the long centre pew in the second back row at the 11.00 a.m. service at Vulture Street Baptist Church.

Grandfather and Grandma sat on the left, and then came Mother and the four of us, with Miss Annie Wakefield (Grandma's companion for thirty years) on the right aisle. Auntie Daisy often sat behind us.

At the right-hand end of the pew in front was a mysterious box, the purpose of which I could not fathom at the time, though I now believe it held fans and bibles. It created a problem for a small boy's swinging leg, for if they swung too far, a hollow sound reverberated throughout the large but mainly empty auditorium. I remember that prayers were much longer than they are now and that Annie used to pass us jelly beans during the sermon.

Grandfather died when I was nine. After his death, I was promoted to sit beside Grandma who never stood during hymns. I still remember the calm of those early services, which always closed with the singing of the hymn, Drop Thy Still Dews of Quietness till all our Strivings Cease.

After the service, there was a ride home with Grandfather in a yellow cab to Folkestone for lunch. If I was lucky, I rode in the dicky seat at the back. Grandfather never owned a car. He was frightened of cars and was a most anxious passenger, even putting his hand out of the window of the back seat to signal a turn.

Lunch was a happy, if somewhat solemn, occasion at the long table, set with a starched white linen cloth in the dining room. Even though a lad, I could not remove my jacket until Grandfather gave permission and did so himself. Lunch was usually a roast or joint carved at the table with ceremony, accompanied by mashed potatoes and beans. It was normally followed by stewed fruit and custard.

After lunch, I was sent to the study to do my Sunday School homework, though I often spent the time hunting treasures in the many drawers of the roll-top desk. Joan remembers being somewhat frightened of Grandfather, who always expected answers to his questions about the Sunday School lesson or the morning's sermon. Joan and I then accompanied him to Dunellen Baptist Sunday School, of which he was Superintendent, after which we returned home.

Sundays were special days during which special stories were read. No dice games were allowed and play had to be quiet. I do not recollect it as boring because it was accepted that this was what Sunday was for."

*

Folkestone, Gladstone Road, Dutton Park
(The last home of David and Clara Webster)

"The house was always fascinating to me. It was set opposite Dutton Park at 282 Gladstone Road, between Denbigh and Maldon Streets. In the park, until 1939, there was a pensioner shanty town with houses made of galvanised iron, beaten-out four gallon drums and bagging. These disappeared during the war. The park was also the place where Grandfather's 30-40 horses (used for bread delivery) were driven each Friday night. The park was a forbidden area, into which we were rarely taken, partly because of its bareness, partly because of the pensioner undesirables and partly because the river lay beyond it. It was unexplored.

Trams clattered up and down Gladstone Road. Stop 21 was directly outside Folkestone and the terminus was two stops further on. Across the barren footpath lay the well-cared-for garden, bright in season with poppies, stocks and dahlias.

At the front door was an electric bell, powered by a Leyden jar. This was installed because the doctor who called when Grandfather was ill could not make anyone hear. Inside the door, across the verandah, were two large fern plants with aspidistras.

Beyond, along the red carpeted hall, one was faced by two large fern plants with aspidistras and two large plaster figures of cavaliers, which always fascinated me, and which I later inherited.

On the left was Grandfather's bedroom with his special bed. Prominent in the room was a marble-topped washstand with its large china jug and washbasin. On the far wall was a chest of drawers in which Grandma kept Christmas presents for the grandchildren, which she purchased throughout the year. Occasionally, one had a sneak preview. In this room, I was once sick for a month and was first introduced to jigsaw puzzles. In this room, on 3 July 1937, Grandfather died and to it we were taken to see his body resting in the coffin.

On the right was Grandma's room, full of fascination. Her bed was surrounded by a u-shaped carpet. On the right, above the washstand, was a medicine cabinet with the carved head of Hippocrates on the door. Beside this, hung a framed citation and medals of Uncle Roy, who was killed in France in 1918.

The verandah ran around two sides of the room. In each of the two walls were French windows. Through them, endless games could be played. In the corner between the two windows stood the dressing table on which stood a fascinating bottle filled with green smelling salts. Grandma used to retire to bed at 8pm. In the morning, she used to sit beside the French windows and vigorously brush her long hair before plaiting her bun. Then she would kneel beside the bed and pray. In this room, I spent a month on my back in a second bed which faced the verandah. I had some sort of back trouble and had to lie flat.

Further down the hall, on the left, was a small bedroom, at one time occupied by cousin Cedric and subsequently by Grandma's companion, Annie Wakefield.

At the end of the hall was an enormous sepia print of an American bison. Under this, on a table, rested a case of coral. On the left was the bathroom with its smelly gas geyser, and on the right was Grandfather's study, with wall telephone and roll-top desk. Further down the dark hall, one passed two bedrooms and a chiffonier on which Grandfather always kept a jar of dates, and Annie, a jar of fudge. Making fudge was one of her hobbies.

Then, on the left, was the kitchen with its walk-in pantry, laundry chute and gas stove. A cupboard in one corner contained the rubbish bin and scrap bucket for the chooks. Many a time I remember seeing Annie ironing at the table, using Mrs. Potts irons heated on the gas stove, and wearing a blue petticoat and the headphones of her crystal set. It was not until 1940 that Grandma bought a wireless set which stood in the dining room. There was no refrigerator until even later but an ice chest stood on the back verandah. On the verandah, on a table outside the kitchen window, was Cocky the galah. He would call out as someone came up the stairs, "Pretty boy, Cocky wants a cup of tea", often being rewarded for this display by tea offered on a spoon.

Across the hallway from the kitchen was the enormous dining or living room, in the middle of which was the large dining table covered by a green chenille tablecloth with tassels all around. On the left of the door was a round table on which often rested an enormous silver bowl of Iceland poppies. The memory of their perfume still delights me. Next to it was a sofa in front of which was a mat on whose patterns one could play a counting game. Another sofa was on the far wall. Between the sofas was Grandfather's large leather easy chair where Grandma sat and read Georgette Heyer. Behind this chair was an old brass switch and socket, long since disconnected, but an excellent prop for games involving planes, lifts and trains. Beside it was a bookcase with exciting books.

On the far side of the adjoining sofa was another octagonal table on which sat brass Buddha bookends and a little silver bell. Before the war, Uncle Bert who lived next door, didn't have a telephone (Grandfather had an extension from his office in the factory), so when Uncle Bert was wanted on the phone, the window would be opened, the bell rung and someone would come running up the long flight of stairs to the study.

Grandfather's death and the war changed this. Beside this table was a door which led out to the fernery which was Grandma's pride and joy, and a fascination to us. Beside the door was Grandma's chair where she sat to sew beside her sewing table.

Next to this was a very large sideboard with crystal and silver. On the fourth wall was a china cabinet on which stood a marble clock which never worked but was a fascinating ornament.

Beside the sideboard, French doors opened into the drawing room between the living room and the study. This was a large room rarely used. One fascination was the Aeolian (later given to Mervyn) on which, on special occasions, one was allowed to listen to records of nursery rhymes or of Dame Clara Butt singing The Last Chord or The Holy City. Surprisingly, a foxtrot or two, the origins of which were never divulged, were also in the collection. In one corner was a tiled gas fire which never worked. This room seemed to have little use. The only occasion I recall it being used was on the occasion of Grandma's funeral service with an open coffin.

From the back verandah, one could look down twenty feet to the garden below with its bushhouses, chook yard and war-time air raid shelter. Grandma spent a great deal of time sitting on this verandah. She used to suffer from oesophagitis which she described as a thousand knives being thrust in her chest.

Grandma was a great gardener and there were always delights in odd corners. Beside the house stood the garage which didn't house a car but various odds and ends of dusty old furniture.

It was a house full of interest and delight to a child and I spent many happy hours there."

John *I did my apprenticeship as a Pastry cook in a small bakery in Moorooka. When I finished my time, I went to the Webster's Factory at Annerley Road, South Brisbane. It was a very manual business in those times.*

I remember starting early in the morning when you had to go down the pits to light the ovens. You had to give the grate a good rattle to chase off any unwanted vermin that might surprise you. I wasn't there long when I was selected to go to the new factory built in Chermside to test out all of the new equipment.

The two places were like chalk and cheese.

South Brisbane being all manual and the new factory so automated with all of the ingredients going in one end and the finished product coming out the other. Huge travelling ovens produced tons of fruit cake per day. The mixture was put into tins at one end of the travelling oven; then when it came out the other end, it would be put into coolers and the other side of it was taken out cut, wrapped and packed and then out the door the same day. The rollette machine was amazing – one continuous piece of cake some 40 to 50 metres long.

It would be put on the oven band at one end and come out baked at the other then transferred onto a wire conveyor belt. It would go up and be turned over to receive the cream and jam, then cut, and the girls would stand there all day rolling them up and putting them into boxes and packed for delivery.

They used to do tours in those days – I don't know if they still do that as it was 40 years ago. I ended up assistant Production Manager but the world was calling me so I left and went to live in the USA for 6 months came back had a snack bar for 5 years then opened my own Travel Agency which specialised in Motorsport tours to the USA for the next 32 years.

Thomas Webster (Arthur's Uncle)

Thomas was the youngest son, being born in Ipswich on 26 December 1865. In 1889, he married Mary Amelia (Minnie) Osmond.

Like his brother, David, Thomas became a baker, setting up his business in Fernberg Road, Rosalie. He suffered from lung disease and, despite a visit to Europe for medical help, Thomas died on 16 May 1899, aged only 33.

Mary carried on the business for a number of years but, following the tragic deaths of all three sons in the course of a little more than three years, she sold the business to MacDougall's. The premises at 115 Fernberg Road, on the corner of Stevenson Street, are still identifiable though no longer used as a bakery.

Minnie retired to the slopes of Mt. Coot-tha and died on 11 May 1949, just five days short of fifty years after her husband.

Jessie Webster

The only daughter of John and Margaret, Jessie was born in Ipswich on 18 June 1868, and died of a convulsion five days later on 23 June 1868.

John Webster (Arthur's Dad)

Last, but not least, it's time to introduce you to Arthur's father, John Webster, or John Jnr, for the purposes of not getting him confused with his father, also John... honestly, with all the names in this world, you'd think people would get original and not cause us historians so many headaches!

John Webster (Jnr) was the first surviving child of his parents, John and Margaret. He was born in Ipswich on May 25, 1859 and lived until his seventy-fourth year.

John was a schoolteacher for a short time and then joined the  Queensland Railways. Not all the details of his service are known but it is understood that he was Station Master at Cabarlah (on the now-closed Toowoomba to Crows Nest line) in 1885; at Beenleigh from 1886–1889 (the line from South Brisbane was opened to Beenleigh on 25 July 1885); at Grandchester (1890–1896); and at Corinda from 1901 until his retirement in 1924.

John Jnr married Sarah Jane Waters on 19 December 1882, and in the years that followed, they had six children:

Thomas John (TJ) 14 April 1884
Sarah Jane (Tot) 1 October 1886
Elizabeth Margaret (Maggie) 20 March 1888
Arthur William Joseph 24 August 1890
Elsie Christina Amy 21 April 1895
Edith Stella 11 November 1896

While working as the Station Master at Corinda, John Jnr chose not to live in the stationmaster's house, but in *Westhaven*, a large house in Donaldson Street, Corinda. His wife, Sarah, died on 5 Jun 1926, aged 67, after which time he was looked after by his four unmarried daughters. John Jnr died on 16 Dec 1933.

The 'Westhaven Story'
by Louis Carter

'Westhaven', at 81 Donaldson Street, Corinda, is a lovely old family home that has belonged to my family since we bought it at auction in 1975.

The land on which 'Westhaven' stands is part of a 50-acre purchase by Robert Donaldson in 1869. Various allotments were sold off over time, and on 14 March, 1892, one acre of land was acquired by George Theodore Bell.

That land was subsequently divided into two half-acres. The land upon which 'Westhaven' now stands, was bought by Sarah Dunlop in 1901.

Sarah was the wife of John Dudley Dunlop, a prominent builder of the time.

In fact, the Dunlop family were very influential around the district with many places bearing the family name (Dunlop Park, Dunlop Terrace etc.). John Dunlop built the Corinda School of Arts, which is now the Corinda Library.

'Westhaven' was built by the Dunlops between 1901 and 1906, and given they had six children at the time, they required a large family home.

The Webster Era

Jack Dunlop, died on 31 October 1906 after suffering a severe workplace accident. Sarah Dunlop, now with seven children (the eldest only 15) must have struggled for a while and sold the property to Sarah Jane Webster on 18 December 1911.

Sarah Webster was the wife of John Webster, the Station Master at Corinda Railway Station.

The Websters, with extended family, had been living at the Station Master's Cottage in Browne Street, Corinda, near the intersection of the two lines, from the City and Yeerongpilly.

Since the railway line had been laid over the newly completed Indooroopilly rail bridge in the mid-1870s, thereby linking Brisbane and Ipswich by rail, the whole area had become more important.

Arthur Palmer (later, Sir Arthur Palmer, Premier of Queensland) bought land between the railway line and Oxley Creek.

The railway station and suburb were names in 1886. John and Sarah lived at 'Westhaven' with their daughters, Elizabeth (a music teacher), Sarah, Elsie and Edith. When their mother died in 1926, the property passed into the hands of her four daughters, who continued to care for their father until his death in 1933.

Elizabeth died in 1959, and Elsie in 1967, after which the two remaining sisters stayed in residence at 'Westhaven' as unmarried ladies until 1975 when the property was auctioned off.

Ross told me that Arthur may only have lived in Westhaven for a short time, since it was bought in 1911 and he married in 1913, but his brother Thomas (TJ) never did. Ross's father wrote in his diary about visiting Westhaven in about 1914 (as a lad), and again in 1954, "the first time for 40 years". He later refers to visits in 1959 and 1961, and it's one or both of these visits that Ross can recall, when three of the sisters were still alive.

The above picture is Westhaven as it looks today, fully renovated.

The Third Generation:
The Children of John Jr and Sarah Webster

Thomas John Webster (Arthur's only brother)

Thomas (TJ) was the eldest child of John Jnr and Sarah, and the eldest grandchild of John Snr and Margaret. Born in Ipswich, TJ lived for some years with his Uncle David at "Beulah" in Gladstone Road, while his parents lived in Grandchester. He entered the Commonwealth Public Service and, at the time of his retirement in 1949, was Chief Commonwealth Auditor in Queensland.

Thomas is the only one of the John and Sarah Webster union with descendants remaining today.

I was contacted about nine months into the UTL Project by a woman called Darcelle Hegerty (née Webster), TJ's great-granddaughter. Darcelle belongs to the only living strand of relatives of John and Sarah Webster, Arthur's parents. Her grandfather was Mervyn Webster, and Arthur's nephew. Her father, Douglas, Arthur's great nephew, is still alive at 85, and would have stories to share about Arthur. Douglas is Morgan's first cousin, once removed. Had Morgan had children, they would have been Douglas's cousins.

Darcelle described Arthur and TJ's sisters as very tight knit, having met them when she was a little girl. As a small child, she had also met her great-grandfather, TJ. She described the family as being very close, keeping in regular touch with each other and the extended family. They all went on holidays to Sandgate and Redcliffe together.

Roberta (Bobbie) Edes, one of the Under the Lino Team, is Darcelle's father Douglas's first cousin, and a family historian who works on the Queensland Genealogy blog.

Bobbie *We're descended from John Webster Snr's elder brother, James b. 1829.*

As well as John Snr (who went to Qld), and James (who went to Windsor, NSW), there were siblings Margaret (who also went to Windsor) and William (who went to Vic).

Additionally an uncle of theirs, another William (generation above) went to Victoria. My grandmother Elizabeth Agnes White was the daughter of Euphemia Brown Webster.

Grandma came to Brisbane to live when she married. The couple lived in 'Merkara', a wonderful old home on Old Cleveland Road, Coorparoo, and their next door neighbour was David John Webster (son of George M. Webster) and his wife Olive (née Thorne) who were a big help during the depression. The family was very close to Mary Amelia (née Osmond) and Thomas Webster – he was the youngest son of John Snr and Margaret (née Ramsay). Thomas was born in Ipswich on 26 December 1865. 'Aunty Minnie' lost her 3rd surviving son in WW1, his 'Penny' was passed to my Dad.

I'm also the niece of the wife of the nephew of Arthur. That is my relationship via my other side. My first cousins on my maternal side are direct Webster descendants of John Webster as the children of Mervyn Thomas Edward Webster. And yes, we've all got a strong DNA confirmed link on two sides.

TJ and Laura Webster (née Jarrott), with their grandchildren C. 1945 – Douglas and his sister Audrey (from Mervyn) and Desmond (from Eric)
Photograph courtesy of Darcelle Hegerty

Sarah Jane (Tot); Elizabeth Margaret (Maggie); Elsie Christina Amy; Edith Stella (Arthur's spinster sisters – *The Corinda Girls*)

These four sisters were known collectively in the family and elsewhere as "The Corinda Girls". The four daughters of John and Sarah, they never married, spending all their lives at "Westhaven" in Donaldson Street, Corinda, after the family moved to Brisbane.

Sarah Jane was named after her mother. She was known by her nickname 'Tot' throughout her whole life. She was below average height and was often described as "painfully thin". Tot was a member of the City Tabernacle, working hard for the Senior Girls' Missionary Union and the Wartime Soldiers' Teas. She was, for part of her life, a dressmaker.

Two of the Webster sisters

Elizabeth Margaret was known as Maggie, and worked as a music teacher. Elsie Christina Amy was the housekeeper of the family. Edith Stella worked in the Commonwealth Public Service in Brisbane like her older brother, TJ.

"The Corinda Girls" maintained close contacts with other members of the extended family.

And then, of course, we all know Arthur by now…

Arthur William Joseph Webster

Maternal Grandparents: William Waters (B. 1828 Londonderry Northern Ireland, Arrived in Australia 1855, D. 1904 Ipswich) and Jane Smith (B. 1836 Londonderry Northern Ireland, Arrived in Australia 1855, D. 1916 Ipswich)
Paternal Grandparents: John Webster (B. 1833, Crail Fife Scotland, Arrived 1857 Australia, D. 1901 Brisbane) and Margaret Ramsey (B. 1830 Crail, Fife, Scotland, Arrived 1857 Australia, D. 1893 Brisbane)
Parents: Sarah Jane Waters (B. 1859 Qld D 1926 Brisbane) and John Webster (B. 1859 Ipswich D. 1933 Brisbane)
Siblings: Thomas, Sarah, Elizabeth, Elsie and Edith (Arthur was the 4th child)
Born: 24 August 1890, Grandchester
Educated: Taringa State School and the Normal School (Cnr Adelaide and Edwards Sts, Brisbane City)
Career: Worked his way up in QR from Engine Cleaner 1906 to Fireman to Locomotive Driver, retiring in 1955, on his 65th Birthday
Married: 1913 to Eleanor Murphy
Home: Bought Eleura, later 86 Heussler Terrace, Milton Heights, 1914 and lived here until 1976
Children: Morgan 1914–1989; Colin 1918–1918 (10 months)
Widowed: 24 August 1958, on his 68th Birthday
Died: 1976 at 86 Heussler Terrace Milton, left a will with over $60,000 to Morgan, plus the house.
Buried: Toowong Cemetery with Eleanor and Colin

Part 6

The History of the Murphy Family

The History of the Murphy Family (Eleanor's family)

Hamish and Lyn were very active in the early days of discovering who the Websters were, forever updating the ever-growing family tree, however, there was never a lot of information available to us about Eleanor.

We knew Eleanor was a housewife, was married to Arthur in 1913 and that she had given birth to two boys; Morgan in 1914, and Colin, in 1918, who died at 10 months of age. We also found out that her maiden name was Murphy.

Meg *This seems to be Eleanor's father (if I'm reading that right)*

Mr. James Murphy.

Mr. James Murphy, of Brisbane Road, Dinmore, one of Ipswich and district's oldest natives, died on Monday night. He was a son of the late Mr. and Mrs. Michael Murphy, and was born at Upper Bundamba, 79 years ago. The late Mr. Murphy, in his early days, followed the occupation of mailman, carrying the mails from Ipswich to Nanango and other places on the head of the Brisbane River by

Late Mr. James Murphy
The Courier Mail 2 Nov 1933

Lyn *The Ancestry tree is now up to 184 people. Still trying to find an Edwin Murphy who was bequeathed money in 1989 from Morgan Webster's will.*
Kym *This cousin, Edwin, and Morgan might not be close in age – some of mine are 20-odd years older than me. Just a thought*
Lyn *Christabel was only a year older than Morgan, being born in 1913. There was no Edwin born around that time that was still alive in Jan 1990 when the will was finalised. Therefore I am looking for an Edwin born after 1917 but probably not too far later because Morgan would have had to be fairly close to him to have left him any money.*
Brenda *Edwin Murphy may have been a nephew of Eleanor's? She had a brother called Edwin who died in 1963.*

Lyn *Yes, it could but because of privacy laws, I haven't been able to find any yet!*
Brenda *He could easily still be living... I haven't found him on electoral rolls yet.*
Lyn *Perhaps. He would have had to be at least 21 years old in 1989, which gives him a minimum age of 49 years. I have a feeling that he would have been older.*
Brenda *Ethel May Cowell was quite a bit younger than husband Edwin James Murphy... there may have been a child. Younger than the cemetery records indicate, if this is accurate?*
Nicole *Do we know if Christabel had any children?*
Lyn *She didn't have any children.*

The Search for Murphys

As a result of this research, Lyn and others were able to build up a solid Murphy family tree of over a hundred members. We were doing the same with the Webster branch of the family, but because their historical information was so much easier to locate, a lot more time and effort went in to Arthur's side.

It was more than six months into the project before I thought it was time to start looking into the Murphys. I was becoming desperate for photographs of Eleanor and Arthur, and having had no luck on that front from the Webster's extended family, I thought I'd have a dig around for contact details for the nearest living descendants on the Murphy family tree. Something was bugging me about Edwin Murphy... I thought he may still be alive having re-read the above conversation. Kym certainly hit the nail on the head when she suggested that Morgan and his cousin may have a large age gap.

A simple online search tracked down a phone number for Edwin Murphy Jnr, the closest living family relative to the Webster-Murphy clan. Edwin was Eleanor's nephew (her brother, Edwin Snr's, son), and therefore, Morgan's first cousin.

As luck would have it, he was home when I called. It was a delight to speak to such a friendly man who is so closely related to Eleanor!

Edwin Jnr's father was much older than his siblings when Edwin was born, so he is technically of the next generation – Morgan would be 104 were he alive today, so to find a first cousin was nothing short of a miracle.

As is my way now, I invited myself to visit Edwin for an interview. It was a beautiful autumn day when I arrived at Edwin and Gloria Murphy's neat and attractive home, in one of the outer suburbs of Ipswich. I'd driven past some of Ipswich's most historic homes on my way, and was in a great mood for family history!

Edwin was warm and welcoming, inviting me in for a cup of tea and a long chat. He was eager to hear my part in his family's story, and listened eagerly to what I had to share about his Auntie Nellie. I was just as curious to hear about his family story!

Sitting at the kitchen table, we were so excited to share stories, that tea was forgotten for some time. Edwin was ready with a Murphy family history book that had been collated by extended families in 1999 before their last Murphy reunion. This hand-typed book was filled with wonderful family trees, photographs and information pertaining to most of the branches stemming from an Irish-Australian pioneer called Michael Murphy and his wife Mary Ann (née Potter). It was, for me, like finding a pot of gold.

There'd been an ad placed in the local newspaper calling for relatives to step forward for a reunion, as well as to collect money to build plaques for the unmarked graves in Ipswich Cemetery.

Family seeks Ipswich history

THE number of descendants of Ipswich historical figures Michael and Mary Ann Murphy is unknown.

The hundreds, perhaps thousands of people spread throughout Ipswich, Goomeri, Maryborough, Mackay, Rockhampton and Cairns are all invited to a family reunion to pay tribute to the pioneering couple.

Edwin confirmed that his father had indeed been older at his birth, thus the disparity in age between him and Morgan. Born in 1946, as opposed to Morgan in 1914, there was at least a generation separating the two cousins. Edwin recalled visiting our house as a young child in 1958, when his parents stayed there for a Salvation Army congress at City Hall, as was their usual custom for Brisbane events.

This would have been shortly before Eleanor's death, when Morgan would have been in his mid-40s.

I loved how Edwin referred to Eleanor as Aunty Nellie. It was the first time I'd heard that name, and loved the familiarity and comfort of it. His memory of his Aunty Nellie was poor, however, as he was only 12 years old when she passed away, and he'd only met her a few times.

He recalled that Eleanor's father, James, had remarried after the early death of his first wife, Agnes. Eleanor's stepmother, Magdalene (Lena) Weimer, married James in 1904, when Eleanor was about 20 years old. To Edwin, Lena was always known as 'Grandma Dinmore', as he had never met Agnes. Lena was born in 1866, and was 18 years older than Eleanor.

Edwin's own mother had passed away when he was only 9, and later, his father when he was just 17, in June 1963. He lived with a maternal aunt after he lost his parents, maintaining a loving relationship with her and his extended family thereafter.

After Edwin married Gloria and started their family in Silkstone, Morgan became a regular visitor on Sundays. He described Morgan as a kind man, who kept to himself, with few, if any, friends. He was very involved with the Anglican Catholic Church, and had worked hard to rise through the ranks of the Commonwealth Bank (CBA) from his first role as a teller. He described Morgan as a slight fellow, with his mother's build, dapper and well-presented at all times, in a dark suit.

Edwin recounted a time, in the mid-1960s, when he'd just left high school and was going for a job, in Moorooka, as a coffin makers' apprentice. He'd been dropped off to the interview, having left the house too late to catch the train back to Ipswich. When he came out of the meeting, he felt in his pocket for his wallet and rail pass to return home, only to realise he'd left it at home. He'd been in such a flap that morning about the job interview!

Edwin knew nothing about the big smoke of Brisbane at the time, but remembered that his cousin, Morgan, worked at the Queen Street branch of the CBA.

He stopped a local policeman and explained his situation.

The officer asked him what he intended to do about his predicament. Edwin told him that he just needed to get into Queen Street and he'd be right – his cousin would lend him the money.

The policeman flagged down a tram enroute to the CBD, explained the situation to the driver, and Edwin got a free trip into town. He found Morgan at work, explained to him what had happened and was given the fare to get home, no more questions asked.

Edwin's Uncle Arthur, however, was a very different sort of fellow. He was very exact, wanting things to go his way and everything had to be 'just so'. He was a big bull of a man, as strong as he was large, and it was easy to imagine him as a locomotive engine driver.

I told Edwin the story that Noel Condon had shared with me about 'Jumbo' Webster, and Edwin was not surprised in the least. Arthur had never behaved like that in Edwin's company, but he was able to recognise these traits immediately. Edwin had been doing a watchmaking course in 1968, and some of the training was at Milton State School. He'd take his lunch up to share with his Uncle Arthur, in that decade after his Aunty Nellie had passed away, and said that Arthur was okay to talk to, but was a very stubborn man.

We compared notes and worked our way through our respective family trees. He showed me that the name Murphy had been changed or misspelled many times throughout the years, as was the way of the times. We had Murfhey and Murfphy to contend with as well.

The First Generation
The Michael Murphy and Mary Ann Potter Story
(Eleanor's Paternal Grandparents)
by David Gould and Dora Griffiths

There are several versions about Michael Murphy's entry to Australia in the 1830s. One oral history tale has it that Michael was born in County Cork in Ireland, and came to Australia as a young orphan lad with his older sister Mary, after their parents (free settlers) died on the voyage over. Michael and Mary were sent to orphanages in Liverpool and Parramatta, NSW.

Michael claimed on his marriage certificate that he was a native of Campbelltown and Parramatta NSW. Some research suggests that Michael was the accompanying son of a female convict and was placed in the Liverpool Orphanage while his mother was in the Female Prison Factory at Parramatta.

Mary Ann Potter's mother and step-father were convicts. Her mother, Elizabeth Martyn, worked in the Female Prison Factory where young Mary Ann was born on 16 May 1837, but she was christened Mary Ann Taylor (possibly after her father, although there's no evidence that Elizabeth was ever married to a Taylor). A few years later, while on a 'ticket of leave' with her young daughter, Elizabeth married William Potter, a convict gardener. Whatever the beginnings for both Michael and Mary Ann, they had an interesting, arduous and adventurous life in the pioneering days of the colony.

The Parramatta Female Factory

The Parramatta Female Factory was located in the grounds of Cumberland Hospital, in the former penal colony of New South Wales. It was one of 13 female factories in the colonies of New South Wales and Van Diemen's Land. The factory idea was a combination of the functions of the British bridewells (reform schools), prisons and workhouses.

The first female factory was above the Parramatta Gaol, commissioned by Governor King in 1804 for convict women. By 1814, there was mounting pressure for the local authorities to manage over 200 women and children who could not be adequately accommodated at the factory, which only had room for 30 people. More than 9000 women passed through these 'factories'.

Courtesy of the National Library of Australia
Painting by Augustus Earle (1793–1838)

When Governor Lachlan Macquarie arrived, he proposed a solution after choosing four acres of William Bligh's 105 acre grant further upstream on the Parramatta River to build a new factory. He instructed Francis Greenway, a convict architect, to design a building that would accommodate 250 women, and in 1821, the first purpose built female factory in the Colony was opened for business, becoming a model for the others.

The success of the Parramatta Female Factory at the time lay in its many purposes – as a hospital, a marriage bureau, a factory, an asylum and a prison for those who committed a crime in the Colony. Being a factory, it also manufactured cloth – linen, wool and linsey Woolsey, which was exported. The inmates also did spinning, knitting, straw plaiting, washing, cleaning duties, rock breaking and oakum picking.

In 1827, the women rebelled with riots, after their rations were cut, and in response to the terrible living and working conditions. It was eventually turned into a Convict Lunatic and Invalid Asylum in 1848.

Wikipedia: The P'matta Female Factory

On the 30th March, 1854, Rev. John Dunmore Lang, who ran the Liverpool Male Orphanage at the time, married the young couple at Sydney Scots Presbyterian Church.

NB: Lang Park (what we now know as Suncorp Stadium), Dunmore Park and Dunmore Terrace are named after John Dunmore Lang, at the end of Heussler Terrace... watch out for more cameos from Dr Lang.

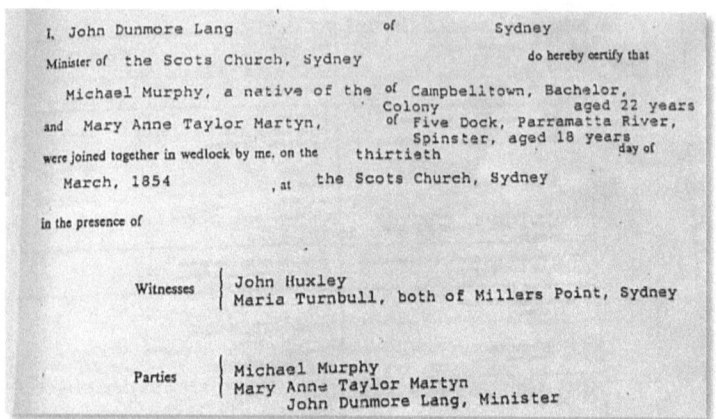

Two children were born in NSW – James in 1855 and Elizabeth in 1857. A short time later the young Murphy family moved to the new colony of Queensland (1859) and were blessed with seven more children – Henry 1861, John 1863, Charles 1865, Susannah 1868, Emma 1870, William 1872 and Arthur 1876.

For many years, the Murphy family lived in the tiny Cothill Cottage, Silkstone. Mary stitched and sewed long into the nights, given that men of the day wore pin-tucked shirts and women, frilled petticoats, so Mary's eyes and fingers were kept busy. As schooling was not free and money was scarce in the Murphy household, Mary home schooled her elder children, while Michael taught them all Irish songs, poems and stories.

Michael, meanwhile, worked as a Cooper, making barrels, and was one of the first men to attempt to grow tobacco in the Ipswich area.

Tragedy struck the Murphy family on 6th June, 1880, when a relatively young Mary, aged 43, died of paralysis, having been ill for a year beforehand. She was buried in Ipswich Cemetery.

> **Mary Ann Murphy (née Potter, Martyn-Taylor)**
> **Born:** 16 May 1837
> **Died:** 6 June 1880
> **Buried:** 8 June 1880 Ipswich Cemetery
> **Religion:** Church of England
> **Mother:** Elizabeth Martyn
> **Father:** Unknown Taylor
> **Stepfather:** William Potter
> **Marriage to James Murphy:** 30 March 1854
> **Children:** James, Elizabeth, Henry, John Thomas, Charles, Susannah (Susan Ann), Emma, William, Arthur

In 1884, the Queensland Government organised for Michael and his four youngest children to travel north to the new village of Cairns to try to grow tobacco. Malaria fever was prevalent in Cairns and district at the time, which had Emma and Arthur laid low with fever. The tobacco would not be grown successfully in the humid climate on the banks of the Barron River, so Michael decided to take his family south again. His daughter Susan refused to leave and found work at Mayoress Severin's place, and later that year, married a young drover called William Mason who had settled on an adjoining property.

Once back in Ipswich, Michael worked on Bell's property at Coochin Coochin, as well as taking on the role as caretaker of the Ipswich Show Grounds. The Murphy family members took on many different jobs such as Cobb & Co Mail delivery (James), horse-drawn cab and bus driver, coalminer, railway worker, farmhand building sheds and fences, and contractor for building roads and bridges.

Many resided in the Ipswich area, while others ventured to Goomeri, Maryborough, Mackay, Rockhampton and Cairns.

The descendants today number many hundreds, perhaps thousands.

Michael Murphy
(Eleanor's Paternal Grandfather)

In his later years, Michael moved to Maryborough where he lived with his eldest daughter Elizabeth (Telfer) until his death (aged 86) on 7 November 1918. He is buried in Maryborough Cemetery. One of the difficulties in tracing Michael was the way his name was spelled on the death certificate – Murfphey.

> *Michael Murphy (aka Murfphey)*
> **Born:** *1832 Kilkenny Ireland*
> **Died:** *7 November 1918*
> **Place of Death:** *Maryborough General Hospital*
> **Buried:** *Maryborough Cemetery with his daughter, Emma (Griffiths)*
> **Occupation:** *Farmer (tobacco), Cooper (barrel-maker) and Caretaker, Ipswich Showgrounds*
> **Religion:** *Church of England*
> **Mother and Father:** *Unknown*
> **Marriage to Mary Ann Potter:** *30 March 1854*
> **Children:** *James, Elizabeth, Henry, John Thomas, Charles, Susannah (Susan Ann), Emma, William, Arthur*

Just to be clear, Michael Murphy and Mary Ann Potter were Eleanor's paternal grandparents. Their firstborn son, James, was Eleanor's father.

James Murphy (Eleanor's father)
by Edwin Murphy, grandson

James Murphy was born at Five Dock, Sydney, NSW, on 31 July 1855. He was the oldest child of Michael and Mary Ann Murphy.

He was educated in Ipswich and later followed the occupation of mailman, carrying the mail, by horseback, from Ipswich to Nanango and other places on the head of the Brisbane River.

It was while he was engaged in this occupation that the historical massacre of the Fraser family at Hornet Bank Station took place. James was at the scene of the massacre shortly after it took place.

The Hornet Bank Massacre

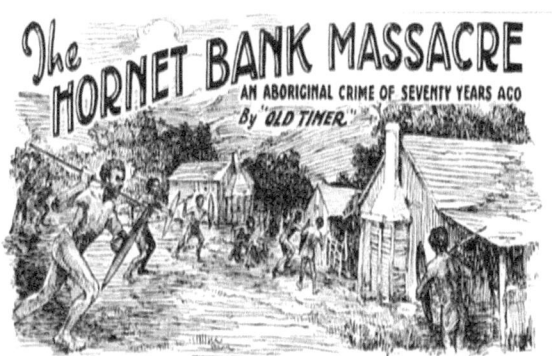

1 August 1925, The Daily Mail

The Hornet Bank massacre of eleven British colonists (including seven members of the Fraser family) and one Aboriginal station-hand in direct retaliation to the deaths of twelve Iman people by members of the Fraser clan, occurred in the early hours on the morning of 27 October 1857. It took place at Hornet Bank Station on the upper Dawson River near Eurombah in central Queensland, Australia.

In subsequent punitive missions conducted by Native Police, private settler militias and by William Fraser, as many as 300 Aborigines may have been murdered in counter-retaliation. Indiscriminate shootings of Aboriginal men, women and children found within a wide radius of the station were conducted.

The result was the believed extermination of the entire Iman tribe and language group by 1858, but this is however not true and descendants of this group have recently been recognised by The High Court of Australia to be the original custodians of the land surrounding the town of Taroom.

Wikipedia: Hornet Bank Massacre

James Murphy

James married Agnes Morgan, a daughter of Mr Morgan Morgan, a well-known wheelwright of the town of Ipswich and father of Mr E. G. Morgan, who for many years was the secretary of the Qld Woollen Manufacturing Company. James and Agnes settled in Ipswich where James was employed by such well-known produce firms as John Pettigrew & Sons, and G. R. Wilson. James lived for some time on Mr Wilson's property at Raceview. Afterwards, he was on the Ipswich Station cab rank, and worked for Messrs J. P. Bottomley & Sons butchers.

Later, he secured employment at Whitwood Colliery, where he worked until his retirement in 1929. His first wife, Agnes, died in 1896, and he married Lena (Magdalene) Weimer, from Dinmore in 1904. James always led an active life and enjoyed good health until a sudden seizure, when he became the victim of a stroke. He lived at Brisbane Road, Dinmore and Murphy's Gully was named after him.

Magdalene Murphy

James Murphy
Born: 1855 NSW
Died: 1933 Buried Ipswich Cemetery
Occupation: Mail Rider
Married: Agnes Morgan on 1 January 1879
Children: Edwin James (died); Agnes; Fred; Frank; Eleanor; Gwendoline; Sidney; Edwin James
Agnes died in 1896
Remarried: Magdalene (Lena) Weimer 1904
Their children: Rosa, Henry Gustav and Charles Whitwood
Lena died 3 April 1954

There are many, many relatives of the Murphy family, but there are only two strands that we need to know for this story. James is one. Henry, his brother, is the other.

Henry Murphy (Eleanor's Uncle)

Henry Murphy, born 12 March 1861, and died 18 January 1907, buried in Mackay Cemetery, was a Railways Engine Driver or Fireman who lived in Mackay. He married Jane Gillespie in 1889. Their children were Eileen, Muriel, Robert and William.

Make sure you take note of the children's names for later – at least one of them comes up again – no prizes for guessing which one ☺.

Thanks to Kay Dieckmann, Michael Murphy's great-great-granddaughter, who was responsible for organising the 1999 Murphy reunion. The history and photographs were shared by members of the extended Murphy family with the additional help of the Queensland and New South Wales State Archives, and the State Library of Queensland.

What happened in Edwin and Gloria Murphy's Lounge Room?

So, as you can see, my off-the-cuff phone call to the only Edwin Murphy I could find, was really fruitful!

As we finished our cup of tea, Edwin's wife and daughter arrived home. Gloria and Penny were welcoming but curious, so I quickly caught them up with who I was and why I was there, showing them the bank books and money. Gloria weighed in with memories of Morgan's Sunday visits, and took me for a wander through the house. The walls of their home were lined with beautiful family photographs of their children and grandchildren, as well as older, sepia portraits of their ancestors.

As Gloria was explaining who was who to me, I suddenly remembered that THIS was the family whom Morgan had nominated as one of his two beneficiaries.

"Oh," I exclaimed, "I know who you are now! Morgan left you money in his will!"

As I saw Edwin and Gloria look startled, I quickly apologised, and said that it must be quite disconcerting to have a stranger know so much about their family. They were very forgiving and understanding of my faux pas, having built up a level of trust in me and the Under the Lino Project by this stage.

"Yes, that's right," said Edwin. "He looked after us after he died, as was his way."

"He also left us his parents' lounge suite, Caylie," said Gloria, leading me into their sitting room. "Shame I can't really use it anymore – it's too low to the ground for me to get out of easily."

And there, in front of me, was Arthur and Eleanor's fully sprung and restored silky oak lounge setting... three beautiful pieces. I ran my hand over the broad, wooden arms and imagined Eleanor and Arthur sitting there of an evening, respectively sewing and reading the paper, in my house, a hundred years earlier.

"It used to be brown velvet, but we had it recovered and restored, so we could sell it. It's been for sale for some time now, but no bites."

My mouth went dry, my heart started to race and I just had to ask, "How much do you want for it?"

Two weeks later, David and I were driving home with the kids from Ipswich, having just spent a very pleasant morning with the Murphy family. In the back of our Ute was Arthur and Eleanor's couch, heading back to its original home, as part of our family now.

David had taken a little convincing to part with the money, but he's watched me fall in love with this project over the course of the last year, and knew it was yet another synchronous event.

All he said was, "You'd better sell some of those bloody books!"

The acquisition of this beautiful old settee was nothing in comparison to the new relationships I had built with the Murphys of Ipswich, the Websters of Milton and the greater Brisbane community, but honestly, I smile every time I walk past that settee, and disappear back in time every time I sit down on one of those low, low chairs. I only curse the Websters and Murphys when I have to get up out of the damn things!

Arthur and Eleanor's Silky Oak Lounge Suite, bequeathed to Edwin and Gloria Murphy, by their cousin Morgan. It's now back where it started 100 years ago at 86 Heussler Terrace, Milton

*

Cothill Cottage

Until I came along, the Murphy family believed that James and Agnes Murphy's house, Cothill Cottage, was on Blackstone Road, Silkstone.

After I drove away from my initial meeting with Edwin, I had just enough time to visit the home where Eleanor Murphy and her many siblings had grown up. I pulled up in front of a dear little wooden workers cottage on Blackstone Road, Silkstone, and jumped out of the car with my camera. The neighbour was in his front yard, and I explained that I was just going to take a few pics of the house.

He said, "The owner's at home – he's just out the back, if you want me to get him."

Next thing, a man called Dan was standing at the gate, asking if he could help me. 'Salt of the Earth' is how I'd describe Dan. A retired journalist, in a flannel shirt, jeans and boots, he looked as if he had been born to live in this house. He was reminiscent of a swagman, and could have been a descendant of the Kelly gang, had he been born a century earlier.

Dan was immediately interested in the Under the Lino story and happily walked me around the house, telling me what he

knew about its origins. The houses in this area of Silkstone were in a Heritage precinct, having been built in the 1800s. His cottage was built between 1887 and 1897.

He had bought his house from two sisters who had run the old Booval Post Office. There were rumours that Ned Kelly's brother, Dan, had lived in the house in the earliest days. Funny for me to think that this Dan also looked like his namesake from the Kelly gang then!

Dan told me about the Coonawarra Historical Centre on Redbank Plains Road, and Picture Ipswich, part of the Ipswich City Council's Historical Section, which I filed away in my notes for future reference, loving his buy-in. He invited me into the cottage, after promising me he wasn't an axe-murderer... I am a pretty good judge of character, and had already marked Dan as a good guy, so I laughed and said, "Yeah, that's good, because nobody knows I'm here...!"

The cottage had been lovingly cared for by my host, kept in as original condition as was possible, given the council rules on heritage-listed properties.

I left Dan with my details and suggested he take a look at the Under the Lino website to get a better picture of the project. He did one better and joined the Facebook group, where he became an active member almost immediately.

Because he's got an investigative background, some of my story about the house hadn't rung true for Dan, however. He'd had a proper look at the photo I'd sent him that Edwin had given me of Cothill Cottage,  and just couldn't see his house as being the same place. He called me a few days later to say he'd visited the house he knew as Cothill Cottage on Cothill Road, just around the corner and the pics were the same as the pic I'd shown him.

After all that, I'd been oohing and aaahing about the wrong house!

Dan *Just confirming, went to titles registry and there are No Murphys on my title deeds... I went back as far as the New South Wales Deed of Grant in 1855... also no Kellys listed anywhere... sorry for you and even sorrier for me!*
Caylie *What a shame for us both Dan! It was very exciting to walk through your home, though, with even an inkling that a Kelly had lived there, and for me, that a Murphy may have lived there!*

Eleanor Webster née Murphy

Maternal Grandparents: Morgan Morgan (B. 1820 Pembrokeshire, Wales, Arrived in Brisbane, Australia 1873, M. 1879, D. 1894 Ipswich) and Ann Adams (B. 1829 Pembrokeshire, Wales, Arrived in Brisbane, Australia 1873, M. 1879, D. 1901 Ipswich)

Paternal Grandparents: Michael Murphy (B. 1832, Kilkenny, Ireland, Arrived 1854 Australia, M. 1854, D. 1918 Maryborough) and Mary Ann Potter (B. 1837 Parramatta NSW Australia, M. 1854 D. 1880 Ipswich)

Parents: James Murphy (B. 1855 Sydney D. 1933 Ipswich) Mail Rider and Agnes Morgan (B. 1857 Pembrokeshire D. 1896 Ipswich)

Born: 10 July 1884 QLD

Siblings: 5th of ten siblings – Edwin (died as an infant), Agnes, Frederick, Francis, James, Edwin, Elizabeth, Vandelyne and Sydney

Stepmother: Magdalene Weimer, married James in 1904

Half-siblings: Rosa, Henry Gustav and Charles Whitwood

Educated: unknown Ipswich area

Career: Housewife

Married: 1913 to Arthur William Joseph Webster when she was 29 and he was 23

Children: Morgan 1914–1989; Colin 1918–1918 (ten months)

Death: Sunday, 24 August 1958, aged 72 years old at the house of the O'Donnell family, 47 Montpelier St, Wilston on Arthur's birthday

Buried: Toowong Cemetery with Arthur and Colin

Part 7

Who is Muriel White?

The Mystery of the Third Bank Book Owner

So, who *was* Mrs Muriel White, whose address in the back of the South Brisbane Commonwealth Bank pass book was Bristol Street, West End? There was over £1,000 in her account and the last transaction was in June 1958, just six weeks before Eleanor's death.

For the first few days of research into who Muriel White was, many names were put on the table by people in the group, who had used Trove, Billion Graves and Ancestry.com to seek her out. Lyn even frequented the registry of Births Deaths and Marriages, spending money from her own pocket in the process, going above and beyond in the quest for answers.

People found wedding notices, music teacher ads, obituaries and race day articles. Many had relatives with White as a surname, several of them also called Muriel! Whites Hill on the south side of Brisbane was carefully considered for a while, but it all came down to matching dates and addresses.

The bank book transactions were dated from 1951–1958, for a married woman called Muriel White.

We ascertained that the name 'White' was a name a bit like 'Smith' or 'Jones', designed to make our job more difficult!

We also went down a few rabbit holes from time to time forgetting some of the pertinent facts, such as Muriel White was a married name. It took Meg, who has an ancient history degree with a particular interest in social history and tombstones, to remind us all that the name on the bank book said *MRS* Muriel White. People continued to forget this, however, but others were quick to remind us all and keep us on track.

But then Diana threw in, "Don't discount the fact that Muriel may actually not be a 'Mrs'. My husband's grandmother used 'Mrs' and her maiden name due to having an illegitimate child. The child's father (who was engaged to my husband's grandmother) came back from war married to someone else. To avoid the stigma attached she put on a fake wedding ring and anyone who didn't know her thought she was a widow."

In amongst these theories, another cropped up that would have made a wonderful story... One of the people Arthur ran over while he was a train driver was a man called White so we had several conversations about whether the Websters were helping out the family after the accident.

Janelle *So Arthur was involved in at least two tragedies at work. Poor man. Back then hopefully most were accidents. These days such a lot of deaths on the rail network are deliberate and it is devastating for drivers, other staff and customers as well as the family and friends of the deceased, of course.*
Lyn *Yes, the post mortem/inquest was deemed an accident. The train ended up 90 feet further down the track before it was stopped. It must have been traumatic for Arthur as well, as it still is today.*
Michelle *I don't know whether anything here may be relevant, but may be worth checking? Has anyone else seen this? So, Bailey we know was killed by a train and Webster was the driver and a witness. White was also killed by a train (his second run in). Webster isn't listed as witness. Are all five men witnesses or something else? Mary White is listed as relative and is actually his wife. May Webster is his niece. Could there be any connection to Muriel White and May Webster? I agree it is possible there is no Muriel White, as suggested in a recent post, but checking every avenue is what we do eh?*
Lyn *I had a look at this inquest last week and feel that the surname White is just by chance. That poor old William and his family had nothing else to do with our lot. Mary White was his wife. They lived at Geebung. He was deaf and started crossing the rail lines without looking about him and although Arthur Webster sounded the horn several times, Mr White didn't hear it. The inquest was closed as being an unfortunate accident.*
Shar *Could Mr White have had a daughter that Arthur and Eleanor felt responsible for after the death of her father?*
Felice *The bank account was created before the death of old man White.*
Caylie *That blows a fascinating theory out of the water...*

Hamish and Lyn were the real drivers behind the Muriel White mystery. Between them, and several others, they discovered scores of Muriel Whites buried in Brisbane cemeteries.

From the very beginning, people theorised that Muriel and Eleanor were one and the same person, so we really needed to get our detective hats on and start to think critically. Electoral roll records, marriage and birth certificates were the only way. We still struggled to match any of them to Bristol Street. Not having a house number made the search more difficult.

It was getting very frustrating but Hamish and Lyn were always there to give us a laugh and relieve the tension...

Hamish *Found Muriel.*
Lyn *You're terrible Muriel!*

Steve Webster *To further the intrigue, a Mrs Muriel White was my brother-in-law's mother! I know she was of Irish decent so it possible she was a Murphy as was Eleanor. They could have been sisters? I'll check with my b-i-l.*
Caylie *Oh my God Steve! She is the missing link! 500 people are hanging on my every word waiting to hear who Muriel White is!! Why was her money book here??!! If she was Eleanor's sister then that solves the mystery*
Linda *Hi! I've just joined this group so am trying to catch up on the story. I'm really intrigued as, not only am I Steve Webster's sister, but Muriel White was my husband's mother's name. She was Muriel Devine and married Laurence James White (Jim), we think in 1940. They would have been in Brisbane at this time, but we have no knowledge of where they were living then and whether or not they had any connection to this house or family. Fascinating stuff!*
Some hours later...
Steve Webster *Muriel not my b-i-l's mother.*

Caylie *Because of you, we know that she was Muriel Murphy and was possibly the child of Eleanor who may have been married to a William Murphy no relation in early 1900s*

Steve Webster was the one, ironically, who gave us the idea that Muriel could have been a Murphy. Hamish was the one to discover electoral roll records on Ancestry.com and found a Murphy family living on Bristol Street in West End: The 1905-1925 electoral roll showed a Muriel Murphy to live in a house called Cooran on Bristol Street.

Caylie *Hey, Steve Webster is suggesting that Muriel was a Murphy and potentially Eleanor's sister?*
Hamish *OMG*
Caylie *I KNOW!!!*

Picture Hamish here, typing furiously with this new-found knowledge, looking now for Muriel Murphy...

Hamish *OMG MURIEL MURPHY BRISTOL ST 1919 TEACHER*
Caylie *Omg you are a legend!!! You found her!!*
Hamish *Need to make sure though. Muriel Murphy in 1925 still at Bristol St... Cooran is house name. Late 1920s Muriel Murphy drops off electoral roll records at Bristol*
Caylie *Maybe she moved in to our house then?*
Hamish *Still can't figure out why use Bristol St and take on White. Whole bunch of other Murphys at Bristol St in same house: Jane Murphy Muriel Murphy Robert Cleveland Murphy William Henry Murphy... 1934 Robert was still at Cooran Bristol St, Muriel wasn't. William was listed as Bristol St, but diff house. Perhaps, Jane and Robert were Muriel's parents? We sure this is the right Muriel?*
Caylie *James Murphy and Agnes Morgan are Eleanor's parents*
Hamish *1928 Muriel Murphy goes to Muriel Hill, still at Bristol St. I think it must be her. She must be hiding from something. To go from Murphy, to Hill, to White.*

Caylie *Oh! Muriel Hill. THEN White...*
Hamish *Lost a hubby in the war methinks. After 1928, who knows where she went.*

Hamish to Old Brisbane Album
We have a Muriel in Bristol St, just trying to figure out if it's the Muriel we are after....
Emma *Did Muriel pass away and Eleanor was being both Muriel and Eleanor?? Could Muriel and Eleanor be the same person??*

So now we knew that this Muriel, who lived in Bristol Street, West End, was a Murphy. We'd already worked out that Eleanor's maiden name was Murphy. So I put it to the group that we had to find out if Eleanor and Muriel were related in any way.

Meg *So did we rule out niece?*
Caylie *No that's definitely on the table.*
Meg *I found Miss Muriel's teaching advert.*
Lyn *Wow. Mandolin. That's an unusual one.*
Rob N Suzanne *Could they have been related in some way? Or perhaps good friends during the war time.*
Vivianne *Illegitimate daughter? Murphy is Eleanor's maiden name...*

In 1928, Muriel Murphy turned into Muriel Hill, according to the electoral roll. We lost her after that and didn't know how or if she became Muriel White. Was there a Mr White before Mr Hill? Did Mr Hill die in WWII? Was there ever a Mr White?

Hamish *Nope, she appeared out of nowhere on the electoral roll records in 1919; matching Bristol St.*
Emma *Wow... so Muriel and Eleanor could be mother and daughter??*
Caylie *We just need Muriel's date of birth... Eleanor was born in 1884. If Muriel was born after 1900, then we can suggest she was her daughter...*

Lyn *Muriel Murphy born in Qld – parents Henry Murphy and Jane Gillespie. She was born in 1892 in Maryborough. I got her marriage cert and death cert this morning.*
Wendy *Muriel Murphy married Horace Hill in 1927*
Hamish *Name: Horace Hill; Spouse Name: Muriel Murphy, Marriage Date: 18 Apr 1927. 1927 would make sense. 1926 electoral roll has her last name as Murphy. 1928 electoral roll as Hill*
Lyn *Horace Hill died: 1969*
Caylie *So Horace died 1969, but Muriel became Mrs White somewhere between 1927 and 1955...*
Grace *Maybe the White person may have been an American when they were in Brisbane during the war years and took up with Muriel?*

As we discovered facts and ruled out dead ends, Lyn updated the family tree on Ancestry.com. A splinter group, run by Hamish, looked into marriage and cemetery records for Muriel's parents, and found that Jane Murphy (née Gillespie) died in 1951 aged 83.

Lyn also bought Muriel (née Murphy) Hill's death certificate, and discovered that she'd died on 7 July 1969.

Benita *I reckon Muriel's family was loaded and they didn't trust Hill so they left her financials with the Murphy family. When did she marry Hill?*
Hamish *Marriage records obtained by one of the members show that she married Horace Hill in 1927, aged 34.*
Lyn *Okay. Just spent the last of my life savings. Horace Hill died 10 May 1969. Only two months before Muriel. They both died in Mt Olivet. They married 18 April 1927 at St. Peters, West End. These are the children of Henry and Jane*
1890 Eileen Murphy; 1892 Muriel Murphy; 1894 Robert Cleveland Murphy; 1898 William Henry Murphy

Slowly but surely, we built up the family tree, looking at BDM records, cemetery records and TROVE notices.

We still couldn't find a link to White from Muriel Murphy-Hill, despite the fact that the family tree was growing! What we were trying to do was to find a connection between Eleanor and Muriel. To do that we needed to go further back in both women's family trees.

Benita *James' father was Michael Murphy. Has anyone confirmed if Eleanor Webster née Murphy was part of Muriel Murphy family? Muriel Murphy's Sister, Eileen, had a child, who has had children whom should be alive today. I haven't made the connection of Muriel to Eleanor yet. There are just so many Murphys.*
Caylie *If we know Muriel's father and Eleanor's father and could see if they were brothers... I can't see the Murphy siblings from Eleanor's parents*
Hamish *Muriel's father was Henry Murphy. But I don't have any Birth or Dates for him*

Right from the very beginning, we believed that there was a relationship between Eleanor and Muriel.
1. The bank books were hidden together at Eleanor and Arthur's home and,
2. Eleanor died six weeks after the last transaction (a deposit) in Muriel White's bank book, and there was cash within the book awaiting the next deposit

Our research thus far had given us this...
- Eleanor's parents were James Murphy and Agnes Morgan.
- Eleanor was born in 1884
- Muriel's parents were Henry Murphy and Jane Gillespie
- Muriel was born in 1892.

So what was Muriel's relationship to Eleanor, who was only eight years older? The only way to find out was to find a relationship between Muriel and Eleanor's parents. Of course, there were many Murphys living in Brisbane in the late 1800s/early 1900s, but we had the street name as Bristol Street.

There was a huge flurry of activity one night, where several of us were up until 3am, so close to finding the answer, yet so far. Lyn, Hamish, Missy and Benita were the drivers behind this particular investigation, looking at the huge Murphy family connections in Brisbane and trying to find who was related to whom.

By 1:30am, we knew Eleanor's parents and siblings, noted from Trove records. James Murphy and Agnes Morgan had four sons and three daughters...

>Frederick Murphy (married Emma)
>Edwin Murphy (married Ethel)
>Francis Murphy (married Elsie)
>Eleanor Webster (née Murphy)
>Sydney Murphy (married Constance)
>Gwendolyn Hegerty (née Murphy)
>Agnes Besgrove (née Murphy)
>plus half-siblings from her father's second marriage to
>Magdalene Weimer
>Rosa Berry (née Murphy)
>Henry Murphy (married Mabel)
>Charles Murphy (married Marie)

There were no Muriels in that lot, so Muriel Murphy could *not* have been Eleanor's sister – different parents and not in her sibling group. Eleanor therefore may have been her cousin or Aunt, given that both women's fathers were Murphys.

Benita *Hmmm the James Murphy I'm looking at died in 1911*
Hamish *Yeah, Mary Ann Potter... his death notice is 30 October 1933 and has Mary Ann Potter listed*
Benita *Does it have his dad as Michael though? I saw all their transport to Australia. Pretty cool. I think I found Michael's death notice. And James would have had lots of siblings if that's the case. The census lists them all. His father I reckon is the one from Maryborough.*

Does anyone know where we got Henry and Jane from re Muriel's parents? I can't remember now and I can't seem to find anything that matches that info, so just want someone to confirm what and where we saw that

Lyn *Yes, it was on Muriel's marriage certificate. Just bought another one... Marriage certificate of James Murphy and Agnes Morgan, Eleanor's parents. Date: 1 Jan 1879. James' parents (Eleanor's paternal grandparents) are Michael Murphy and Mary Ann Potter. James was born Sydney.*

Benita *Yup got that. No marriage certs for Henry and Jane by any chance?*

Lyn *The witnesses at James and Agnes' wedding were a Henry Murphy and Elizabeth Murphy.*

Benita *Maybe his mother and father? I'll look up Elizabeth. I have her address here I think: 179 Kent St, But she wasn't living with Henry. Found her photo. I think she became Elizabeth Prow*

Lyn *Ha ha! Bingo!!! I just got the marriage cert for Henry Murphy and Jane Gillespie and tada! Just as I was wondering!!*

Benita *What does it say?*

Lyn *No, probably brother and ?? The parents are.....*

Benita *Yup. Tell me!*

Lyn *Michael Murphy and Mary Ann Potter!*

Benita *So Henry and Elizabeth are siblings, at the wedding. Wait. Is that the link made?!*

Lyn *Yes!!!!*

Benita *Woot! Ok. Let me add it.*

[2:45 AM]

Lyn *Henry Murphy married Jane Gillespie 8 July 1889 at Maryborough. Henry was born at Ipswich and Jane was born at Maryborough. He was 28 years and she was 21 years. One of the witnesses was a Charles Murphy. Henry and James were brothers. Eleanor was the daughter of James, and Muriel was the daughter of Henry. That makes Eleanor and Muriel first cousins!*
Caylie *Well, Lyn is a legend for piecing the evidence together and working out that these ladies were cousins! I knew if we went back far enough and proved their fathers as brothers, we'd have an answer! We still don't understand where the name Muriel White comes from and why were the bank books together.*
Lyn *Her husband Horace, was a widower from Luton, Bedfordshire. At the time of the marriage he lived in Kurilpa Street and he was 32 years. His occupation was rubber worker! His parents were James Hill and Charlotte! So, the Horace who died in 1969 is the right Horace. Leaves me with another question – where did White come from??? Argh!!!*
Caylie *yes. Somewhere between 1927 and 1955 she became Mrs White.*
Lyn *I don't know! Maybe Horace and Muriel divorced?*
Caylie *Would have had to as he died in 1969 after 1955 Mrs White bank book.*
Lyn *I have just got Muriel's death cert. So sad. The informant was the Public Curator. She died at Mt Olivet on 7 July 1969 and was cremated at Albany Creek two days later. It shows that Horace was her only husband and they had no children.*
Hamish *Where'd the 'White' come from??? How'd you find info re: her death?*
Lyn *The BMD lists. That's where I've been following all the batch, match and despatches.*
Wendy *My grandmother lived with a man but was married to another, she used the second man's name till she died. Horace and Muriel were still listed in Bristol St in 1958 and still in 1968.*

Hamish was the one who found a Muriel Murphy on the electoral roll from 1903 onwards living in Bristol Street and Lyn discovered she was Eleanor's cousin through marriage records of their parents. She was the closest we came to finding Muriel White in Bristol St.

Hamish *1968 electoral rolls... 19 BRISTOL ST! GO GO GO!*

till. Muriel, Cooran, 19 Bristol st., home duties, F

Shelley *Looking at 19 Bristol Street. It's been renovated beyond recognition and has been bought and sold four times just since 1990.*
Michelle *Interesting, that they seem to live at "Cooran, Bristol St" up until 1954 when Muriel and Horace were at "Cooran" listed as number 6. Must have moved their house or the numbers changed (more likely).*
Allan *6 may have been a Lot number in the early days of the street getting houses, changing to number 19 later. This practice still continues to this day.*
Michelle *PDOnline has them as L115 and L107 for 6 and 19 respectively. Don't know if they would have changed over the years too?*
Kym *You'd have to investigate if Council still have old parish or subdivision maps that would show the lot numbers. Street numbers often changed but don't think lot numbers did*
Diana *Would lot numbers had to have changed through subdivision?*
Kym *They could have, you'd have to look at Council maps and rate records. The original paper records would hold much more info than current computer records.*
Allan *If you go to the Antique shop on Ipswich Road at Annerley, there are literally hundreds of old BCC subdivision maps for around $10 each. I have bought quite a few of my local northside area.*
Michelle *Thoughts on trying to contact owners of 6 and 19 to see what information they may have?*
Caylie *I am getting historical titles records on that property, as well as mine.*

Some excellent advice to look up historic land titles may have saved us all some time, and I eventually did do this six months down the track! Jay suggested that most of the Queensland school enrolment records are available with many of the Brisbane school records digitised and viewable online. The enrolment records usually recorded home address and father's occupation etc., sometimes with additional notes. This can be a useful source of corroborating evidence and timelines.

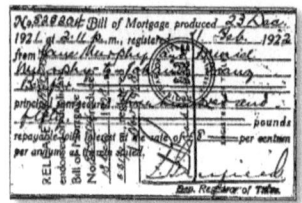 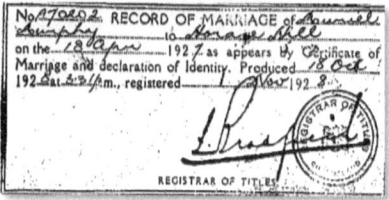

Again, it took some time, but Magnus Eriksson's cadastral map from 1919 was helpful in finding out more information. The land upon which the 19 Bristol Street house was sitting originally was owned by John George Cribb – Jane and Muriel Murphy became joint tenants of the property in 1922, after Jane was widowed.

They bought it from Johann Franz Benfer in 1922, presumably having rented the house from him for several years, as they'd been listed as living at Cooran since the early 1900s.

Excerpt from 40 Chain Moreton Cadastral Map 1919

Brenda *According to electoral rolls, Muriel's mother Jane, Muriel and brother, William Henry, were living in Maryborough (after father Henry died in 1907 in Mackay) until 1917. Jane was a dressmaker, William worked for the Railways. In 1919 Muriel, Jane and William were living at "Cooran", 19 Bristol Street, West End. According to this advertisement in the Courier Mail February 15, 1928, someone in the house had enough money to own a 1924 Maxwell Tourer and was selling it! In the 1928/1929 Electoral Rolls, Muriel's husband Horace Roland Hill had moved on from being a straw worker (?) to a tyre repairman...*

Shar *Quick question Brenda... If Janes hubby (I'm gathering that would be Mr Murphy) died, did Jane ever remarry? If so, who?*

Brenda *I haven't seen anything to indicate that she did remarry. There's nothing on the electoral rolls to indicate another man living with them in Bristol Street and she is recorded as Jane Murphy when she died.*

Shar *That could be very true and Lyn is by far more experienced at this than I am BUT I can't give up on Muriel White until she is completely ruled out as being someone (don't ask me why, but I just have this unequivocal belief there is a link we're overlooking or hasn't become apparent)... It's a bit odd tho', don't you think that Maryborough was the land of the Whites and the Murphys... and no link exists*

Brenda *It might be of interest is this advert for the sale of "Cooran" in 1913, which gives a description of the house*

> Under instructions from the Owner.
> To INVESTORS, SPECULATORS, and OTHERS.
> TWO WELL-BUILT and comparatively NEW COTTAGES.
> BRISTOL-STREET, WEST END.
> "COOROY" AND "COORAN."
> These houses will always command good tenants, and fine returns on investment.
> 3. BRISTOL-STREET, WEST END.—Situate on rise between HARD-GRAVE-ROAD AND BOUNDARY-STREET. TWO VERY DESIRABLE COTTAGES, well and faithfully built, each containing sitting and dining rooms, half hall, 3 bedrooms, kitchen, bath, gas and water, pantry, described as Subdivisions 106 and 107 of W.S. Allotments 81 and 82, each 16 perches. At present occupied by Messrs. Phillips and Smith.

And then this happened...

Rebecca Levingston ABC Radio National Life Matters

Hi Caylie, My colleague in Conversations passed on your email for Under the Lino – it sounds fascinating! I'm wondering if you'd like to come on my Weekends show and share the story (and hopefully get some more people on board to help with the investigation).

Would you be available to come into the studio this weekend? I have an interview slot available at 8:30am. Feel free to give me a call to chat in more detail.

Rebecca

8:30am ABC Radio Brisbane Interview with Rebecca Levingston

It was quite an excursion for Will, Kitty and I when we headed into the ABC studios at Southbank on a rainy Saturday morning in October. They'd never seen me do a radio segment live before, and I loved being able to show them how it all works. Not that I'm an expert, of course! I was just as curious and excited.

I was also very nervous, because so many of the UTL Team, family and friends were listening. It was important that I spoke confidently about the project.

Just before the show started, I handed Rebecca the bank books and money. She needed a few minutes before we went on air to familiarise herself with the documents, and was genuinely fascinated by my discovery. Rebecca Levingston is extremely good at her job, and she made me feel very much at ease, so I knew the show would be just fine.

As the on-air discussion progressed, Rebecca continued to flick through the bank books. I saw her pause and frown when she got to the back page of Muriel White's bank book. I was explaining to her that Muriel was our missing link, that we'd found out plenty about the Websters, but couldn't work out who this Muriel person was.

As she stared at the back of the book, she mentioned that her husband had once lived in Bristol Street, which was quite a coincidence. Then while we were on a break, she texted her hubby to check what number he'd lived at.

As the next segment started up, Rebecca's husband texted her back. He used to live at No. 19 Bristol Street, West End.

At that moment, I actually felt a strange sensation come over me, like electricity crackling through my body. It was such a surreal moment and one that really reflects so much about this story. For it to be captured on air for others to hear, though, really gave kudos to the other stories I'd been telling about serendipitous events.

Nicki *Muriel White was not a real name in my opinion. Maybe Eleanor was helping her escape her real husband or something?*
Lyn *Then why did Muriel and Horace stay together until they ended up in Mt Olivet together and died within two months of each other?*
Caylie *True... but you never know? We have to consider all possibilities until the truth is revealed?!*
Helen *Muriel White I would guess was definitely a fake name. It used to be so easy to have a fake name, you got paid in cash and to open up a bank account you just said I want one. I remember one person told me once that you always kept the First Letter of your last name because that way it would look like a normal signature – I was told that in the '70s. The reason the bank books may have been hidden under the lino – is to hide them from her husband and also because of death duties – I remember my grandmother telling me about TV licences and them hiding the radio and the TV*
Shar *Maybe Eleanor didn't tell her about the money and when she up and died there was no longer anyway to help Muriel*
Carolyn *My grandmother had many bank accounts under false names, which was very easy to do back then. She did it to hide income and savings so it didn't affect her pension.*

Lyn *I concur totally with you Caylie. I really don't think anyone else knew about it. I still can't get my head around the White. I keep thinking about and can't come up with an answer. I believe she was the only one who knew about it otherwise the pounds would have been converted to dollars – both the cash and the books.*

Diana *I am of the same opinion. But I keep asking why were the other two books also hidden? They both belonged to real people. I can't find a Muriel White with any kind of connection to any part of this family. I have been wondering if she was already deceased (and maybe without a will and leaving no indication she had a bank account) and someone was using her account.*

Katrina *I agree, I think it was perhaps a bank account under a false name. The more interesting question to me is where the money came from in the first place – quite large sums on a regular basis. Maybe some research around a potential source (typical wages of the time, how much one could earn if a property was rented out, given the era what a war widow's pension was) might shed some light on what kind of activity might generate that kind of cash??*

Brenda *Perhaps the women found the money somewhere and instead of reporting it as lost property, created bank accounts and deposited smaller amounts to make it seem legitimate.*

Benita *Also it might be relevant that Morgan Webster was a bank officer... maybe he was involved somehow with the bank books*

Franki *Sounds to me like mum was saving money for son (in a false name) but didn't want son to know (I like the initials matching theory, Muriel White/Morgan Webster). The addresses match Muriel in West End but maybe they just used her details. Could son not be trusted with money or was the account started from when he was too young to have an account in his name (sum carried forward)? I set up account for each of my children (and have been saving a little sum of money each week for them since they were born) which they know nothing about so if I dropped dead, it would be a similar situation although the accounts are at least in my name!!*

Or maybe because Morgan worked at the bank he didn't want his fellow tellers to know how much money he had/was saving. Maybe when mum died he couldn't find the bank books? Couldn't withdraw without them – especially the fake name one – all got too hard – forgot about it?? Legal costs involved in the will etc...

Caylie *Trying to find out from the bank if the family could have found out from them if there were accounts and accessed the money without them after her death...*

Franki *Do we know whether they had wills? Maybe we could do a search at the Supreme Court to get a copy I'll also try to do some looking into property records to see how property passed from mum/dad to son*

Sue *They would have been able to. People lost their bank books all the time.*

Lyn *I've got several wills on order from the archives.*

Eleanor's Estate and Historic Title Searches

Arthur bought the house from Alfred Richer on 27th January, 1914, with no mortgage, but he may have had a loan from his father, John.

John Webster, Arthur's father, died on December 16, 1933, and shortly thereafter, Eleanor Webster became a joint tenant on the title (19 January 1934).

Morgan took over his mother's title share three weeks after his mother's death.

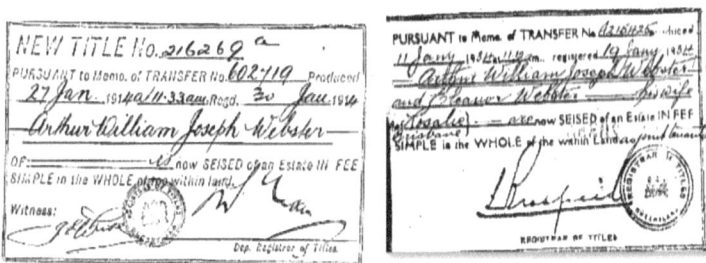

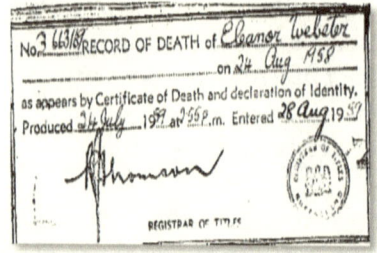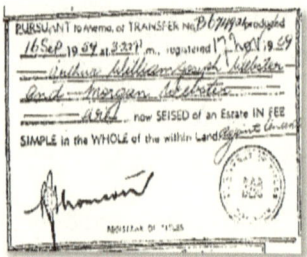

Caylie *Why would Eleanor have become a joint title owner after John Webster died? Do you think his will might have stipulated that whatever money that was left owing to him from Arthur should be just given over to Eleanor as the title owner?*

Cheryl *On your original title deed it showed that there was no mortgage, paid in full at purchase. I guess that Arthur's parents gave it to Arthur as a wedding present. When Arthur's father died Arthur added Eleanor as a joint tenant.*

Caylie *Why would he give half to her after his dad died?*

Cheryl *Arthur's father may have been old school and women weren't put on the title deed.*

Caylie *Aaaah, so this also makes me think that Arthur and Eleanor were relatively close then?*

Cheryl *Also no probate tax on the property when a joint owner, the title is automatically transferred to the other party. That is what 'joint tenant' means.*

Caylie *So it was a financial decision not an emotional decision, both times*

Cheryl *Could be both. He wouldn't have added her if he didn't care for her. It also shows he probably loved Morgan as he did the same when Eleanor died. Remember Arthur's father left the Corinda house to the girls. He seems to have provided a home for all his children.*

Caylie *Excellent! I totally agree. Arthur's brother TJ was a self-made man according to one of his relatives and she doubted John would have given them anything to start them off. I am not so sure though.*

Both Eleanor and Arthur had cash in the bank when they died, so it may be that their bank books were redundant, and the money was located without them. I am very interested in Morgan's relationship with his mother. I like to think that Morgan had his mother's interests in hand. Muriel's account opened in Oct 1955.

Cheryl *Hiding anything under the lino in the kitchen which is the woman's domain, leans toward Eleanor being the only one involved. If a man was to hide this under the lino, it would more likely to be the living room or main bedroom. A man would tend to hide something under the house. My deep feeling is that Eleanor hid everything during wartime and managed the money of the house. When she died suddenly, I'm thinking that it sent a shockwave thru the house. Has anyone considered that the name White is simply 'pure as snow, white and clean' not black. Just a thought. Sometimes the simple answer is the way to look at it. Why should it link back to a real person, it was a secret deposit account.*

Caylie *It possibly doesn't... a thought that has been considered briefly by some. I like your train of thought*

Muriel Murphy-Hill's Will

Lyn *Muriel's will was dealt with by the Public Trustee and they have a closure of 75 years (according to the Archives) so we can't get a copy! Why they keep them closed for longer than the archives (10 years) is beyond me.*

Felice *It would probably be to protect the beneficiaries' privacies. After 75yrs, it is likely the beneficiaries have also passed away.*

Helen *Normally if Public Trustee's involved it's because no next of kin that they feel they can trust to execute the will. Or person was under guardianship of the Public Trustee and considered not capable of handling own affairs, my grandmother died under their guardianship*

Lyn *Yeah, but why so long. The archives, which is the State department for keeping records releases the ones they have after about 10-20 years.*

Helen *Don't know they operate in a law unto themselves. A lot of elderly people get caught up in the free will thing and then of course Public Trustee is involved and that's a whole different ball game. I've seen them do some interesting things. In retirement villages the common saying is you don't let them into your affairs and you don't get them to do your will. But the more frugal are the ones who get caught*
Deidre *Wills are free from them if you nominate your own executor – if you name them as executor that's when all the fees come in*
Helen *Although most people I know who deal with Public Trustee to get their wills done – they end up being their executor as well*
Jenny *You should be able to get the wills, probate and letters of administration from the Supreme Court. When I worked there, we had them all and anyone who paid money for searches, we gave copies to.*

September 3
Caylie *Just recapping... am surmising that the bank books' whereabouts was only known by Eleanor. Eleanor's sudden death at 72 meant she was unable to bank the last saved £20, nor was she able to tell Arthur or Morgan about the money and bank books. If Muriel White, whomever she was, knew there was a bank book being held by Eleanor for her, surely she'd have told her where it was. Then after Eleanor died, she would have paid a visit to the house to get it? I reckon only Eleanor knew about all three bank books. Is Muriel White real or a made up account by Eleanor? Muriel never took out one penny from that account. Only deposits.*
Hamish *Maybe Muriel was using White so Horace couldn't find the money?*
Lyn *So why were they last used in 1958 and found at Heussler Terrace, when Muriel lived in Bristol Street until just before she died 11 years later?*
Lou *Maybe they were stolen and hidden in the house at Milton and the 2 ladies aren't connected at all?*

Cheryl *My thoughts... Re: the Muriel White name and address in the bank account is Eleanor's and she used the name 'Muriel' and address, probably with Muriel's knowledge so that any mail e.g. bank statements could be passed on to Eleanor without anyone else knowing. After Eleanor's death, Muriel wouldn't go looking for the bank book because it wasn't hers. Also the account being at South Brisbane, the bank tellers wouldn't recognise Eleanor Webster.*
Re: where did the money come from? At 72 years of age Eleanor probably wasn't capable of too much physical work and wouldn't be conducting business from Heussler Terrace to avoid attention from neighbours. Therefore, this income was generated away from home and obviously in cash which had to be hidden.
Caylie *Cheryl, that's a solid view of what could have been going on. There's been some discussion about whether Morgan may have been paying her rent as well? She never had a known income, as you say. Regarding Muriel, your view would be the clearest I've seen yet. Cousins are better than siblings at keeping secrets.*
Cheryl *If Morgan was paying Eleanor rent, why would it be hidden? Besides the house was in Morgan and Arthur's name so no need to pay rent. Even if Morgan was paying his mother for washing and ironing, no need to hide it and that would have been very expensive domestic charges to her son.*
Caylie *Perhaps he was paying off his part of the mortgage... and maybe she wasn't hiding it from anyone in particular, just from any marauders, and each month, did her banking from her stash?*
Cheryl *If a title search showed Eleanor as a previous joint tenant with Arthur, then it could be considered that Morgan was paying her back in instalments. But that wouldn't explain why the need for a secret bank book unless it impacted on her eligibility for an aged pension. If this were the case, we could assume that Arthur and Morgan were aware of a bank account.*

If the home was only in Arthur's name when it was changed to Arthur and Morgan, then maybe Morgan felt that his mother was poorly treated and he was paying her secretly.

Hence Arthur wouldn't know about the bank account but Morgan would. In this scenario it would be easier for Morgan to deposit directly into an account for her. Does a title search on the property show if Eleanor was ever registered as an owner before title shows Arthur and Morgan? In those days and up into the '70s, property was often only in the husband's name. When a husband died his will would state that the remaining wife had the right to live there until her death or left her the house in its entirety. What date did the Muriel White bank account open, did it coincide with the home title change to Arthur and Morgan?

If Eleanor was hiding the bank books from possible break and enter, she would tell either or both Arthur and Morgan where they were hidden.

The deposits were not that regular and the amounts varied, not consistent with Morgan paying off this mortgage.

The Bank Books, again...

The bank books were the key to a wealth of information for those who were willing to look. I am not a details person, so I was fortunate to have several of these in the team, who made up for my broad brushstrokes. In my defence, my focus in this project has always been about the psychology and the people. I stopped caring about figures when I failed Business Principles in Year 9...

Catherine *I've liked looking at old account books etc. from centuries ago... And old bank books give a spy into C20 transactions. Wonder what our mishmash of electronic statements will give future generations puzzlement? Put your old credit card statements and bills that still come in paper under your lino NOW* ☺

How to Open a Bank Account in the 1940s

Roxy *As a side note, what identification is needed to open an account back then?*
Janelle *I worked for the Commonwealth Bank from 1973 till 1982. Was just talking to friend who also worked there. We don't remember the customers needing any identification to open an account. I thought maybe a birth certificate but Martine was still working at the bank when they brought in the 100 points identification and she remembers thinking, 'gee they've gone from nothing to all that'.*
Joanne *An "extract" birth certificate at most!*
Janelle *Which is really no id anyway. No signature or photo. You could borrow anybody's birth certificate. With Morgan working in the bank, he could have vouched for his mother opening as many accounts as she wanted to anyway. Life was so much more relaxed back then. Bank managers actually knew their customers.*
Sharon *I hate to say but my Dad opened accounts in different names with no identification. After he died we would have had no idea where or what he had.*

Jane *Maybe the bank officer had just written "White" and Mrs Muriel filled in the address and 1st name?*
Lyn *But why White?*
Joanne *A familiar name, close relative, mothers, grandmother's maiden name?*
Lyn *Nope. Don't think so. Certainly not family.*
Meg *Super common name. My maiden name is White and there were 3 'Megan Louise Whites' at the Commonwealth in early 2000s at Indro alone!*
Lyn *Okay so Muriel or her cousin Eleanor could have opened the account in that name and no questions would have been asked. Funny that it was never picked up by the bank.*
Allison *Yes it is, perhaps it was never presented to the bank afterwards? My gut feeling is that Muriel has changed the name; I guess I only think that because the bank book was hidden. Someone else could have stolen the bank book, altered and then hidden it? Eleanor? I wonder then if the bank book was reported lost or stolen by Muriel and replaced? In those days she wouldn't have forgotten she had £1,000, I'm sure. So the CBA would issue another bank book with a new number, transfer the balance across according to their ledger balance and continue on as usual. That seems likely given the timeline above.*
Kym *If you lost your bank book (or hid it from yourself, like I hide things so well I can't find them again) you'd just rock into the bank, you wouldn't sit there wondering where it was*
Allison *When I joined CBA in 1981 there were no photocopiers faxes etc. You went to your local branch and opened a bank book account. When my mum and I opened our accounts in the 1970s, our signatures were recorded in the bank books and were visible to the bank staff via a black light. I'm not sure this technology was around in the forties/fifties though – one avenue to check. Caylie when you took the bank book in did they see if there was a black light sig in the back?*
The world was a smaller place then, you opened an account at your local, most folks were paid in cash and had no need of a bank account except to save money.

Accounts had a new account form and a signature card, cheque accounts had a history card and a signature card. If you wanted to travel to Sydney, you 'made arrangements' with the Bank well prior to – but in those days you could also write a cheque which places would cash for you. A vastly different world to the one we know now!

Caylie *No, they didn't have the black light signature... it was well before that time.*

Hamish *It's good getting an insight into operations when it was easy!*

Allison *Yeah the good old days ☺ If you travelled away, you organised an encasement authority so you could front up to Pitt Street and Martin Place branch and cash a twenty quid cheque, but if you didn't 'make arrangements' it was a can of worms.*

Sue *I joined the bank in the '70s. Prior to black light we had boxes of signature cards. When a customer opened an account we filled out two cards*
1. Details – name, DOB, address
2. Signature card
No ID required to open accounts, everything was bank books and cash.
Customer would drop bank book down a chute, staff would get the book, go to signature card box and verify signature on withdrawal and give it to the teller. You could only withdraw from your own branch unless you asked your branch to send another signature card to another branch

Allan *I remember those chutes now! I talked to an old crim in the '70s who had done lots of time. His last stint at the time was for defrauding the bank. His scam was to use the top of a round wooden clothes peg as a bank stamp for fictitious deposits. He got away with it for ages and made a fortune even though the bank knew how he was doing it. Their systems at the time and the state of communications worked against them. He came undone when a teller from a branch that he had embezzled recognized him when she was doing holiday relief work at a country branch.*

Hamish *Are wills public info or?*

Lyn *Yes, they are after 30 years. IF they are public trustee wills. If they were executed by a private law company they may have been kept but they certainly won't ever be at the Archives.*
Hamish *Have we ruled out fraud?*
Allison *No I don't think fraud has been ruled out. I think it's the top contender...*
Maureen *The money may have been given to the executors (s) by the Commonwealth Bank without the bank books. The executor contacts the bank with copy of will and account is closed and bank passes money to the executor. So there is a possibility (if the executor knew about there were bank accounts) that the money was given to beneficiaries and isn't in the unclaimed accounts vortex. Are we able to check the status of unclaimed money at a time close to the deaths? How long can bank accounts go untouched before they are closed? When did the banks policies change on this? There must be a Commonwealth Bank "librarian" who is across the policies on untouched bank accounts...*
Allison *Used to be seven years inactive and CBA sent a letter to last known address, bank kept it another seven years and then off to consolidated revenue. I still suspect Muriel's big account has been reported lost or stolen and replaced. And another question is how far back does unclaimed money record go? I doubt it would be far enough back for these accounts?? Any ideas anyone? If executors knew beneficiaries had CBA accounts, yes proceeds could have been direct deposited. But not entirely likely given the era. Cheque deposit a whole lot more likely.*
Allan *Arthur would have known at least about their joint account. I would assume he would go to the bank and tell them the missus has died and he can't find the bank book. They would also be aware of Eleanor's own account in her own name. In those days banks employed people to scan Obituaries so I am assuming Arthur eventually got his unexpected nest egg from both accounts (depending on what her will, if any, stipulated). The puzzling thing about Muriel White is that she was a Mrs in the bank book before her surname was later added.*

If she did exist, at some point later she would have wanted to know where her money was.

Sue *One of my first jobs in the bank was to check the obituaries each day. Would then check these against our account holders. If they matched we had to put a red sticker on their account card and signature card. If anyone tried to use the bank book the red sticker indicated deceased account*

Kim *People used to hide things under floorboards but hidden bank books would not have prevented the executors of any will from accessing the funds – solicitors, public trustee and the bank would have worked together to find money.*

Maureen *Records begin in 1857. Queensland has more will and probate records online than any other Australian state or territory, courtesy of the Queensland State Archives. Detailed information is available in their Brief Guide 19: Will and Intestacy Records. Someone will have to put in some shoe leather with the State Archives – maybe for Muriel and Eleanor's parents and Morgan of course. Subject to 30 year rule it looks like the QLD Supreme Court and or State Archives may bear fruit*

Lyn *It would be at the States Archives now. Unfortunately, we have to wait another two years before we can see if there was a will for Morgan Webster.*

Caylie *Three different branches, accounts opened 7 October 1955; 1 March 1943; 18 October 1948. All different hand writing.*

Hamish *How did they confirm correct person?*

Sue *Just if all details matched. Name, address and DOB. It was more a case of us stopping any transactions on the account. If I recall correctly I think a beneficiary could ask for funds to be released to cover costs of a reasonable funeral – bank cheque was given direct to the Funeral Company. After that, money was frozen until will etc. went through process.*

Also, for every bank book there was a corresponding transaction card.

Helen *That's still the case today with probate – with the exception of the transaction cards.*

Allan *Maybe they put that ad in Public Notices as a last resort before declaring it a dormant account and effectively freezing it. More puzzling as there was no correction fluid in those days and the banks were sticklers for correct procedure.*
I could not imagine any situation where a bank manager or supervisor would allow a bank book to be issued in such fashion (a surname to be added later). The bank book aspect is the most puzzling.
Barry *I spoke to my retired bank inspector friend about the 'White' account and he said the name at the top of the book was never written by the account holder especially surnames as it could be copied/forged on a withdrawal form... if it was copied it would not match the account holders signature on their card in the withdrawals tellers' section... he said this was a regular occurrence... and you could only withdraw at the branch that issued the book... so the name on top was the account holders identity only, not their signature. He said the same system applied even after the black light system came in around the early 1970s, but then you could withdraw any branch and the name was type written... He said never ever was there visible signatures on book... also, the only persons authorized to write on or change anything on pass books were bank employees.*
Caylie *No money was ever withdrawn from Muriel's account which is interesting. We do think two different bank employees wrote on the bank book though as two different nibs used and two different hands.*

The Handwriting

My neighbour was the first one who noticed that there was different writing in Muriel's bank book. Being able to touch and see the actual documents made this discovery a lot easier, but I'd had them in my hands for months and never noticed it!

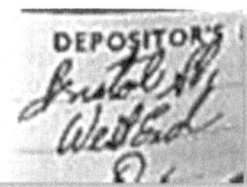

'White' is written in a different hand to the rest of the text, using a different pen. If you compare the *W* of *White* with the *W* of *West End*, you can see it's a different hand using the pen. Curiosity piqued, I asked for possible explanations…

Eve *The bank clerk would have written the name at the top and maybe Muriel wrote her address?*
Caylie *Same hand wrote Mrs Muriel and the address… someone else wrote 'White'*
Robyn *To me White almost looks like it could have been written by a younger relative perhaps practising their 'running writing' as we called it at Stafford when we got our pen licences…*
Gordon *Yes, it looks 'hesitantly' precise? Not free.*
Allison *Looks 'very careful' – like you would when it's important…*
Karen *I think they were differentiating the surname. Similar to making the font bold as we would today.*

Caylie *No, different person wrote 'White' for sure as the W is different – see 'West End'*
Janelle *Wasn't Morgan a bank teller?? Did he write it?*
Leanne *Need something with his hand writing?*
Allan *Maybe the surname was changed to White after a marriage and that is why the bank book surname was left off until after the ceremony in case things went wrong? I can't see the deposit record but was it a wedding gift initially of a sum of money?*
Caylie *£425 initial deposit, could have been a carry-over from a previous bank book...*
Meg *I think 'Mrs Muriel White' was written by the teller, with the "bold" format of their handwriting. I think they probably hesitated before the 'White' part, like checking it mentally. I do this a lot in my line of work, I'll write the student's first name then pause, check, surname. I think Muriel herself wrote the address.*
Allison *Respectfully disagree, nothing about the White reflects the other writing. White is written very deliberately, the rest of it is written by a busy teller – note the differences in the 'I' and 't' particularly.*
Meg *Intrigued by this – do you think the teller would have issued the bank book without seeing ID or without a full name?*
Allison *Yes quite possibly, back then people were who they said they were. Banks had no reason to believe anything but what the customer said!*
Caylie *Agreed and there's some speculation that Morgan may have set up the account... I was thinking that the original surname could have been written by Morgan, the back teller, in pencil and later erased. The handwriting is a different generation too, much younger than the one who wrote 'Mrs Muriel'.*
Allison *Pencil would explain it, but not bank policy by a long shot. Yes agree on the 'White' penmanship – very high-schoolerish – not like the rest of the bank book where the writing reminds me of a cousin I have aged in his early seventies, flowing hurried but still legible and uniform. But why would Morgan do that?*

Caylie *Now we come to the possibility of fraudulent behaviour...*
Jan *It looks different to me but maybe Muriel wasn't used to writing White and it didn't flow as such. She might have had to think about it if it was new or an alias.*
Maureen *#RedHerring Wouldn't the bank teller have written the name of the account holder? Interesting that the address doesn't include the house number*
Valerie *I am not a writing expert, but I spent 10 years as a ledger-keeper in a trading bank in the 1940s-1950s. If a document or cheque had been presented to me with the writing as shown in that pass book, I would have immediately questioned it. The surname "White" appears to have been written by a much younger person than the rest. There may have been an explanation for the change.*
Caylie *I agree completely Valerie... I think that Eleanor has opened a bank book in Muriel's name, but didn't have all the details she needed, like a street number or her new married name...*
Jodie *Can you tell on closer inspection if it was perhaps rubbed out and rewritten.*
Lyn *Couldn't rub out fountain pen ink.*
Allison *As an ex-CBA bank teller I should have picked that up! Everything about the White differs from the rest of it. Someone has doctored Muriel's bank book. I'd be interested to see Muriel's handwriting now!*
Hamish *Can you compare the signatures? Lyn would have sent you the marriage certificate, I know the last name won't be the same but compare the 'M'.*
Janelle *Her marriage certificate would have her signature.*
Maureen *To my eye the e's i's r's and capital letters M MW look as though they were the same hand...*
Also changing the surname written in ink would have made a hell of a mess of the bank book. They both may have been beneficiaries of a will that provided for annual stipend/income to be paid.
Diana *Have you looked at the hand writing on the other two bank books to see if they are similar?*

Kym *Probably the clergyman? Hamish, in the past when you bought a Queensland certificate it was a typed copy of the original and therefore had no signatures. That was all that was available. If you wanted to see the original you had to go into the Registrar of BDMs and ask to sight it. That's why I asked if it was the "actual" certificate.*
Janelle *Different people completed the certificate and the bank book. The "White" of the bank book is a different hand to the "Muriel" too. The "White" is very neat and carefully written.*
Lyn *When the details of whatever birth, marriage or death arrived at the department a clerk entered all of them in great big books. That's why the hand writing is all the same.*
Hamish *I think the marriage dude/woman wrote out the whole certificate*
Joanne *Written with different pens. The nib sizes are different the inks looks slightly different as well*
Caylie *Different ink, different nib and different hand. Handwriting was very specifically belonging to a person like a fingerprint, and the scripts are absolutely different. Agreed Joanne.*
Brenda *Going back to the bank book of Mrs Muriel White, I think the entire name was written by the bank teller who did the first entry. His (I'm assuming he's male, I'm not sure if there were female tellers in the '50s) handwriting is a bit inconsistent but there are a few similarities and I think he was trying extra hard to be neat for the surname which is why it looks different. His writing is pretty terrible otherwise. My reasons for this assumption are... The curl and horizontal bar in "Mrs" and "Muriel" is the same as that for the "M" in March for March 19, 1955. There is a small hook on the cross bar of the "t" in White, similar to that on November 24, 1955 on the written entry for the "t" in twenty one £. The dot over the "I" in White looks like an inverted "v" similar to where thirty five is written on November 30 1956. Still no clue about the surname White...*
Cheryl *Yes, I think the same teller who wrote Mrs Muriel did do those transactions but this doesn't mean he wrote White. More importantly, now that I look at the transactions the first 3 date entries are very odd.*

1. OCT 7 has no entry but is date stamped by that teller
2. NEW 9 (not Nov) first deposit £425 – Initialised and date stamped upside down
3. OCT 19 deposit £12
4. NOV 24 deposit £21.

I think the bank book was written out and no deposit made, then someone wrote White and E went back 2 days later and made the first deposit. Maybe Eleanor took the book with her on some pretence or other e.g. disabled cousin.

And then one night, at my art class, where I always discussed the project...

Caylie *Okay, a friend at my art class just had a thought that Muriel Hill could easily be changed to White with a different pen... she showed us. What do you reckon?*
Diana *You know, I wondered about this too. Hence the thicker nib?*

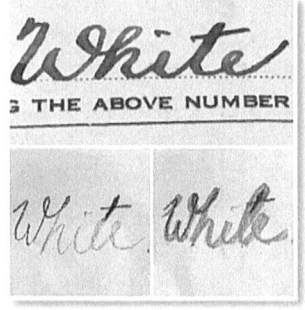

Lyn *Nah. Don't think so. White has been written in one swoop. And there is nothing showing a change.*
Eve *Wouldn't the 'h' have been capital H?*
Caylie *Yes we think so, but it was an interesting take that only an artist or a naughty child who forged her parents' signatures a lot would have picked up*
Diana *I did try it using the capital h as it would have been written and it is possible to turn that into a W. But I couldn't get the 'I' of 'hill' to morph into an 'h' in 'white'.*

Caylie *Nice try. We spent half of my art class trying to work it out and my husband even looked at the lettering under a magnifying glass to see if he could detect an original name underneath. We do need a handwriting expert!*

Diana *I did some work on transcribing ships passenger lists a while back. Learned a lot about how they used to write. Not much changed till Queensland cursive became a thing in the '80s. Had to get to know how letters looked back then. We weren't allowed to guess either. If we couldn't decipher a letter we had to put a ? even if we knew what the letter could be. Saw a few overwritten ones where errors had occurred at the time of writing. But you could tell it had been corrected.*

Caylie *It looks like it may have been overwritten but maybe not either. So much info wrapped up in that name that would solve so much of our mystery! Arghhhh!*

Brenda *I'm wondering if the name White has been written after erasing the original name? Before correction fluid etc. it was possible to use a razor blade to carefully scrape off a word, then run your fingernail over it to flatten the paper. There may have also been other ink removal processes...*

Caren *I used to do that if I made a mistake on my homework. Interesting thought, but wouldn't the bank keep a record of the bank book account number against the name of the person who opened the account? If the intention was to one day take money out of the account the bank would have picked up the discrepancy.*

Brenda *Good point. I still think Morgan had much to do with this and could easily have fudged records at the bank I'm sure...*

Caylie *November 26, 2017 Update on Muriel White... There have been several theories and ideas floating around about this account – who is Muriel White, is she the same person as Muriel Murphy, who lived at the 19 Bristol Street, West End address, did Eleanor open a bank account using Muriel Murphy's address but change the name? Cheryl, Brenda, Allan, myself and several others, have been working hard to decipher bank account books and signatures.*

Caylie *I have all the rewards I need here Jennifer! And if some of the thoughts about fraud are correct then that money doesn't belong to anyone else but the government... there are no living heirs.*

Narelle *Could it be the clerk was called away and someone else finished opening the account?*

Leanne *I'm starting to think Muriel had no knowledge if the account and it was all set up by Eleanor as a secret account from her husband. As there was only deposits she could have done this at local branch where she was known, saying it was her cousin's account??*

Caylie *Yes, I believe Muriel Murphy Hill had no idea... so why South Brisbane then? When the other accounts were George Street and Brisbane City Branches?*

Allison *To keep them secret. Still relatively accessible, but no-one would have thought of an account in a neighbouring or nearby suburb. And no computers then so it would need to be known by family that a person opened an account apart from local branch. Quite crafty!*

Brenda *If it wasn't a secret account for Cousin Muriel, why even use Bristol Street? Or the name Muriel? Could it be that Eleanor had envisioned needing to deflect blame if a false bank account was discovered?*

Caylie *Possibly, with the name Muriel White's mail coming to that address being a 'bank error'*

Allison *You wouldn't want bank mail going to an address other than your own if the account holder was false. Lady of the house at home, could vet the mail and man of the house would be no wiser. I am growing a fond appreciation of Eleanor and her talents.*

Narelle *I believe Muriel White did exist. She doesn't show on the electoral because she was too young to vote, then she probably married and was no longer White. We can't search her birth because it was after 1914. As Trove only displays Qld news up to 1954 we need to wait another 30 years. Were all deposits for all three bank books made at the same branch on the same day?*

Brenda *I wonder if banks ever wrote to their customers? Were bank statements issued back then?*
Pauline *Not for bank books.*
John *I don't think the name in the bank book has been fraudulently altered. It would not match the branch ledger card and the holder would not be able to withdraw funds.*
Allison *Correct. But if the account holder reported the bank book as stolen the branch would reissue it (in the original name). With respect, the bank book shows all the signs of alteration, and by an amateur. So let's say Eleanor opened the account as Muriel Hill (just saying). Caylie's art group has come up with a scenario where Hill morphs to White. Muriel knew a White from her Maryborough days I believe. To anyone's eye, White is quite deliberately written and stunted, and is certainly not the script of a busy bank clerk. Remember the account bank book has one handwriting throughout – apart from the surname White. Who opens an account knowing everything except their surname? And in a suburb not their own?*
Meg *Did Eleanor have the secret account for Morgan?*
Caylie *It's possible but he worked at the CBA! Why would he need one?*
Meg *I mean, parents have always been worried for their kids?*
Diana *I was looking through old articles on bank fraud. It was far more common than I expected! And I found quite a few that did include bank staff. But as I said, everything in that book stops at Eleanor's death year. I have been curious too Caylie, as to how far under the lino these books were? Were they somewhere accessible?*
Caylie *Easily accessible on a monthly basis. At the edge next to the stove. Meg, true but Morgan was in his 40s when that bank book started although it could have been a second book as it started with £425 possibly carried forward.*

At this point, we were fairly convinced that Muriel White was a fictional character Eleanor made up based on her cousin Muriel Murphy who lived at the 19 Bristol Street address.

Lyn *As far as we have worked out, Eleanor never knew a Muriel White. Besides, the one we found didn't leave Brisbane. No signature on marriage cert. It's because it's the official one and not the one signed at the church.*

Allan *Presumably Muriel White would have to be a close friend or relative of Eleanor in order to have possession of her bank book. The fact that she does not crop up at all almost confirms that the bank book name is false. On Eleanor's death, you would think Muriel would be looking high and low for her bank book and money. Did the bank help her out? Did she make a claim on Eleanor's estate? You would think Muriel would have attended her funeral and asked everyone if they knew where Eleanor hid her bank books. So many questions!*

Caylie *I think that's where we're coming to. Muriel Murphy was Eleanor's cousin, and a 'safe' address for her to set up a false account in a slightly different name. Muriel may have got letters from the bank from time to time for a Muriel White, which she'd have probably chucked in the incinerator... We don't think anyone but Eleanor knew about the bank book so nobody searched for it.*

Cheryl *Maybe we are missing the main point re Muriel's account. If Arthur or Morgan knew or found out later that this account existed, they and the bank would have the same problem as us, finding Muriel or proving that she was in fact Eleanor. This money would have gone to unclaimed money and the government would have spent it wisely on its people (us) ha ha. As the Muriel White account was only showing Bristol Street West End with no street number it is unlikely that any correspondence from the bank was ever delivered and returned to the bank as 'unknown at this address'.*

Shar *Oh oh oh oh... Muriel was a music teacher but could she have also been a performer? A lot of performers take on another name. Could Eleanor have been managing her gigs so to speak and taking a bit off the top as a fee? Could the dates match up with war time where maybe the ladies had to be resourceful in making money?*

Hamish *this is the best suggestion!*

Patterns in the Deposits and Withdrawals

Bob *There will be a pattern in the banking. I think these women will be related... it is not just the losing/forgetting of their bank books because there was cash there as well, insinuating that banking was going to happen soon due to the amount of money*

Maureen *Were there any withdrawals on Muriel's accounts at all Caylie? There was only one withdrawal of 300 from Eleanor's account correct? There were annual deposits made in December in Eleanor's bank book and one withdrawal of £300... maybe to buy a property or pay off a mortgage.*

Caylie *Only deposits in Muriel's account...*

Nicky *Can you briefly plot the Muriel White account activity? Was there a weekly amount (wage) deposited? Was it a regular deposit?*

Maureen *Have you seen a pattern of deposits – was I correct that they are annual deposits in December?*

Shane *Did you notice the same bank person signed both Muriel and Eleanor's books on the 19th June 1951?*

Maureen *Miss (Maureen) Marple here... can you tell us the frequency of deposits withdrawals and amounts? Trying to see what was coming in/going out to fuel more speculation!!! Thousands of pounds have been moved thru the two accounts #somethingwasgoingon*

Heather *Were funds just moved from one account to the other?*

Caylie *Monthly deposits in Muriel's account between £12 and £35, starting with £425 in Oct 1955 and ending with £1013 by 1958; interest only accrued in Eleanor's account over three years starting at £510 ending at £469; Arthur and Eleanor's joint acc had regular deposits of £20-£40, sometime £100, starting with £100 and ending with £500*

Maureen *Thanks for this info... The large deposits could have been rent from properties... the big variations e.g. £12-£35 suggest income different/additional to rents or from a business like a shop which usually have a reasonably stable monthly revenue...*

If you do a spreadsheet of the transactions monthly for both accounts you might see a pattern even the day of the week deposits were made could tell you something. Were there any/many withdrawals. Is there a pattern there? It is big money in those days for a couple of women to be banking into their accounts #whatweretheyupto

Hamish *Where was the first deposit made and date? For Mrs White?*

Caylie *First deposit £425 9th Oct 1955*

Helen *That was a lot of money back then.*

Caylie *The £425 may have been carried over from a different pass book*

Ray *An amount of £425 deposited in 1955 was a lot of money. Being deposited in Oct I thought it could possibly be a tax refund.*

Caylie *I wondered about this too but perhaps it was rolled over from another bank book? She was, after all, in her 50s?*

Hamish *What if the book was forged?*

Meg *Have you matched up when Morgan moved to Bris (1941) with when they all died? And the last transactions with Eleanor's death?*

Caylie *So, Eleanor died Aug 1958, her last transaction was July 31 1951, withdrawing £50 leaving £469 from her personal account and depositing £10 into her joint account with Arthur. Muriel White (relationship and personage as yet unknown) was a £27 deposit a month before Eleanor died in 1958. Who was Muriel White?*

Brenda *Lyn were you able to get copies of wills for Eleanor and Arthur? What about records of death duties?*

Allan *Do we know how much money Eleanor left in her estate, or rather how much was actually distributed? That might indicate whether her accounts were accessed without the books being found and whether Muriel's account was included. As Eleanor died in 'mid-deposit' so to speak, the cash amount of the estate should be exactly the combination of one or several books. Maybe the Muriel White account was a nest egg for Morgan that he got a fellow bank employee to set up.*

I think Morgan knew what Mum was doing (though we don't know yet and not necessarily illegally). Mum has told him to set up an account in a false name so Arthur doesn't find out about it. Whether Eleanor's secret account was for her future benefit or her and Arthur's we will never know. Could or did Morgan access Eleanor's or Muriel's secret accounts after her death as he could not find the bank books? He could be certain of not being found out as only he knew of their existence.
Lyn *We know that Eleanor died intestate, and that Arthur became the beneficiary. Her estate contained the following:*

```
Personalty
Money in Bank                270L.14. 7.
Debentures, War Bonds, etc.  1,007.10. 8.
Other personal property        807. 4. 8.
                             £2,519. 9.11.
```

Thanks to Franki, our resident legal eagle, we know that Eleanor died 'intestate', which means she died without a will.

Franki *When someone dies without a will, her next of kin have to apply to the Court for "Letters of Administration" to allow them to deal with her assets. Most of the documents provided are relating to court procedure which is required to be adhered to on the death of someone "intestate" (e.g. In regards to advertising the death etc.)*
Some interesting points above the court application.
- Her only next of kin recorded are her husband Arthur and her son Morgan.
- Morgan was 44 years old at her death, living with his parents at 86 Heussler Terrace
- Her assets at the time of her death were valued at £2519/9/11. There is an inventory of her assets which amount to
§ Money in bank £704/14/7 [this does not tally to her bank book under the lino, which makes me think she had another account.

Or her bank book under the lino was an old one, as its last transaction was in July 1951 and she didn't die until 1958]
§ Debentures, war bonds £1007/10/8
§ Other personal property £807/4/8
- She had no unpaid debts when she died.

Allan *If they were married then it is part of her estate though it would normally go to the surviving husband anyway, unless she decided to leave it to the cat or something. I was wondering whether that amount included their joint bank account and Eleanor's secret account, or just the joint account.*

Cheryl *With an intestate situation the Public Trustees would have written to every major bank requesting a search for any records in Eleanor Webster's name, hence both Eleanor's and the joint account would have been found plus any registered Commonwealth Loan Bonds she may have still held. Eventually the money would have gone to Arthur.*

If Eleanor's account was left untouched from July 1951 until after her death and compound interest was added to the balance over 7 years at say 2.5% p.a. the balance would be approximately £557, so there is approx. another £166 in a bank account somewhere in her name. This would indicate that Eleanor had a second account somewhere or more deposits were made into this account after the bank book was hidden under the lino

Regarding the joint account I am unaware how these monies were legally regarded, e.g. like a joint property that automatically passes to the other upon their death, or half is regarded as belonging to Eleanor's estate. This account if untouched and compound interest added would be close to £600.

Caylie *Based on the fact Arthur got money from Eleanor's estate after she died intestate, I'm assuming he found her account? I reckon Muriel White is the rogue account too. Eleanor's Heussler Terrace address was in the back of her book so assuming the bank would have sent mail here after a time.*

Kym *Even if Arthur was unaware of the account she kept in her own name, then eventually the bank would have tipped him off.*

What did the Bank Book Transactions tell us?

Allan *As far as I can see, Muriel's transactions seem to be all or mainly at South Brisbane; The Webster's joint account at Brisbane City; and Eleanor's secret account at George Street, Brisbane. All are reasonably handy to Milton. Was this part of the deception so no one bank branch or individual knew about the other accounts? I assume Eleanor did not have a car so would have to use public transport and the banks were only open from 10.00am > 3.00pm. It would be nice to profile the transaction dates and locations to see if any pattern emerges.*

Arthur and Eleanor's Joint Account

Arthur William Joseph Webster and Mrs Eleanor Webster of 86 Heussler Terrace, Milton CBA Bank Book #490819 Brisbane Branch
Final amount £500
March 1943 – July 1951
Annual wage £10 a week
Train driver would make £520 a year in the 1940s.

Eleanor's Account

Mrs Eleanor Webster of 86 Heussler Terrace, Milton.
CBA Bank Book #7156 George Street Brisbane Branch
Carried forward £510 18th Oct 1948
Final amount £469 July 1951

Muriel White's Account

Mrs Muriel White of Bristol Street, West End
CBA Bank Book #29618 South Brisbane branch
Account opened Oct 7, 1955, £425
Final amount £1,013 June 1958

Most of us had assumed that I had found three *Savings* Account books, containing amounts totalling just over £2,000.

Several people suggested I do a spreadsheet of all of the transactions in the books, to make it easier for the 'details' people to work out any patterns within the banking behaviour.

While I was doing the exceedingly laborious task of data entry (remind me to delegate this task next time!), I noticed the words 'Commonwealth Loan Interest' in Eleanor's bank book.

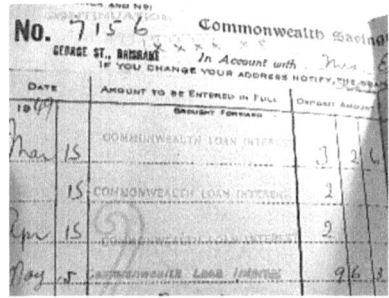

It suddenly occurred to me that these could have been mortgage payment books! The fear I experienced at this point was huge... what if I had got everyone to go to all this trouble for a few loan books, with no money in them at all! There'd be no point searching for heirs, and people would lose the enthusiasm for the project! I shared my fears with the UTL Team...

Benita *It looks like interest on a loan.*
Caylie *It says Commonwealth Loan Interest, yet it's in the deposit line?!*
Sandra *One is a home loan book.*
Caylie *How do you see that Sandra? I can only see regular deposits and accrued interest.*
Sandra *I thought it was a home loan book from the stamps used. I may well be wrong.*
Caylie *Hey, what if these are all mortgage bank books? Omg.*
Hamish *BAHAHAHAHA. No, just no. Please don't be.*
Missymoo *Caylie, it calculates as a deposit account. Maybe it is a Commonwealth ('government' rather than bank) Bond*
Joanne *My hubby works for the bank and he said it is interest paid to Eleanor on War Bonds or similar that she owned, it's not a loan. Hope that helps.*
Caylie *Ok everyone, thanks to Joanne and her wonderful husband, I think we can relax. One of the books – Eleanor's – has war bond interest and the other two are savings accounts.*

This can be seen by the random deposits of different amounts and no monthly interest accrued. The other two had yearly interest added. OMG thought I was going to get attacked by 800 people.
Hamish *That's a lynching.*
Diana *In 1946 the government announced a crackdown on undeclared incomes. Apparently there was a huge spike in luxury items and a huge influx on the banks for war bonds and the like. There is no mention of more accounts than usual being opened. I am wondering if Eleanor was giving Piano lessons and not declaring the income or was declaring it but didn't want to pay tax on it all. Did she open another account for this... hence the money under the lino as well. Did she hide the bank books and neither husband nor son knew where she was hiding them but were aware of them? Since hers had not been touched since 1951 is it possible that Muriel's account goes back further than this book? She also would have been getting a pension by then? And if still working i.e. giving lessons.*
Helen *Death duties weren't abolished till 1979 – which is why there were a lot of fake bank accounts, I remember mum and dad talking about that years ago. It was easy to do as well.*

My mistake was just the thing we needed, though, to realise that Eleanor had been dealing in War Bonds. This could have been part of the answer we were seeking!

A few super-sleuths were involved with the dissection and interpretation of the bank transactions. Cheryl and Allan, in particular, gave us some wonderful insights...

Cheryl *I have been thinking about the three accounts and the dates, amounts deposited and withdrawn and how and where the monies came from. I am looking at Arthur's role as a train driver during the war, how and to whom his wages were paid, war bonds and interest and their maturity dates, pension means test and how this links to 1955 and Muriel's account. Also dates that the government changed pension entitlements etc. It is looking very feasible and Eleanor was a very smart woman.*

I need to see each page of the 3 accounts to try and confirm my thoughts.

Shane *More info in 1940 war loans were available in £10, £50, £100, £500, £1,000 lots interest paid as was shown in bank book Av male wage £5/15/8 female av. wage £3/4/4 so some serious money in those accounts. It's interesting that the page from Eleanor's bank book shows interest from a commonwealth bank loan with interest of £2. I wonder how much was needed to get that interest.*

Cheryl *When you look at Eleanor's bank book, the dates in the left column are not the date of transaction, they are the month and date that the interest was paid to.*

You need to look at the bank seal on the right to determine the date the transaction took place. She didn't go to the bank very often. Interestingly if she withdrew money on the same day the interest was put into the account she would come back later and use a different teller.

This book shows a lot of things.

I have broken down the deposits into Eleanor's account, it shows 5 separate sets of bonds with four paying interest 6 monthly and one paying interest monthly. I will eventually put this all into a spreadsheet colour coding each set.

She had lots of assets, as the spreadsheets indicate to get that much interest. I guess Arthur found them or knew all along about the bonds, because his estate was so large. What if Eleanor was a very family orientated person and over the years had been secretly helping her siblings etc.?

The money she put aside over the years doesn't really match up to what she left in her estate. Maybe this is how Morgan managed to pay for uni fees. Even if he had a scholarship to UQ it still would have cost for all the incidentals. If Arthur was a bully and control freak he would not have been sympathetic to Eleanor's family losses and with the anniversary of her sister's death the day after Eleanor died she could have been very depressed.

I have dissected Eleanor's bank account and it shows some very interesting facts. It looks like C'wealth loan interest (war bonds) were being deposited from 3 separate sets of bonds.

Two were being credited monthly and a third every six months as a bulk sum.

It appears #1 bond for £1,000, #2 bond £1,200/1,500 approximately and the bulk one #3 again £1,200/1,500. This is very serious money...

My thoughts are that two bonds were lodged with the bank and the third was a lot of smaller bonds held at home by Eleanor and she took the interest coupons to the bank every 6 months to receive the interest. How the War Bond interest deposits increased with large deposits not connected to the original £1,000 bond?

1. Purchase small bonds e.g. £1, £5, from accumulated interest withdrawn from Eleanor's account.
2. Remove interest coupons from bottom of bond
3. Loan bond (same as cash) to 'X' to make a purchase on the black market or similar
4. Charge interest on loan to 'X'
5. Eleanor is now receiving interest twice on the same monetary outlay. One from the bond coupons and another from 'X'. She would gather up the coupons interest due date and present them at the bank to be deposited into her account
6. Buy more bonds as money accumulates from 'X' 'Y' & 'Z'.
7. Eleanor still has the capital to be repaid to her from 'X' 'Y' and 'Z' at a later date
8. This would explain the other CLI deposits into Eleanor's account
9. Small bonds probably purchased from theatres as these were basically untraceable
10. Eleanor was doing what the government was asking, being frugal, saving, and buying bonds. She would be seen by an outsider as a patriotic good woman.
11. When war bonds cease to be issued, Eleanor then loans out cash, she continues receiving interest, hence Muriel White account and Arthurs retirement age.

Economy during WWII verifies the frugal lifestyle that the Websters had. In 1901, new social security payments were introduced for the aged, and pension was reduced.

Eleanor kept her account at £500, and probably kept it a secret from Arthur, which was why she opened it at a different branch – Eleanor was also six years older than Arthur and one would assume she had started her own account before she got married? Her sole income could have just been interest payments from War Bonds and rent from Morgan.

What exactly were War Bonds?

War Bonds were debt securities issued by the Australian Government to finance military operations and other expenditure in World War II. They called the bonds called "Victory Loans" and urged citizens to buy them.

> ### War Bonds
>
> *The sale of war bonds was a significant aspect of the Australian home front during the Second World War. Administered by the Commonwealth War Loan Office, the war loans scheme encouraged Australians to buy war bonds which would mature with interest after the war. A total of 12 major Government war loans, variously called Liberty, Austerity, Special or Victory loans were offered to the Australian public during the Second World War. The Fourth Liberty Loan with the slogan '"Back the Attack!" was launched by Prime Minister John Curtin on the night of the 4th October 1943 in the Sydney Town Hall. The target of the loan was one hundred and twenty five million pounds and 750,000 subscribers. It closed on 9 November 1943.*
>
> **awm.gov.au Australian War Memorial**

Allan *Eleanor was clearly the one in control of the books. I can't understand why some of the deposit amounts are so odd like, for example, £6, 3 shillings, and 1 penny. You would think they would be round figures if she was putting money away on their behalf. Also, you would think there would be a pattern of regular branches that she would use. If she was a housewife then she would be constrained by public transport.*

More puzzling and what would be good to know is if the other two persons had other bank accounts (maybe not with the Commonwealth).

They could not use the books if Eleanor had them hidden under the lino. Maybe she was managing their money on their behalves and kept the books hidden for safety. Lastly, how would Eleanor copy the signatures in the books for withdrawals especially, unless she was the one that signed them originally? If that was the case, the other two would have been unable to use the books that were in their names.

For that situation to occur, Eleanor must have had a friend at the issuing branch for the other two books at least. Another thing to look at is the deposit profile across the three books like a spreadsheet.

Look at deposits on same days at same branches for example and the amounts. Why would she for example deposit in different branches on the same day if that did occur?

I'm thinking of the total amount that was deposited across the three books in a given period like week, month etc. A £5 deposit is one thing but three of those in the same week in different books means she actually had £15 spare which is a serious amount of money for a housewife.

Lyn *I don't think that Horace or Muriel ever knew what was going on. It's the surname 'White' on the bank book that we can't understand. And Muriel obviously knew nothing about it because she died 11 years after Eleanor, who had the books. No we think that Muriel had no idea of the bank book.*

Allan *Thanks for clearing up a few things for me! It seems that Eleanor already had her own secret bank book so she would hardly need another one under Muriel White's name. Maybe Muriel had a previous beau (surname White) that she was keen on marrying and Eleanor set up a sort of marriage account for her?*

I wonder what Eleanor's husband earned? Did Eleanor have a job at all? Bank hours in those days were rather limited (10 > 3 I think) so she hardly had time to flit around to different branches by public transport. Did Eleanor and/or her husband have a car and did she have a licence?

Was her husband on local trains or long-distance trains like the Sunlander or freight trains which would pay a lot more and require frequent stays away from home?

I'm just thinking of abstract theories to try and eliminate where Eleanor got this money from. If her husband was bad with money then it wasn't him. Was Eleanor a good looking sort and are there any photos of her? Lots of schools have their old records on-line nowadays.

Caylie *Arthur earned about £5-6 a week, and did mainly local work, with no stays away. Arthur had a car, but neither of them drove. Morgan did all the driving, and even then, it was only on weekends. There are no pictures of either of them, and no evidence that Eleanor had a job, or that Muriel Murphy/Hill had a beau...*

Allan *No worries. The answer to these mysteries must lie in where Eleanor was getting the money, and why she was able to put away so much of it given her husband's wage. An important part of that is to factor in where and when deposits or withdrawals were made relevant to her position as an average housewife, unless she could drive. I think the Muriel White aspect may be secondary?*

Lyn *Eleanor certainly would have been handed her husband's pay packet each time. She would have kept what money she required to pay any bills and for food etc. Anything spare would have been banked. Seems a bit funny that she had her own account, let alone the third one.*

Why did they have so much Money?

It's not often we get to look into people's bank accounts. In fact, it's often felt intrusive to be seeking such personal information about the Webster family and their goings-on. I have been able to justify this part of the investigation as background knowledge. To know how they made so much money might explain why they felt the need to hide it.

Knowing that Arthur was a locomotive driver, earning around £5 a week, and that Eleanor was a housewife for her whole life, according to electoral roll records, we figured there was a different reason for there being so much money. They wouldn't have been alone in those days, earning money on the side doing different things.

Other possibilities for 'under the table' income were put forward...
- Eleanor gave music lessons
- Eleanor had a large vegetable garden and could have been selling her produce locally. Darcy said that the Toowong Cemetery used to grow flowers to sell to mourners...
- Eleanor may have been a dressmaker, working from home

Diana *A thought I had over the weekend while trawling Trove was maybe the money came from a win? While I was reading articles that pertained to Bristol Street, besides the fact that a lot of bad, sad things happened to quite a few residents of that street (the sad story of the man who was talked down off the roof of his house only to turn around a few minutes later and succeed in his suicide attempt while his wife and doctor were in the kitchen discussing his problems.) there were quite a few golden casket and such wins in that street. Did they also bet a lot on the horses? It seems to have been the favourite pastime of many of all classes back then. My grandfather was a terrible gambler on the horses and the family were fairly destitute because of it. But this didn't stop my grandmother from doing the same whenever she could find spare money to do it. Was the Muriel White account where the winnings went?*

Caren *Just thought maybe Arthur was a loan shark? That would account for the deposits and no withdrawals. Avoiding tax? My father had his own business in the Brisbane CBD for 36 years from the mid '50s and it was all cash. He had 2 sets of books, 1 for the tax man 1 for his records. Maybe something like this? I just love this stuff.*

- The Websters may have always taken in boarders before the ones we already know about after Eleanor's death.

Caylie *They could have been renting out the front of this house?*
Brenda *Don't know when it was split into flats. Perhaps. Many people rented out a single room, or space on a built in veranda. There were many itinerant men after the war.*
My grandmother in Corinda used to make tea and scones for any who turned up at her house, but they had to stay at the bottom of the front steps. I asked my Mum who was responsible for directing returned soldiers to homes where they could be fed etc. Mum says it was the head of the local Red Cross in Corinda who had a list of names and addresses of volunteers. There were also centres in the city where the different armed forces could go if they had no family in Brisbane to visit and wanted a bit of home cooking etc. She remembers the RAAF had a building called Osman House somewhere near All Hallows'.
Helen *My grandmother used to have "boarders" according to my Mum that could account for the money unexplained and also the bank accounts*
Caylie *Yes Helen, this was a big house and at some point it was divided into a few different areas with two kitchens, possibly in Morgan's time 1980s etc. when we moved in, many people had been living here in squalor.*

- Morgan may have been paying for his keep

Frankie *I had another thought – maybe the money was rent from Morgan if he was still living at home at 44! Or paying off his part of a shared mortgage, hence the large amounts deposited.*

- When their respective parents and elders passed away, they may have been bequeathed money. Arthur's father died in 1933 and left the house to his four daughters, but may have left his sons some cash. The month after John Webster's death, Arthur put Eleanor's name on the title as a joint owner.
- Perhaps the money was an annuity paid in cash each year at Xmas, as a possible condition of a bequest. This bank book wasn't being used for everyday use.
- Given that Arthur bought the house on Heussler Terrace, Milton, at about the same time his mother bought Westhaven, we might be able to assume he had financial assistance from his parents for the purchase. This could explain Arthur and Eleanor's ability to put aside so much money over the years.

If he'd had little or no mortgage, then his wages would have added up so that by 1945, after working for nearly 40 years, he'd have accrued a tidy sum in his bank accounts...

Maureen *It was hard to buy a house back then... you needed 50% deposit at least and a good job. Some parents loaned 100% the price for block of land so couples could build. Sorry I've lost track of the whole story but did Morgan and his dad buy the house or did Morgan give him a mortgage thus ending up on the title?*
Bank employees paid almost zero interest for housing loans back then.
Diana *Not sure if you saw my post of Arthur father's death notice and probate, Caylie. This is the death notice. The other photo is the probate. It was quite a sizeable sum of money (£2,451).*

> John Webster, late of Corinda, Brisbane, retired stationmaster (realty nil personalty £2451).

Courier Mail, Monday 18 December 1933 Trove

- Arthur sold chook eggs locally in the late 1950s, after Eleanor's death. We know he had a lot of chickens...

- Arthur and Eleanor were 65 and 72 years of age, respectively. Could this have been a fair amount to have in one's bank account after a lifetime of being frugal?
- Muriel Murphy's father died in 1907 and her mother died in 1951. It is possible that Muriel got some money from her mother after she died. She certainly inherited some or all of the house from her, as her name was already on the title deed.
- The Websters could have owned another property and been collecting rent (although there was no evidence of other properties in any of their wills)
- Arthur was given money by his father to buy shares in Castlemaine XXXX for him, but he put those shares in his own name instead of his father's, and some years after John Webster's death, Arthur sold them and bought a new car.

I contacted the archivist at the XXXX brewery, and at the time of writing this, he was still looking into the history of the company's share sales, position on the stock market from the 1930s-1960s, and any other information that might shed some light on Arthur and his father's money.

Castlemaine XXXX Brewery

In 1870, the Queensland Distillery was established in Milton. The original owner, W. Samuel was hampered by failure of the sugar crops in the early 1870s, and in 1872 Robert Forsyth purchased the operation and renamed it Forsyth's Distillery. Forsyth's produced rum and acted as an agent for the sale of wine.

The distillery was not a success and in 1877, the business was purchased by Fitzgerald Quinlan and Co. with the intention of building a brewery.

The first product of the new Milton Brewery, produced in 1878, was called 'Castlemaine XXX Sparkling Ale'. X was the standard symbol of purity for alcoholic beverages, first used in medieval times when brewing was confined mainly to monasteries.

By 1887, a limited liability company called Castlemaine Brewery and Quinlan Gray and Co. Brisbane had been formed. In 1916, 'Castlemaine XXXX Sparkling Ale' was first produced when the brewery changed its formula to emulate lighter German style beers.

The 'Mr Fourex' character first appeared in advertising in 1924, possibly modelled on Paddy Fitzgerald the company's general manager.

In 1928, Castlemaine merged with another Brisbane brewing company to become Castlemaine Perkins Ltd. The company continued to expand and develop with major building works taking place in the 1940s and 1950s. The buildings currently on the site date from this period of construction, apart from the former brewing tower building and brick cold-stores which date to around the 1920s.

In 1959, a neon sky-sign comprised of the four Xs was built by Claude Neon and positioned on the brewery tower to maximise visibility from a distance. This sign is a rare survivor of this once popular form of advertising. The brewery is listed on the Brisbane City Plan Heritage Register.

2002 Milton Brewery.
Unpublished Brisbane City Council Heritage Citation.

We recently went on a XXXX brewery tour with our kids, and the chat I had with a parent at St Peters' Netball the following morning went a little like this...

"You totally have to do the XXXX tour!" I say to Tom.

"Oh yeah, I've always wanted to. My grandfather was Paddy Fitzgerald, so I really should go!" replies Tom.

I fall off my camp chair onto the dew-covered grass, once again struck down by the UTL serendipity.

Why did Eleanor Webster hide the money, then?

I'll save you a lot of time by saying up front that the majority of us believe that Eleanor was the one who hid the money. It was in the kitchen (her known domain), and the last transaction was just six weeks before she passed away. The money lay undisturbed for nearly 40 years.

Bob *If the bank books have all their last deposits around the same time, it would be correct to assume something 'bad' happened to the women at the same time. It would have happened quickly as the cash found would be the next deposit going by the amounts usually banked by Muriel White... (Or someone else doing it AS Muriel White)*

Eleanor died without a will (intestate) but money was retrieved from her bank accounts by her executors that added up to more than her account balance.

Sadness and fear were the underlying feelings when we discussed the theories and possibilities behind WHY she hid the money. Sadness that she felt she had to hide money at all – either a person or a situation was frightening for her. Who was she hiding it from and why? What did she sacrifice to hide it? What was the rainy day she were saving it for, but never realised?

There were several factors discussed pertaining to this subject...

Did Eleanor use the lino as her 'safe'? Many people across the world had been hiding their money since the 1929 stock market crash, but this was in 1958, nearly thirty years later.

Narelle *I think people who lived through the depression found ways to hide money, they lost all faith in banks. I am sure a lot of old homes would have money hidden in them including members of mine however I was told about it before they died. Not a huge amount but enough for a rainy day.*

Jane *My Nana had 1, 2, 5 dollar notes stashed in so many books on her shelf... money for the milkman, bread man, poultry man. Even though a habit that kept on even years after the last home delivery!*
Heather *Memory – I was working in a bank when these types of bank books became redundant (with the introduction of computers-years after your little mystery). Many elderly were unbelievably upset and would start crying if asked to stop using their book as it was no longer needed. I honestly think they may have thought the book was currency. I also worked in a big hospital where we tried our best to have patients hand over any cash they brought in. There ARE bad guys that prey in hospitals. These lovely seniors would hide actual bundles of notes under, in and around their beds. It was SO important that it was near them. That was NOT that long ago.*
Lyndall *My mother and my aunt found quite a few old notes stashed away under their old family home in Northgate after their father died. Grandpa was always said to not have faith in banks after the Great Depression. Maybe these notes were hidden away because of similar fears.*

Perhaps it was an old World War II behaviour related to the Brisbane Line. People in Brisbane often buried things around the stumps of their houses, and even had cyanide tablets to be used if the Japanese invaded. Australia was a very frightened nation. Townsville girls were even taught how to cook Japanese style food in the belief that this skill may save them in the event of invasion.

Helen *Start looking at the Brisbane Line – if they were from Qld country, possible they've come down with that – if he was originally from Brisbane, it would make sense for him to come back when they were evacuated.*
Lyn *I don't understand you in the sense of being evacuated.*
Helen *The idea was to give the top of Australia to the Japanese – so anyone living above Brisbane either had the choice of going to Brisbane, Sydney or Melbourne.*

My Dad's family lived in Halifax, which was North Qld and they opted to go to Melbourne. My grandmother thought there was more advancement in Melbourne – they never went back. A lot of people didn't. My grandmother was very ambitious for her kids – and it used to drive her nuts that my Grandfather couldn't give a bugger, so when the opportunity came she jumped at it, apparently, packed them all up, and they were off. My parents met at St Kilda Town Hall, built a house at Avondale Heights (where Dad was councillor), and then moved back to Townsville – Dad's heart was always in Nth Qld. From what I know, they were all packed up and stuck on trains.
Kym *It would be interesting to know how many people opted to move south because of the Brisbane Line. None of my family on both sides (and there were a lot of them) left Townsville.*
Judith *I remember Air-raid sirens going off in the '40s and my mum hiding valuables in the house, so she wouldn't leave them on the table as she hurried us to the shelter. (Once she left her diamond ring on the kitchen table and was so relieved that it was still there when the All-clear was sounded). My dad was in Enoggera Camp. We lived in Mitchelton.*
Jo *During WWII, the people of Brisbane were told that if the Japanese got into Australia, or looked like they were going to take us, that they were to burn off anything that would be used against us by them. China and silverware were buried in the back yard for the same reason. "Scorched Earth Policy"? Soldiers on retreat from a place left nothing there to help the enemy. Relatives of someone who lived in Miles buried all her jewellery and then forgot where it was after WWII! Needed a metal detector!*
Rachael *I just had a talk to my nanny! She lives with me! She was born in 1925. My nanny said, "It was war time, the girls probably got a call up. They could have been nurses. When you got a call up everybody hid their money and books so they were there when you got back. They just quickly locked up and went! The girls may have been renting the house, got their call up and went! There was a hospital ship that went down outside of Caloundra, near Fraser Island somewhere, call the Centaur. The war office will know whose names were on the ship.*

All the staff went down with it, doctors nurses etc. maybe why it's never been claimed." Nanny also said the girls could have been in the land army. She asked was it in the years when Darwin was bombed. Could be that too! Just some suggestions!
Michelle *My grandmother in those days worked like three jobs when my grandfather was in the war, to have money like that she must have had a great job... to have that much money in those days is a bit suspicious I reckon.*

*

Constant fear of living next to the Brisbane Line in WWII
by Margaret Henderson

The term "Brisbane Line" will mean very little to most people in Australia today. However, at one time it was a very controversial term and one which directly had repercussions for the Northern Rivers.

Those who are still here and remember the bad old days of the Second World War may also remember the rounding-up of all males to form groups which would defend our area against Japanese invasion, or to drive cattle over the Tablelands or help in the evacuation of women, children, and the elderly.

Tank traps were built in many areas. It is not clear whether these would have impeded the cattle drive, or the evacuation. Apparently there were 10,000 or more troops stationed near Tenterfield to protect the area once the evacuation had taken place.

It should be remembered that it really was a very frightening time, though children were often not aware of this unless they had a father or other family member in the armed forces. Aeroplanes could be heard every night as there was a large base at Evans Head and there were several crashes reported. Wardens patrolled the streets each night in towns, especially those near the coast, and residents were warned to keep lights to a minimum.

The trains were full of soldiers so most people preferred to travel to Sydney by the daily shipping lines, either from Ballina or Byron Bay, though several ships had been attacked by enemy U-boats and a few had been sunk.

Most people in our area who were not in the Armed Services were involved in agriculture. It was a booming time for the farmer as England needed to be fed as well as servicemen. It must have been a confusing time for people making important decisions and trying to plan for all eventualities.

No wonder the Brisbane Line became an idea, then a plan, then a disaster, and eventually no-one wanted to believe that it really existed. It seems likely that the original idea came from our own General Iven Giffard Mackay who, in early 1942, was involved in proposals to prepare Australia for its defence against the Japanese. At that time the Army was under-manned. He was trying to prepare plans using the five divisions under his control. However, the manpower he had could barely provide three divisions.

He, therefore, proposed to concentrate his forces in locations between Brisbane and Melbourne. Areas such as Northern Queensland would be barely manned. This was in line with government thinking which was that the Port Kembla and Newcastle areas were vital and as long as they were held Australia could continue to fight. Mackay later stated that he at no time called his plan "The Brisbane Line".

The "plan" became a political football, however, and a Royal Commission was held. It found there was no such plan but people still seemed to think there may have been. In 1943 General Douglas MacArthur added fuel to the fire by referring to the plan in a press conference and calling it "The Brisbane Line". When asked, he stated that he believed that all documents concerning it had been destroyed.

We will probably never know the exact sequence of events but it is likely that a small part of a plan got blown up by someone else and as it bounced around it grew into something much bigger.

Cheryl *If Eleanor was hiding the bank books from possible break and enter, she would tell either or both Arthur and Morgan where they were hidden.*

The more we found out about Arthur 'Jumbo' Webster, through our research with Queensland Railways, the more people started to lean towards a possible domestic violence situation. The fact that Eleanor was still hiding money when she was 72 years old, however, led us to believe she was either in the habit of hiding it from years past, or had some other reason. She didn't seem to be about to cut and run, and the more I learned about this family from relatives, the more I opposed that idea, as did many others.

Allan *We might assume that whatever Eleanor was doing was for her own future benefit, unless of course future revelations show her to be cut from the same cloth as Arthur. You would think domestic violence would be a likely possibility in the household.*
Caylie *I am definitely thinking along those lines Allan. The more I hear. Remember Eleanor lost a baby too and raised Morgan pretty much by herself as well. A lot going on here.*
Allan *More likely that she was ensuring the future of Morgan. He may have known about her hidden stash but not Arthur and I assume Arthur would have gone ballistic to find out his wife was hiding money (a large amount!) from him. I have the funny feeling Morgan may have been complicit in the bank book situation (and Muriel White) but he never knew where they were hidden. They had death duties then.*
Caylie *I always felt Morgan was complicit esp. after the Year 6 boy at Milton State School noticed the initials Muriel White matched Morgan Webster. But perhaps Arthur adored Eleanor and took out his pain and suffering from losing his first born son on his co-workers? Maybe he loved Eleanor but was unkind to his remaining son, a son who was more interested in books and numbers than learning a trade? Eleanor could have been the meat in a sandwich trying to care for both her husband and her son.*

Margaret *Poor loves were dependant on their husbands solely and had to ask them for absolutely everything so I guess they wanted just a little of their own.*
Jay *Raises the question of what happened to stop her from putting the stash to good use? Another era related point is that a husband had legal claim over a wife's possessions. So if she wanted to keep an emergency fund out of his hands (for whatever reason e.g. gambling), she'd have to go to great lengths to keep it quiet. We've known banks, gov't dep'ts etc. to separately (quietly) call up a husband to get approval for a wife's request.*

Maybe Morgan, being a whiz with maths and figures, could have advised his mother about investments. He may have been privy to her personal bank book/s and war bond activities.

Pension Fraud

Cheryl was the one who was finally able to back up the fraud possibility (and most likely scenario) for the third bank book in Muriel White's name. She posed many questions, one after the other, to get us thinking about what was happening for the Websters over the years.

Not only was she capable of getting into the details, but once she had enough of them, Cheryl was also able to look at the family's situation as a whole. Such a critical evaluator was hugely valuable to the UTL Team, and we were regularly awed by her contributions, and Allan's corresponding thought processes.

Allan *I initially thought Arthur may have needed the joint account book to access cash while he was away, hence Eleanor needing her own book. If that were the case Arthur's withdrawals would have been shown in the book. Be interesting to find out the billing cycle for electricity, rates etc. at that time to see if any withdrawals might have been for that reason.*

Also curious why she used three different CBA branches for three different accounts. Why not a Wales or National Bank account to be really secretive?

A totalling of all the Bonds comes to a minimum of £2,630 or 375 weeks of average pay or 7.2 years average wages. A lot of money for battlers and they could seemingly have lived off the interest. It would have made more sense to buy more houses. The Bond interest would be a great safety hedge for repayments in case of tenant problems or use the interest to pay off the houses(s) faster. The old age pension would not be such a concern in that scenario.

Was their house bought through a War Service loan, bank loan, or owned outright? Were some of the withdrawals to make house payments or pay extra payments to pay it off quicker? You would not think there would have been any period renovations with only one child and presumably a spare bedroom. I wonder if there may have been a fourth bank book in Arthur's name that he retained? These bank books don't really indicate day to day life but rather investment accumulation.

Cheryl *The starting point I am looking at is Arthur's occupation as an engine driver for QR.*
- *Average weekly wage 1943-4: £6/12/0. 1946: £6/9/7 QR would pay wages directly to a wife if the husband declared her as next of kin. Larger monthly deposits could be due to overtime and penalty payments.*
- *July 1944, start of new financial year – £1,012 withdrawal. I would suggest War Bonds for £1,000 was purchased and the interest paid directly to Eleanor's account. This could be for tax purpose as Eleanor had no other income.*
- *Eleanor turned 60, pension age in 1944.*
- *War bond interest paid into accounts is in keeping with a £1,000 bond earing 3.25% interest paid monthly*
- *Joint account – only the accumulated interest was withdrawn in most instances. Larger withdrawal £300 possibly another smaller bond purchased.*

This would account for the increased interest paid by CommBank war bond interest.

- *Eleanor's account – only interest withdrawn except June 1950, £110, maybe more bonds purchased*
- *Both Eleanor and joint accounts kept to around £500 balance, was this for tax/pension reasons. See Federal Gov't web site for pensions in that era.*
- *The smaller, interest-only withdrawals could have been small war bond purchases not held by the CommBank but could be used as black market cash transactions. Bonds were still being issued in 1950, maturing 1960. These small withdrawals could have also been used as cash loans to a third party.*
- *If the war bond had a 10 year maturity, it would have been cashed in around 1954/55*
- *August 1955 Arthur turned 65, pension age.*
- *October 1955 Muriel White account opened with £425. Was the war bond cashed in and some of the money used to open this account to hide assets to be eligible for the pension?*
- *Did Eleanor retain balance of war bond money and loan out amounts privately, charging interest which she collected and banked into Muriel's account? Did she change coins and small notes into £5 notes as the money accumulated, which would explain the coins under the lino and some odd amounts deposited?*
- *Arthur either never knew about this, or just couldn't find the bank books. A man probably wouldn't think to lift the lino in the kitchen.*
- *Eleanor's and joint accounts were probably found through a probate/intestate search, but Muriel's account never found because there is nothing to link it to Eleanor.*
- *Arthur's will had a lot of value – $60,000 plus the house. I think they found the main accounts but not Muriel's.*
- *If Eleanor was doing private loans she probably kept a book/ledger. Arthur could have called in the loans over time and this would account for his large estate.*

> A gradual accumulation of money was often put down as 'a big win on the races' or a win on the casket (Qld lottery) and nobody questioned it in those days.

- Eleanor appears to be a thrifty woman, saving not spending money. I can't see that the withdrawals would have been spent, more likely 'invested' elsewhere.
- All this would mean no 'dirty' money, just 'black' money, just tax and pension fraud. Loan Shark would be too harsh a term, a 'Canny' Irish descendant, who knew how to survive, but apparently didn't consider her mortality and kept the secret too close to her heart.

I think this scenario makes sense.

Pension Scheme

By 1940 Australia was one of about thirty five countries with social security programs for the aged and the disabled. By 1997 at least 166 countries of the 185 in the United Nations had some sort of program in this area.

The Australian pensions were modelled in part on the New Zealand scheme and were similar to the NSW scheme. The pensions were non-contributory, non-discretionary and means tested. They were available from the age of 65 years for men and 60 years for women.

aph.gov.au/About_Parliament/Parliamentary_Departments/Parliamentary_Library/pubs/BN/1011/SSPayments1

Do you see what I mean about Cheryl being an amazing critical thinker?

She, and others, worked hard to come to these conclusions – the gathering of evidence with facts and anecdotes gave us all the opportunity to form opinions and theories. This is the most probable scenario for the Webster family's hidden money, accumulation of wealth and third bank account belonging to a Muriel White we have never found.

So if the above is in any way true, Muriel White never existed, and the Webster's excess earnings came from War Bonds and loan interest accrual, selling chook eggs, selling shares that didn't originally belong to them, and taking in rent from Morgan and/or other boarders.

If the money in Muriel White's account was deposited to avoid paying tax, and the money was never claimed by anyone else, the Government would have absorbed that money back into consolidated revenue.

Cheryl *There's something very Karma-like about the way, if Eleanor was committing pension fraud, that the government got her ill-gotten gains back in their hot little hands anyway!*

My personal belief is that this is the Universe's way of maintaining balance. If the above scenario proves correct, then the money that I found never belonged to the Websters, it belonged to the tax department.

And that's exactly where it ended up.

Part 8

My Place in Milton

The History of *My* Place

There's a wonderful children's book called *My Place*, written by Nadia Wheatley and Donna Rawlins which was made into a miniseries by the ABC. It starts in 1988, painting a picture of a tree and the life that surrounds it on a street in Sydney. Every page goes back another decade until the dawn of time. The blurb says, "Everyone is a part of History, and every place has a story as old as the earth."

It took eight months of research before I got to the point of going back to the time of white settlement in Brisbane.

Why would you need to do that? What's that got to do with bank books and money from the 1940s? I hear you ask.

Well, history gave us answers and backstory to many of the issues and situations we asked at the beginning of this project. It's amazing how one event or incident in history can have a massive knock-on effect into the present. For want of a nail, the horse was lost, sort of thing. I believed we could win this battle with the bank books by going back in time.

The story of 86 Heussler Terrace has a wonderful timeline dating back to the 1850s, when George Farquhar Leslie bought the parcel of land that this house currently sits on. Before that, the lands belonged to nobody, but were the home and hunting grounds for the local aboriginals.

I juggle quite a few activities in my life as a mother of two, and doing tuckshop once a month is one of them. It's always a busy day, feeding hundreds of starving boys, but I love it – the chats with Barb, Zophia, Mr T and the other volunteer Mums is always interesting, and we have spent many hours trying to work out who Muriel White is while toasting sandwiches!

After tuckshop, I have a few hours to kill before the kids finish for the day, and I sometimes headed over to the Brisbane Boys College Junior Library to do some work. DJ, the teacher-librarian, was really helpful on my first visit, pointing out the local history books which, of course, encompassed the area I've been writing about.

The first book I pulled from the shelves was *Toowong, A Community History*, a collection of 16 essays by different authors, edited by Susan Leggett and Roslyn Grant. The authors used their personal memories and research to paint historical pictures from their own perspectives of one of the oldest parts of 'settled' Brisbane. The very first essay was called *Aboriginal People of Toowong*. Just what I was after.

Thirty second later, I nearly slid off my chair when I realised it was written by one of the Dads at soccer – Arthur Palmer. I mention soccer friends here because they continue to make cameos throughout this book. You've already heard about the netball XXXX Dad!

I was fascinated by Arthur from the moment I met him – we swapped contact details so we could organise play dates with our sons, Will and Beau – and just reading Arthur's business card was an illuminating history lesson in itself! A pilot and anthropologist, Arthur has a plethora of stories to tell about Queensland and is always up for a good yarn.

I was also delighted to discover that Arthur is the great-grandson of Sir Arthur Palmer, the 5th Premier of Queensland (1870–74), who makes another appearance later in this story. Do you recall that he bought the land around Corinda where Arthur's parents lived?

After reading his essay about the native Aboriginal inhabitants of this area, I asked Arthur to contribute a piece for this book.

The Aboriginals of Toowong
by Arthur B. Palmer

Aboriginal ownership of this estate area, now known as the suburb of Toowong, began around 30,000 years before present (BP) [Hall 1990:176]. At the beginning of human occupation, the sea level was some 90 metres lower and the shore line would have extended 30 kilometres further East of its present position [ibid: 176]. Between 15,000 and 6,000 years BP the coastline gradually retreated inland, as the last great glacial (Wuerm) ice age came to an end [Laseron 1969: 215, Map 24].

Australia lost approximately one seventh of its landmass [Blainey 1975: 85], forcing coastal salt water Aboriginals inland to intermingle with the land owning subcoastal hinterland groups. This drastically effected language, marriage patterns, food resources, religion, ritual, ceremony and conflict. There is evidence that this area once had a much moister climate [opcit]. Vegetation and fauna also changed markedly during this period.

About 6,000 years ago Moreton Bay and the Brisbane River took on their modern form, population density increased and the pace of economic and technological change intensified [Gregory 1996: 2]. A diverse and rich economy developed and flourished, providing the Toowong traditional owners with an impressive standard of living. Aboriginal collective knowledge meant they were masters of the profundity of their environment, ensuring that a vast range and variety of food resources were exploited; one hundred and forty species of vegetable foods and in excess of fifty marine, river and land animals. Seasonality delivered as regular a harvest as cultivated gardens or domesticated stock.

The hunter gatherer economy involved the technique of 'firestick farming'; regularly burning off the grass and undergrowth to facilitate access, mobility and regeneration of food plants and grassland to attract larger game. This practice gave parts of Toowong a 'park like appearance' as described by the early European explorers. Indeed Oxley's 1823 chart of the Brisbane River describes the area between Longreach and Glenmorrisson Range (Mt Coot-tha area) as "fine open grazing country" [opcit: 17]. Oxley also noted low open forest and good grass near the site of the present Regatta Hotel [Gregory 1970: 22]. The utilisation of sophisticated technology for food gathering afforded ample leisure time. Elaborate and complex ceremonial and ritual life, intergroup gatherings and extensive trade routes were well established.

Like all Aboriginals, the people of Toowong were multi-lingual and even small children would have spoken up to five languages. Had Governor Brisbane returned to England with a Toowong Aboriginal as a tourist in the 1820s, and taken the visitor on a tour of Scotland or Ireland, the 'savage' would have returned to his family at Jo-ai Jo-ai, to describe what he had seen in the third world with all its poverty, hardship, slums and famine.

The first recorded interaction between Toowong Aboriginal clans and Europeans was with the "lost castaway" convicts Pamphlet, Finnegan and Parsons in 1823, who were eventually rescued by Oxley. They had spent several months living with and moving between Aboriginal groups, clearly enjoying both their hospitality and protection [Gregory 1996: 6]. There is some indication that the convicts may have picked up sufficient Turubul language to ask the Jagara land owning group [Tindale 1974: 169, Petrie 1904: 4] for a cooked meal of fish. This contact is recorded when a Jagara fishing group apprehended the convicts with an appropriated canoe [Gregory 1996: 6]. Gregory describes the language as Yugarabul [1996: 2].

The only other Europeans known to have spoken turubul and lived with the Jagara, apart from Tom Petrie, were three escaped convicts; James Davis (Duramboi), Bracefield (Wandi) and Fahey (Gilbury) [Petrie 1904: 12]. Davis lived with Aboriginals for seventeen years (approximately 1825–1840), was scarified, a noted hunter and presumably had an Aboriginal family, but after returning to Brisbane and becoming a blacksmith, refused to disclose any information on Aboriginal society or culture [ibid: 135-141]. On 2nd December 1823 Oxley returned to explore the Brisbane River with Finnegan as guide [Gregory 1996: 18]. Oxley records in his journal 27th September 1824 that he saw a large group of Aboriginals at a favourite hunting ground near the river at Toowong and describes them as "about the strongest and best made muscular men I have seen in any country" [ibid:6].

However, after camping the night on the flat below the present site of 'Moorlands', they noticed amongst "a very large assemblage of natives" a man who had "taken" Oxley's hat at Breakfast Creek on 17th September. The man refused to return it. How it was relayed that the hat wasn't a gift, or how its return was demanded is a mystery. Perhaps Finnegan clumsily interpreted the request, perhaps not. In any event, a member of Oxley's party fatally shot the man immediately, flagrantly disobeying Governor Brisbane's order that the Brisbane River Aboriginals were to be respected and any ill treatment or injury was to be severely punished. The irresistible Jagara conclusion must have been that a hat clearly outweighed a human life. The Aboriginals retreated in confusion and during the night Oxley and Cunningham heard "the most dismal howlings and wailings" [Gregory 1990: 23 –24]. It's uncertain whether Oxley regained his hat, as it probably would have been passed or traded on as a curiosity through many hands in the intervening period.

Although Aboriginals were not unused to violent confrontations resulting in death, this must have come as a serious shock in return for hosting a group of strange men deep within the Jagara estate. Nothing leading up to this event could possibly have given the traditional owners the vaguest anticipation of the repercussions of not returning what must have been perceived as a gift in reciprocity for the obligation the Europeans had incurred for travelling in and living off their land. The Aboriginal perception that groups of men travelling without women should always be regarded as threatening and suspicious, would on this occasion, have been reinforced. Thus the period of conflict and retribution began.

The establishment of the convict settlement at North Quay in 1825 and the opening of the Brisbane River area to free settlement in 1842 did little to change the nature of White/Black contact. Both events introduced hard men with hard attitudes in hard times. Also introduced was grog, a range of irresistible and desirable items, venereal disease and various pan epidemics; chicken pox, small pox, TB, measles. The conflict of interest was immediate, as was the litany of misunderstandings on both sides. In the end, it was only Aboriginals who were capable of adaptation.

The Toowong confrontation with Oxley set the bench mark. The complexities of Aboriginal language meant that Europeans rarely acquired fluency, and even less frequently sought Aboriginal opinion or their vital knowledge. There was to be no meeting half way, no going company. The Toowong traditional owners had to display one hundred percent flexibility and accommodation in all dealings with Europeans. It was a constant and ongoing struggle. The pantomime of 1788 between Governor Philip and the Port Jackson Aboriginals was repeated.

Alternating experiments with expulsion or assimilation, with no one in authority ever thinking to consult with the traditional owners. Consequently, of the hundreds of Turubul Jagara named localities, the only remaining recorded sites in Toowong are a corruption of Tu-wong (Djuung) purportedly the name for the river bend near the Indooroopilly Bridge, meaning the call of the black goat sucker bird. Mt Coot-tha a corruption of Ku-ta, meaning dark, native bee honey. Baneraba as a named site near the Toowong Railway Station, of unknown meaning and Jo-ai Jo-ai for where the Regatta now stands.

All these names were recorded by Tom Petrie who was as perplexed then, as we are now, by our resolve and inability to absorb so little from such a rich and generous culture which offered so much to many generations of Traditional Owners. Perhaps precisely because Aboriginal linguistic markers in the landscape denote land tenure systems (Palmer 1984: 86-94), amnesia was an imperative for the new owners to comfortably take possession not only of Toowong but large portions of the continent.

Bibliography

Blainey, G. 1975 Triumph of the Nomads: A History of Ancient Australia. Melbourne: MacMillan.

Gregory, H. 1990 Arcadian Simplicity: J.B. Fewing's Memoirs of Toowong. Brisbane: Boolarong.

State Library Board of Queensland. 1996 The Brisbane River Story. Meanders through Time. Yeronga: Australian Marine Conservation Society inc.

Hall, H.J. 1990 20,000 Years of Human Impact on the Brisbane River and Environs. In Davie, P. et al. The Brisbane River. A source book for the future. Brisbane.

Palmer, A.B. 1984 Sacred Sites: The Focus of Aboriginal Land Ownership. Simply Living, Vol. 2 No:3

Petrie, C.C. 1904 Tom Petrie. Reminiscences of Early Queensland. Brisbane: Watson Ferguson.

Tindale, N.B. 1974 Aboriginal Tribes of Australia. Their Terrain, Environmental Controls, Distribution, Limits and Proper Names. Canberra: ANU Press.

Canning Downs Station Homestead 1875
Photograph courtesy of State Library of Queensland

Newstead Cottage built by Patrick Leslie, Darling Down's pioneer
Dixon Galleries, State Library of NSW

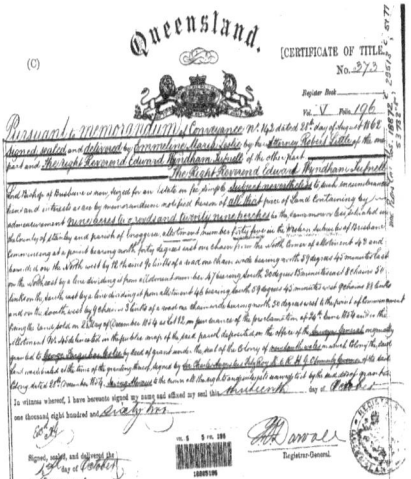

The Title Deed transfer to Bishop Tufnell 1862
John Oxley Library

The NSW State Library Archivist, whose surname was coincidentally, Leslie, was very helpful in my research, and e-mailed me a copy of this letter, sent in 1838 by George's father William Leslie, the 10th Laird of Warthill, to his son asking him to stay safe in the colonies. I love this letter because I can imagine David writing something like this to Will in ten years when he takes off on his first overseas expedition! Fathers who love their sons are the same century after century...

Letter to George Leslie from his father, William Leslie, 1838
Courtesy of the State Library of NSW Archives

Transcript

Warthill, 14 September 1838

My Dearly beloved George,

   I hope you have been sometimes thinking, already, of the cautions, admonitions and recommendations contained in a letter addressed to your Brother Patrick, when similarly situated as you now are. They will be found generally applicable to your own case, and the copy you have taken, will save me the pain and trouble of addressing you and Dear Walter on the same subject, amidst the hurry and bustle of parting with you both.

   You will soon, my Dearest Boy, be far removed from the personal superintendence, and watchful care of your affectionate Parents, but, while you continue to discharge your duties aright, the Great Parent of all will be ever ready to point out the paths wherein you ought to walk, and to afford you not only his merciful protection but also the gracious assistance of his Grace and Holy Spirit, in all the various vicissitudes of life –

   I can form but a very imperfect idea of how you will be situated upon your arrival in N. S. Wales, but I am certain Dear Patrick will not be wanting in doing his best for you both. Most probably, you will, in the first instance, be employed in such departments of his concerns, as he may see fitting for you, however irksome the labour and drudgery may appear to be, rest satisfied that it is all for your future good; and ever have in mind that, to young beginners, no profession is without its drawbacks, and that independence is not to be won but after years of toil and trouble.

   Considering the comforts you have enjoyed in your early days, the privations, and hardships of a Settlers life may, at first, appear difficult to contend with; but you must never give way to the still more uneasy feelings of despondency, should your outset prove more trying than you may have anticipated. On the contrary, you must boldly, and steadily encounter every obstacle that may come in your way, and depend upon it, independence and ease will afterwards follow in due time.

Combined with a very amiable disposition, I know you, Dear George, to be possessed of business talents and attention, which, if properly applied will, under the blessing of Heaven, soon render your services useful both to yourself and others – and when opportunity occurs for their being employed on a larger scale, they will, I doubt not, insure perfect success in all your undertakings.

I must remind you, however, that business and pleasure have ever been found incompatible companions – more especially in the heyday of youth – the one or the other very quickly gains the ascendancy, and many a promising youth's fate has been sealed, by thoughtlessly allowing the latter to predominate.

Your truly affectionate and devoted Father
W. Leslie

And then, of course, there was the completely mind-blowing e-mail from my Aunt Daphne to say that her husband, Dom, had a Grandfather from Scotland called George Farquhar Leslie... at the time of writing this, we haven't been able to make a connection, however, my Uncle Dom is currently trying to claim that HE is Muriel White, and that our house is rightfully his...☺

George Farquhar Leslie, Aberdeen
Family photograph of Daphne and Dom Gonzalvez

Settlement of Brisbane: Milton and surrounds

The new settlement of Brisbane steadily gained momentum after Separation with the main suburban growth continuing in the previously established directions, north, west and northeast of the city.

To the west, development embraced Milton, Rosalie, Torwood, Kelvin Grove and Paddington extended further west. The construction of the first stage of the tramway system between 1882 and 1890 and expansion of the railway allowed working men to live further from their place of employment. They settled in suburbs, often clustered around railway stations, while industry became concentrated in the city area. Whereas the horse and buggy transport of Brisbane's early days produced a pattern of dense settlement on small allotments in and around the city, the construction of tramways and railways dispersed the population into outlying suburbs where the characteristic residence was a single bungalow set on a 16 perch allotment.

By the mid-1890s expansion of the tramways intensified settlement in the near western suburbs of Kelvin Grove, Red Hill, Paddington, Milton and Rosalie.

Local Government Brisbane was declared a municipality in 1859 and, until 1880, the Brisbane Municipal Authority dealt with local matters throughout Brisbane. During that period, local government services were all but absent; drains did not exist and sanitary conditions were appalling. Roads were unformed tracks.

In 1864 the government passed the Municipalities Act expanding council powers to make by-laws and raise money through rates. Gas street lighting was introduced in 1865, and gradually extended throughout the developing suburban areas of north Brisbane. A local water supply was made available from an earthen walled reservoir on Enoggera Creek.

By the 1890s almost all children were receiving some primary education.

Although denominational and private schools continued to function throughout the metropolitan area, over four-fifths of children aged 6 to 11 years attended government schools. The Grammar Schools Act of 1860 provided government subsidies for the building of semi-independent grammar schools. Free secondary education was not provided as it was considered to be a luxury. By the end of the 19th century secondary education remained a patchwork system, poorly integrated with the primary system and available only to a small proportion of the community's children. The only state subsidised secondary education available in Brisbane was at Brisbane Grammar School and Brisbane Girls' Grammar School.

The Southwest district consists of the suburbs of Auchenflower, Toowong, Mount Coot-tha and Taringa.

Prior to white settlement, the suburb of Auchenflower was characterised by its many hills and small creeks running from the ranges in the west into the river. Following the settlement of Redcliffe as a penal colony, Oxley explored the Brisbane River for a second time and his diary describes a chain of ponds watering a fine valley at the site of present day Auchenflower. After the opening of the settlement to free settlers in 1842 expansion to the west saw the development of Limestone (Ipswich) as a commercial and social centre with tracks and later roads to this centre passing through Milton, Auchenflower and Toowong.

Early European Settlement

In 1842, the area of 'Milton' (encompassing future Auchenflower and Toowong) was divided by Deed of Grant into five acre properties, extending from the Brisbane River to the surrounding ridges above. As was the norm, wealthy settlers purchased large tracts of land on the ridges.

Amongst these was Ambrose Eldridge who, in 1851, purchased 30 acres of prime land where he built 'Milton House', from which the suburb derived its name. Overall, the area was comparatively slow to develop, and by the late 1850s it remained mainly pasture and farm land.

Contemporary accounts state that in 1856, 'there were no more than six houses in the district'.

Development of the Suburb

In 1850, the first subdivision west of the town of Brisbane, Portion One of the Parish of Enoggera, was conducted by James Warner. This land was divided into twelve large estates and several families were given original Deeds of Grant from the Crown and established homes in the region of present day Milton, Rosalie, Auchenflower and Toowong.

Despite the fact that the suburb was within easy reach of the city, its development remained slow. The main reasons attributed to this were the location of the Paddington-Milton Cemeteries, and the flood prone nature of the low-lying areas. The slow rise in land values facilitated the purchase by the Church of England of the land where the first Anglican Bishop of Brisbane, Edward Tufnell, built his See house 'Bishopsbourne'.

Tufnell arrived in Queensland expecting to receive support from the government. Soon after his arrival, however, the first Queensland Parliament abolished the official connection between church and state, thereby removing the anticipated financial assistance. Tufnell therefore had to raise his own funds for the establishment of his diocese. The members of the congregation donated generously, but were somewhat nonplussed when Tufnell spent a large percentage of the funds on the construction of his residence.

The opening of the Milton Railway Station on the Brisbane to Ipswich line in 1877, and the immigration boom of the 1880s heralded the intensification of residential development in Milton as the more popular suburbs of Red Hill and Paddington became overcrowded.

However, despite the closure of the Paddington-Milton Cemeteries in 1875 and the construction of the Milton Drain in 1885, the area was plagued by persistent sanitation problems from stagnant pools within the disused graveyards.

Lang Park (as the cemetery site was renamed) was used as a garbage and night soil dump into the mid-20th century, with the resultant stigma adversely affecting progress of Milton as a suburb. Additionally, Milton continued to be significantly affected by Brisbane's cyclical floods. There are six registered heritage places in Milton consisting of the Milton Brewery, one school, a theological college and chapel, a porphyry retaining wall and a fig tree.

Transport

The first public transport to the district was by horse-drawn cab which could be hired from the city. In the 1880s, cheap and convenient transport became readily available through privately operated horse-drawn omnibuses. Proprietors were often local residents who kept stables throughout the suburbs. Horse-drawn omnibuses continued to operate throughout the district in a limited way until 1912.

Milton also benefited from the railway station that opened in 1877. Electrification of the tramways in 1897 saw a rapid expansion of the tramway network. The line reached Paddington in 1897, Ashgrove (servicing Red Hill) in 1901 and Toowong (servicing Milton) in 1904. Increased tram services required the construction of an additional electricity sub-station at Enoggera Terrace in 1929, to assist the Petrie Terrace substation with the provision of power to the electric tramway system.

In September 1962, the Paddington tram depot was destroyed by fire with the loss of 65 trams. Following the fire, Milton was serviced by buses and by the close of 1969 all trams throughout Brisbane ceased to operate and were replaced by buses. Between 1927 and 1969 the Brisbane City Council's tramway workshops were located at Boomerang Street, Milton on a site formerly used as a nightsoil dump. After the closure of the tramway system, the workshops continued to be used to service the City Council's bus fleet until 1979.

Other heritage places related to the area's transport include the tramway substation at Paddington and a porphyry retaining wall on Heussler Terrace, Milton.

The Milton State School opened in 1889. In its early years, this school was on the western edge of the 'tough' area of Paddington. As a result it had a bad reputation amongst the more genteel families of inner western Brisbane. Their children attended Toowong State School and Rainworth State School. However, by the early 20th century the school was described as being amongst the most commodious and best equipped schools in the district. Its proximity to the yet undeveloped Gregory Park assures the children playing grounds and breathing space.

A total of ten religious places are heritage-registered in the Central district of the Study Area, reflecting the Anglican, Presbyterian, Catholic and Baptist denominations. These places include the Old Bishopsbourne Chapel and College at Milton

Extracts from the Cultural Heritage Report 423b
The University of Queensland Archaeological Services Unit by Jon Prangnell, Karen Murphy, Tam Smith and Linda Berry
Auchenflower: The Suburb and the Name by Dr John Pearn 1997, St Lucia: University of Queensland Press.

The Adsett family's land was on the other side of Baroona Road, where the IGA shopping centre and Park Road Chiropractic now sit, and a lot of family history has been researched by the extended family of the Adsetts, which paints a wonderful picture of the times here in Brisbane.

Extract from The Adsett Family: Origins and Migrants
by F. J. Erikson

One may enquire why it was that the Adsetts' choice fell on Moreton Bay, an insignificant outpost in the vast colony of New South Wales; and there can be little doubt that the answer lies in the publicity given to the area by Dr John Dunmore Lang, in England, during the years 1848 and 1849.

There is some merit in pausing at this point to look around, as the migrants must have done, at the small town of Brisbane as it was in 1851. In fact it was not so much a town as a frontier village, with a population of a little over two thousand. The numbers were increasing steadily, and doubled in the five years to 1856; but the great influx of migrants did not take place until after Separation from New South Wales at the end of 1859.

In 1851 Brisbane was a very young town indeed. The census of 1841 showed that the entire European population of the Moreton Bay area was just on two hundred – and of these, 132 were convicts. The area was not thrown open to free settlement until 1842, when the first land sale was held. The only buildings of any substance then were the convict-built structures of the penal colony. Brisbane had experienced just nine years of urban development when the Adsett group arrived in February 1851.

Despite its youth, Brisbane had made some progress, and had facilities to offer. Stores, hotels, blacksmiths, and stables had been established. A boiling down works was operating at Kangaroo Point. A government administration centre had been set up. The town was officially a port of entry, and a customs department had been established. The Moreton Bay Courier had begun publication in 1846. There was a ferry service to cross the river, and river steamers carried passengers and freight to Ipswich, the head of navigation. There was also a regular shipping service to Sydney. Several churches were active in the town, and Lang's migrants had taken steps to establish a School of Arts. In November 1850, a Branch of the Bank of New South Wales opened for business. On the other hand, there were no made roads, no buses, and no coaches. There was no reticulated water supply. No gas works had been built, and there was no street lighting. Services were few indeed. The Municipality of Brisbane was not proclaimed until 1859, and such services as scavenger and sanitary collection did not exist.

adsetthistory.com.au

The Reverend Dr John Dunmore Lang
1799-1878

The man leading the charge to bring 'quality' free European settlers into the region was the Reverend Dr John Dunmore Lang, the namesake of yes, you guessed it, Lang Park (aka Suncorp Stadium)!

Do you remember reading about him earlier? Rev. John Dunmore Lang married Eleanor's grandparents, Michael Murphy and Mary Ann Potter in 1854 when he was the minister of the Scots Church in Sydney.

John Dunmore Lang was a highly influential and often, controversial, pioneer in Queensland's early history. He was a very clever man, known to be impulsive, outspoken and brazenly bigoted, but he had a great interest in politics, education, Colonisation and writing. He loved a good project, jumping in with both feet (a little bit like me!) but his methods were questionable, and he often lost credibility because of his attitude and loose purse strings.

One of his major projects was a massive recruitment drive to bring migrants into the Moreton Bay area. Whilst on a three-year sojourn to the UK from 1846, Lang used his superior marketing, publishing and journalistic writing skills to convince three shiploads of carefully selected people to come to Australia. He sold Australia and its opportunities so well, that in 1848, the *Fortitude,* the *Chaseley* and the *Lima* left the soggy shores of Ol' Blighty filled to the brim with farmers, labourers and tradesmen from a variety of religions, hankering for the beauty, lifestyle and conditions Lang promised would be there for them upon arrival.

He convinced many missionaries to reroute from various Pacific Islands and alternate destinations to get them to come and bolster the flailing Zionists who'd set up a township in the Nundah area in order to bring Christianity to the Jagera and Turrbal peoples.

Of course, I discovered that Zionists were Lutherans, and as my daughter attends a Lutheran school, it was an interesting dinner table discussion one evening here at home.

The mission opened between April and June 1838, the result of joint efforts by Presbyterians, Lutherans and Pietists. It began with an unusually large number of staff for a Protestant mission – two ordained priests accompanied by ten laymen and their wives – a staff size 'altogether unprecedented in the history of British Missions and British Colonisation'. With such an effort in staffing, this mission was clearly meant to succeed. However, it was not really considered a success in its time, and was finally disbanded in 1848 having witnessed the most difficult and destructive decade for the Aborigines of Moreton Bay.

Source: Griffith University, German Missionaries in Australia

Patrick Mayne 1824–1865

Source Unknown

Part way through the project, several people began to liken this story to that of the Mayne family. *Read the Mayne Inheritance!* they said. *UTL is reminiscent of Patrick Mayne and family!* they said. So I bought the book by Rosamunde Siemon, and read it. Well, most of it. I mistakenly thought it was a non-fiction, true account of the actual happenings of Patrick Mayne.

At some point, I realised that some of this story was made up. I had been hoodwinked by some of the blatant suppositions I came across – theories somewhat bereft of historical fact. The author's claim was that Patrick Mayne murdered a sawyer called Robert Cox at the Bush Inn, Kangaroo Point in 1848, taking £350 from him, and dismembering the man's body, like only a butcher could. Another man hanged for the crime Patrick supposedly confessed to on his deathbed.

Yes, it was an interesting tale, I'll admit. For me, it was made all the more fascinating in that the author, Dr Rosamond Siemon, PhD, was able to describe historical localities that I knew so well, but didn't really know at all!

Queensland Uni was my alma mater, but I had no idea that the land upon which it sits was donated by the Mayne family, or that Mayne Hall, Mayneview and Patrick Streets around the corner, Mayne Train Depot, the Brisbane Arcade and Moorlands at the Wesley Hospital are all legacies from the family with this purportedly infamous patriarch!

The facts of Patrick Mayne's known life are as follows: Originally from Ireland, Patrick arrived in New South Wales on the *Percy* in 1841. He came to Brisbane five years later, working as a butcher at the new boiling down works in Kangaroo Point.

He worked his way up the ranks to becoming a businessman, landowner and alderman. He bought a Queen Street butcher shop with room out the back for livestock in September 1849. From there, he grew his portfolio of property including hotels, shops, houses, and of course, speculated in land all over Milton and Auchenflower.

His contributions to the building of St Stephen's Cathedral led to a commemoration in stained-glass windows inside the church, and his appreciation for quality education saw him donating money to help build the National School.

Patrick was an elected officer on the first municipal council in Brisbane and was an alderman and a member of the finance committee until he passed away. He was a practical man, always considering the needs of the community in terms of matters such as water, sewerage, the levelling of streets and setting appropriate rates.

None of the Mayne children married and the last of them donated land for the University of Queensland (UQ), willing their final estate earnings to the UQ Medical School. Quite an enormous legacy to the people of Brisbane, then and now, I must say, guilt money or not.

So there you have it – have a re-read, and look out for the suppositions. I've been mindful of doing the same with this book, by the way. People in ~~glass~~ old houses shouldn't throw stones...

The History of Heussler Terrace
Johann Heussler 1820–1907

Mary *Heussler Terrace would be named for the man commissioned to entice German families and skilled workers to Qld, post separation and Statehood in 1859.*

I first learned about the man after whom my street was named when Ross Webster came over for morning tea. I'd invited Ross over, along with Lyn and Cheryl, because they'd had such a vested interest in the project to date, and shared my enthusiasm for meeting Webster and Murphy family members who might be able to give us some answers.

I found Ross to be a quiet, studious man, who generously shared all of his Webster family history with us, as you read earlier. He had documents, articles, photographs and a memory stick full of useful information that Lyn was able to use to update the family tree she'd put together on Ancestry.com. This made life a lot easier for us all.

Unfortunately, he didn't have any photographs of Arthur or Eleanor, which is a bit of a theme here... nobody has a picture of them that we know about!

Ross also explained the origins of Heussler Terrace to us, which was an added bonus for us, confirming even more synchronicities. It was named after a prominent Brisbane businessman called Johann Christian Heussler, who originally hailed from Germany.

Trudy Bennett, one of the librarians at the State Library of Queensland, has written an article about him that I'll share with you here...

A COLOURFUL CHARACTER
by Trudy Bennett, State Library of Queensland

Queensland history features a large cast of colourful characters. A notable member of this company is one Johann Christian Heussler. He was born in Germany in 1820, and migrated to pre-Separation Queensland in 1854.

He was a merchant by training and occupation, and on arrival, he went into partnership with fellow German immigrant Frederic Alterwicker, establishing a business together in South Brisbane.

Johann Christian Heussler
Photograph thanks to the John Oxley Library Collection

From this modest start, Heussler embarked on an eventful and varied career: as a wine merchant, importer/exporter, an employment agency for Germans, an immigration agent, a sugar planter, a Member of the Legislative Council, and a founding member of the Queensland Club.

According to a notice that was published in the Queensland Government Gazette on Saturday, 19th May, 1862, Messrs Heussler and Francksen informed the public at large that they had become German immigration agents under the bounty immigration scheme.

Johann Christian Heussler is credited with recruiting some 2000 German emigrants to settle in Queensland, thus the ancestors of many Queenslanders of German descent came to the newly-minted colony.

Heussler was an enterprising businessman, and in the course of his career he experienced both boom and bust.

He was bankrupt more than once, though this did not prevent him from serving as a Member of the Legislative Council. In 1864/65, he had built a desirable residence at Paddington; in fact, this house was one of the first houses built in Paddington. The name of this house was Fernberg.

It was here that the Heussler family lived until 1872, when more economic woes forced them to sell the house. A subsequent owner of Fernberg, one John Stevenson, extended the house.

Heussler became the German consul for Queensland in 1880, and in 1895 he became a Knight of the Order of Orange-Nassau, a Dutch order of chivalry. He died in 1907, and is buried in Toowong Cemetery. His legacy lives on, however, as in 1911, the Queensland Government acquired Fernberg as a permanent Government House for the sum of £10,000. It was restored and extended, and it is our Governor's official residence to this day.

Drawing of Fernberg House 1891
Image courtesy of the State Library of Queensland

Fernberg as Government House 2018

Sir Arthur Hunter Palmer 1819-1898

In 1872, Sir Arthur Palmer, the Premier of Queensland (1870–1874), and later Lieutenant Governor moved into Fernberg as his private residence.

Remember Arthur Palmer, who wrote the piece earlier about Aboriginals in Toowong? Well, this is his great-grandfather! I told you there'd be another cameo!

**Sir Arthur Hunter Palmer 1819 –1898
5th Premier of Queensland**

Born *28 December 1819 in Armagh, Ireland*
Occupations *Sheep Grazier, 5th Premier of Queensland, Lieutenant-Governor of Queensland and a Member of Upper House*
Awarded *Knight Commander of the Order of St Michael and St George*
Sir Arthur Palmer died at *Easton Gray*, his home in Toowong, in 1898 after a long illness, and was buried in Toowong Cemetery
The family home, *Easton Gray*, was sold in 1944. The land has since been the home of Toowong State High School, later Toowong College, and now the Queensland Academy for Science, Mathematics and Technology, which is directly over the road from the school where my son, Will attends, with Sir Arthur's great-great-grandson, Beau.

Wikipedia: Arthur Hunter Palmer

Teutophobia

Ross Webster discussed street name changes in Brisbane, after I asked why Heussler Terrace had shrunk after the First World War.

Original Heussler Terrace Map, Courier Mail
Real Estate Advertisement 1911
Image courtesy of State Library of Queensland

Ross explained that during WWI, streets that were named after Germans were changed. For example, the length of Heussler Terrace was reduced and the remainder was renamed after Generals Birdwood and Haig. The process of doing this was called Teutophobia, which basically, is the fear of all things German.

I was also surprised to discover that Ross's father, Phillip Webster, bought a house in Christian Street, Clayfield, in 1945. This house had been owned by Johan Christian Heussler. After WWI, the Hamilton Town Council changed the neighbouring street from Heussler Street to Marsden Street because they were Teutophobic.

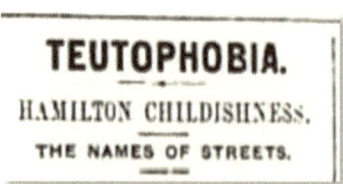

Daily Standard Wednesday 13 December 1916 page 5
trove.nla.gov.au/newspaper/article/181092437

Hamilton Town Council
Re-naming streets, Eliminating German names

Teutophobia: At a meeting of the Hamilton Town Council last evening, presided over by the Mayor (Alderman C. W. Campbell), Alderman Charlton asked about the suggested alteration of some German street names in their area.

He moved that Franz Road be named Alexander Road, Zillman Road be named Kitchener Road, Hecklemann Street to Jellicoe Street, Heussler Street to Marsden Street. Alderman Rees seconded, and the motion was agreed to.

Ross went on to explain that one street narrowly missed the change. The Hamilton Town Council was going to rename Zillman Road in Hendra, incorrectly assuming it was a German name. Local protesters proved it to be a Polish, and they were forced to leave it as is.

Hamilton Childishness; The Names of Streets.

At last night's meeting of the Hamilton Town Council, a letter was received from J. C. Zillman, of Manly, Sydney, protesting against the council's decision to change the name of "Zillman" Road to "Kitchener" Road.

The writer asserted that "Zillman" was Polish, and not German, and that the intolerable oppression of the Poles by the Germans was doubtless known to the aldermen. Mr. Zillman's grandfather, father, and himself were all born in Brisbane, and all the unmarried eligible sons were serving with the A.I.F., and he asked, " Is it to be their reward, and the reward of their mothers, to be dubbed 'German' with all the hateful associations of that name?"

As the council's action would hold his family up to public odium, contempt, and probable financial loss – and was, in fact, libel – Mr. Zillman urged an immediate rescission of that part of the resolution referring to the name of Zillman, with as much publicity as was given the resolution, "thereby removing a gratuitous insult to a loyal and patriotic family."

The road had been named after his great-grandfather, who came to Brisbane in 1830.

The Mayor said the name had been altered at the request of a number of ratepayers, in common with those of other thoroughfares having supposed German names. There was no suggestion of casting odiums upon any individual.

Alderman Charlton considered it very un-British of anyone objecting to having the name of "Kitchener" substituted for his own in naming a street. Personally, he (Alderman Charlton) would have felt proud of such a variation had his own name been in question.

As the alteration had been made at the expressed wish of the residents of the locality in question the council decided not to take any action towards rescinding the resolution, and to write Mr. Zillman to that effect.

Kym *The renaming of places after WW1 must have happened everywhere – the Townsville suburb of German Gardens became Belgian Gardens (half my dead relatives are in the huge cemetery there.)*
Louise *Oh loookee... German Consul... my great-grandfather taught English to German immigrants at Pimpama.*

*

Johann Leopold Zillmann (1813–1892)

Leopold Zillmann was from Neu-Ulm in Prussia, where he was baptised and confirmed in the Evangelical Lutheran Church. He was a blacksmith when he entered the Gossner Mission. He arrived at Moreton Bay with his wife Clara (b. 1817), a Berlin schoolmistress. By 1841 they had two children, one of them was the second child born in Queensland to a free settler.

Zion Hill was part of a plan instigated by John Dunmore Lang to facilitate settlement in the Moreton Bay area. A notoriously brutal penal colony had been established there in 1824.

By 1839 the convict settlement was wound down and the area prepared for civilian settlement, repeating the Port Jackson experience in Sydney. In 1842 the military was withdrawn and Moreton Bay was opened for free settlement. Government funding was withdrawn from the mission the following year.

The Zillmann family also stayed on at German Station after the mission was wound down. Zillmann purchased land near Zion Hill and became a farmer while still being actively involved in the Lutheran, Methodist and Baptist churches in the local area.

Some of the Zion Hill missionaries themselves became pioneer farmers of the emerging state of Queensland, imprinting their names on the modern Brisbane map: Rode Road in Chermside and Wavell Heights, Zillman Water Holes, Zillmere, and Zillman Road in Hendra, Gerler Road in Hendra, Franz Road in Clayfield, Wagner Road in Clayfield, Nique Court at Redcliffe, Haussmann Court and Lane in Meadowbrook (Loganlea) and Caboolture. They are remembered as the first free settlers of Qld, producing the first free-born settler children in Queensland.

Zillman and Carl Franz became pioneers of the Caboolture area, and like August Rode, gave evidence at the 1861 inquiry into the native police, proposing the establishment of a missionary cotton plantation. He had been writing to Johannes Gossner and the German migration agent Johan Heussler about this. This proposal became the only recommendation made by the inquiry, and was ignored. Unlike most of his Zion Hill brethren, Zillmann did not quite reach the age of 80.

German Missionaries in Australia: Zion Hill Mission

Do you remember me telling you about growing up in Hendra? Well, the address of the Hendra house was 105 Zillman Road!! I couldn't believe, out of ALL the possible streets in Brisbane, I had lived in *that* one. And Johan Zillman knew Johan Heussler, of course! And let's not forget our old mate, the Reverend John Dunmore Lang – the one who married Eleanor's grandparents in Sydney – was also the instigator of Zion Hill.

One of Lang's main aims was to facilitate free settlement in the Moreton Bay area and improve relations with the local Aboriginal people! Brisbane was always, and still is, a very small world.

I went for a drive to my old house after I'd had this conversation with Ross – it's had a full renovation since we were last there, which ironically, made it look just like the Heussler Terrace house today – they've even used the same colour scheme. Here are the three main houses I've lived in...

Ross Street, Newstead   **Zillman Road, Hendra**   **Heussler Terrace**

And not only that, but on the same page in the Telegraph Newspaper in 1911, they were selling the Franz Estate land on Zillman Road and the Bishopsbourne Estate land on Heussler Terrace...

The Brisbane Telegraph Friday 2nd June, 1911 Trove

The Old Bishopsbourne

Heussler Terrace originally ran from Castlemaine Street (Suncorp Stadium) to Mt Coot-tha Road. The section of Heussler Terrace (from Baroona Road to Rathdonnell Street) was renamed Haig Road after WWI. The section of Heussler Terrace (from Rathdonnell Street to Sir Samuel Griffith Drive) was renamed Birdwood Terrace around 1918. Heussler Terrace is still so named from Castlemaine Street to Baroona Road.

It is a VERY busy street to live on.

David built a retaining wall and a six-foot wooden fence, while I planted Lilly Pillies in front to green it up and add to the noise cancelling effect of the traffic. Visitors are often a little flustered when they first arrive, having struggled with inner-city parking and the Fort Knox style gates.

Our style of renovation has been very utilitarian with solid structures and clean lines. We are not friendly with curves and architectural special features, because we are both too practical. The house was built towards the front of the property, so we use the front area for parking and entrance space only.

It's obviously an engineer's house, until you get inside, and then, out the back.

People get visibly calmer as they enter our downstairs space – shelves groaning with books, and all sorts of other random things that shouldn't be there (*Ahem, Will and Kitty, that's YOUR stuff I'm talking about*), line one whole wall. The other has a huge map of the world with Australia as the centrepiece (much to the surprise of American visitors!) and big pieces of colourful art painted by people we love.

As you head past the kitchen, you'll find yourself on a large covered deck area, and a view to end all views. Our garden is green, with wonderful play areas, a possum-proofed vege patch, a fire pit and a decked seating area under a huge Poinciana tree.

Beyond that, sits the bush. Yes, less than a kilometre from Brisbane's CBD, we back onto bushland, owned by St Francis' Theological College and the home of the Old Bishopsbourne of Milton.

All heritage listed, we are only a little nervous of redevelopment and entirely delighted with our good fortune that they haven't touched our view since it was first bought as grazing land for George Leslie's bullocks in the 1800s.

The Old Bishopsbourne seemed the perfect place to start my historical enquiries, because they used to own the land upon which my house now sits.

Bishopsbourne 1870s
Photograph courtesy of State Library of Queensland and John Oxley Library

In order to get more information about the Old Bishopsbourne, I approached the Anglican Church Diocesan Archives. Michael Rogers, who used to work at the State Archives, said that I could arrange to come in for a day and get paid access to chapter minutes, property registers and photographs from the 1900s. I also spoke to Eve, the librarian at St Francis Theological College, who said I was welcome in at any time.

Bishopsbourne 1870
Photograph Courtesy of State Library of Queensland

Sharon *It was built for the Anglican Archbishop originally and a chapel built before the archbishop moved residence to Hamilton and St Francis Theology College moved there. Apparently it is open to the public so wonder if they would have any church records*

Gwynneth *A friend's husband studied for the ministry at St Francis College in the late 1960s and I visited them there. I can't remember if there were any records kept there though.*

I was subsequently contacted by Adrian, an historian working at the Anglican Church of Australia's archives, whose wife Mary Ann had been following the UTL Project. After providing me with an edifying history of the Old Bishopsbourne, Adrian suggested I visit the Fryer Library at the University of Queensland to inspect a collection of records relating to the Cameron Brothers' Real Estate firm. He'd done a search of their online database and found specific records about the sale of land in the Bishopsbourne Estate.

"I think, hope, that if you were able to look these records up, you may find correspondence between the Cameron Brothers and the Webster family."

Pictures taken at Fryer Library from Cameron Brothers' Records, University of Queensland

A Visit to the Fryer Library

Established in the early years of the colony of Queensland, Cameron Brothers was a leading Brisbane estate agent and property management firm, whose clients included many of the city's most prominent property owners of the 19th and 20th centuries.

Stuart Cameron, a member of the family which founded and owned the firm, donated many important records to the Fryer Library. The contents of the bound volumes of the Cameron Brothers collection (1868–1996) includes:
- Recordings of clients' estate holdings, real property transactions, chattel sales and rental business, and the financial accounts of the firm itself.
- Legal papers of the Mayne family and
- A plan of the lobby of the Capitol Theatre in Brisbane.

The section I was most interested in was the subdivision of the Bishopsbourne Estate, with lists of buyers from the early 1900s.

After Adrian's suggestion about the whereabouts of the Cameron Brothers' records, I went for a little trip to the Fryer Library, at the University of Queensland in search of these bound copies of the Cameron Brothers Collection.

Wandering through the grounds of my old alma mater, I felt a great deal of nostalgia. I'd loved being on campus at the University of Queensland (UQ), having worked hard to become a student at this incredible institution. I stood a little taller every time I walked through the hallways of those incredible stone buildings, knowing the effort I'd put in to get there.

Over the years, we have spent a lot of time at UQ for various events, not to mention high speed scooting around those same sandstone halls with the children when they were little (shhh, don't tell anyone!). However, it had been many years since I'd graduated and I hadn't been near the libraries since that time.

Now, 25 years later, sitting in the beautiful Fryer Library, away from the shuffle of technograds, I sat patiently waiting for the Cameron Brothers documents to arrive.

There were other studious elders in the room, all absorbed in their own historical retirement research, and I knew I was in excellent company.

I could smell leather, polish and old books, despite the fact that there were no volumes to be seen. The hundred-year-old books were locked behind heavy doors, guarded by efficient librarians, who only asked for my first born child as collateral against what I planned to examine. I felt peace wash over me as I placed the wrapped volumes on the polished wooden tabletop.

Fingers trembling with anticipation, I undid the cotton ties that secured the plastic wrapping, and was delighted to finally get my hands on the 1909/11 volume of the Cameron Brothers land subdivision records. There they were... the copperplate handwritten records, all relating to land sales in the Milton and Auchenflower area. I even found David Webster buying land for his son, John Francis, and Baroona Rd subdivisions of the Bishopsbourne Estate from 1935.

Alfred Richer (Master Builder and future Mayor of Toowong) bought a double block of land in January 1913, built two matching houses side by side, and sold one of them to Arthur Webster in 1914.

Heussler Terrace and the Bishopsbourne Estate 1914
Photograph Courtesy of State Library of Queensland

Matthew Wengert recently asked me to write a chapter about the Old Bishopsbourne, pertaining to my house and its inhabitants, for his anthology called *Within/Without These Walls*. This book is being shared with Brisbane for the 2018 Open Houses event, and my chapter will celebrate the 150th Anniversary of the Old Bishopsbourne.

It was such an honour to contribute this chapter, mainly because of the personal significance the Old Bishopsbourne has for me.

Not only would Arthur and Eleanor have witnessed the new Chapel of the Holy Spirit being built, they were probably members of the congregation – Morgan certainly was. And to top it all off, David and I were married there in 1999 by Gary Smith, a family friend, and head of St Francis' Theological College at the time. It was our place, too.

A meeting with Stephen Clarke, from St Francis' Theological College, cemented my relationship with the property when he offered me the opportunity to launch this book at the Old Bishopsbourne. Matthew Wengert and I spent an afternoon sitting under the warm sandstone and Brisbane tuff arches, discussing the plan for the Open Houses 2018 event and sharing stories of the history of Milton. Historic bliss.

**The Old Bishopsbourne and The Chapel of the Holy Spirit
Portrait by Sue Fernandes**

A small excerpt from my chapter in Matthew's anthology, *Within/Without These Walls*, follows...

2017 The Writer and her Family

It was a perfect spring day when the Jeffery family walked from the Milton Markets towards their home in Heussler Terrace. David and Caylie, with their children, Will and Kitty, had enjoyed a relaxing morning with a hearty breakfast and a meandering walk through the colourful stalls, sharing conversations with friends they met along the way. Not wanting the magic to end, they decided to take a scenic short-cut through the grounds of St Francis' Theological College, next to the iconic Castlemaine XXXX Brewery, to reach the back garden of their home.

As the Jefferys climbed the steep driveway leading up from Milton Road, the rockeries and native trees swallowed up the hustle and bustle behind them, giving their senses some reprieve. Hardly a kilometre from the city centre, they easily forgot where they were as the Old Bishopsbourne appeared majestically before them. It was the world beyond their house.

Always looking for opportunities to share knowledge with their children, Caylie and David pointed out the cloistered sandstone walkways, so like their beloved alma mater, Queensland University, and of course, the halls of Will and Kitty's favourite school, Hogwarts. They showed them the numerous chimney stacks, explaining that the building was said to have a fireplace in every room, which they all agreed was probably overkill, given the climate.

"This is where many of Brisbane's Bishops and Archbishops lived. They were the bosses of the Anglican Church," David explained. "Did you know that they wanted to build a stone chapel to replace a tiny wooden one they'd built, and had to sell off the land on the edge of the property to pay for it? That's how we got our place!"

Much as they loved the grandiosity of the Old Bishopsbourne, David and Caylie were most looking forward to seeing the beautiful stone Chapel of the Holy Spirit. As they neared the tiny church, the couple instinctively held hands. This place didn't just belong to God. This was their place too, and they hadn't been inside for nearly 20 years, despite it being in their back yard.

The number of people milling around the Old Bishopsbourne was curious, until Caylie saw a sign next to the statue of Jesus.

"Hey, look – it's Brisbane Open House! The Chapel's open to the public today... I'd forgotten. We're not trespassing anymore," said Caylie, her body relaxing with relief.

David squeezed Caylie's hand, remembering the first time they had stepped inside the old stone Chapel in 1996.

"Come on kids, I want to show you where Mummy and I were married," he coaxed, taking them into the chapel.

David and Caylie Jeffery, newlyweds November 20, 1999
Chapel of the Holy Spirit, The Old Bishopsbourne, Milton

Before she joined them, a whisper in the wind made Caylie look back towards the Old Bishopsbourne. She thought she saw a stately gentleman, dressed in fine robes, looking down at her from an upstairs window. In his hands he held a delicate china teacup, and as their eyes connected, he nodded at her and smiled beatifically. She shook her head and blinked. When she opened her eyes again, the gentleman was gone.

A shiver went through Caylie as she suddenly understood that two worlds had just collided. Decisions made nearly 200 years ago had all had direct effect on the life she and her family were living today – by the young Scottish pioneer George Leslie when he chose to move to Australia, settle on the Darling Downs and buy acreage in Milton; by his widow, Emmeline, when she gifted the underutilised land to the Anglican Church; by Bishop Tufnell for deciding to build a Bishopsbourne with a wooden chapel; by Archbishop Donaldson for selling off land on Heussler Terrace to build a better chapel; by Alfred Richer for choosing his Master Builder craft over politics; by the Websters to hide their important documents under their lino; and finally, by her husband, David, who'd managed to convince her to move into the worst house in Milton when he was only 23 years old.

David and Caylie Jeffery, newlyweds November 20, 1999
The Old Bishopsbourne, Milton

Part 9

The Writer's Journey

Writing a Book and Researching its Content, Concurrently

Jay *Can see a book evolving out of this tale!*
Pam *Must be a book or a mini-series in this. Start writing and fill out the story!!!*
Allison *Book written over this...*
Lou *This is so intriguing! Better than the trash on the idiot box anyway!*
Beth *Isn't people's Family history fascinating! Well investigated Caylie! I believe you were meant to do this!*

When I started writing my first book, *Bedtime Stories for Busy Mothers (BSFBM)*, I honestly believed that publishers all over the world would be knocking on my door to get hold of my manuscript. All writers think this. If we didn't think this, we would never sit down and write that first page. *This* book will be revolutionary... *This* book is the greatest thing ever written... *This* book is unusual enough to be attractive to an already overcrowded market... *This* book will hit #1 on the Best Seller lists.

I believed *BSFBM* was that book for me. I was wrong.

At the time, I was a member of a wonderful writing group where I watched first-hand how long and hard my colleagues worked on their children's picture book manuscripts of only 500 words, only to be rejected time and time again, despite the high quality of their work. I was on the same path, like a quill to a flame.

Each publisher has their own set of rules, and given that most of us authors are doggedly determined to be 'discovered', we follow the rules implicitly.

You can only send your manuscripts in on the first Wednesday of every second month.
You must submit exactly 500 words (and we WILL count them)
You must use <u>this</u> font and no other
You must have <u>this</u> spacing and no other
You must NOT under any circumstances send your manuscript to another publisher. It is a tight industry and WE WILL FIND OUT.
We might get back to you within three months. We might not. After three months, if you haven't heard from us, DO NOT contact us.

Failure to follow any and all of the above rules will probably result in your manuscript getting filed in the round container under the desk of the work-experience student who gets paid $16 an hour to read your work. No other industry treats their potential clients like the publishing industry does.

And you could have written the next Pulitzer Prize winning novel about Vampire Zombie Aliens, but if Vampires, Zombies or Aliens are out of favour for some reason, your manuscript will be in that receptacle as soon as they read the title.

Conferences and training weekends aren't much better. Together, with our best stories, we would attend these events to listen to 'success stories', learn how to better our craft and reach deep into our empty pockets to pay to have a representative from a publisher critique the first three pages of our manuscript.

Expectant authors would then get a very precious 15 minutes sitting in front of someone who could change their lives forever. One or two percent of the countless hopefuls might have a publisher say to them, "This is really good. Here's my card. Call me on Monday."

The rest will be given, what I like to call, the crap sandwich.

"I love what you've done with this. You've obviously spent a lot of time on it. It's not quite what 'the industry' is looking for at the moment. But keep working on it, and I'll see you next year after you've paid me another $100."

The primacy and recency effects give the writer the courage to continue, but the bad news in the middle saps their self-esteem, like squeezing water out of a sponge.

Back to the drawing board they go, second guessing themselves with every word they write, wondering if this is the part the editor didn't like. It is absolutely and unequivocally soul shattering.

I am a 'here and now' person, and a big believer that we are here for a short time, and a lot must be done in that period to reach our level of self-actualisation, where we are living the life we're meant to live. My husband is the same, and often says when people comment on our *go get 'em* approach to life, "We're not here to drown worms, you know."

I read the most wonderful quote this week from Pablo Picasso that sums up my *raison d'etre* perfectly...

The meaning of life is to find your gift. The purpose of life is to give it away.

I did it once – paid my $100, faced those publishers and had all my hopes and dreams shattered for a few minutes. The worst (and best, in the long run) thing I heard was, "I'll see you next year."

Well, forget that! A year is a really long time, and I didn't have hundred dollar notes flapping around the place to throw at publishers who have found a new way to make money in a dying industry.

After a long discussion with David, who is my best critic, we decided to give self-publishing a go. He had read my manuscript and believed in my writing. He had seen how hard I'd worked to build a following on social media, writing articles for the past three years for free. He knew people liked my work, and had confidence in my ability to do what it took to recoup our investment. So he asked me to draw up a business plan, and a budget, after which he bankrolled the project.

Long story short, it cost $17,000 to self-publish my book. I made $21,000 in return.

So David got his money back, I sold books *and* made a ~~tidy~~ tiny profit – just enough to fill my petrol tank for a year. But most importantly, I learned a new trade, so I guess it was cheaper than going back to uni. I researched all there was to know about creating a book from earliest conception to its arrival on the bookshelves.

There's a lot to do – self-editing, formatting, hiring like-minded editors, finding a printer who was on the same page (forgive the pun), choosing fonts and paper that people would like, working with an illustrator and studying effective marketing techniques. I did a PR course, a Social Media course, a Manuscript Development course, and a Marketing course.

After the success of the book (selling more than 1000 copies of a book for a self-published author in Brisbane is considered successful), I was invited by the Queensland Writers' Centre to be a keynote speaker at the *Brisbane Writers' Festival*, to share my self-publishing journey. It was a relatively new thing at the time, and writers were just starting to get interested, after many frustrating years of traditional publisher rejections.

I attended the pre-Festival meet-and-greet, and was shy, but very happy to be there in the Green Room, amongst many accomplished local authors, (Isobelle Carmody, Nick Earls, Matthew Condon to name-drop a few), who were all there that year, along with many new authors who had found success with their books.

On the opening night of the Festival, all of the workshop presenters were invited to attend a drinks function. I took a copy of my book and some business cards, in case I found a networking opportunity.

Soon after arrival, I found myself in a small group of yuppie writers, who were all talking about their book tours. Two of them even had their publicists with them. I stood quietly, listening with interest to their exciting lives on the road, until someone finally noticed me and asked what I'd be speaking about at the festival.

I was the only self-published author at this event, mind you, but until this moment, I had felt like an equal to these people, believing in my book and my new-found abilities.

"Oh, hi, I'm Caylie Jeffery and I wrote *Bedtime Stories for Busy Mothers*. I'm presenting a workshop on self-publishing tomorrow."

"Ohhh, bless," gushed one of the young women, with a saccharine smile, as she reached out for the book I held up. "*You're* the one who published her own book. Oh look, is this your little mummy book? The cover is *so* cuuute!"

A more classic floor-swallowing moment had never existed. I smiled at her, and said, "Yep, that's me. Oh, is that the time? I must be off, have a good night everyone," before grabbing back my little mummy book and slinking out into the night on a wave of self-doubt and mortification.

I turned up for the workshop the following day, with my head down and teeth gritted. I barely had the courage to face the one or two people I thought might be there to listen to the silly Mummy blogger who couldn't make it in the real publishing world so she published her own book.

The first person I saw in the room, up the back in the shadows, was my husband. He'd dropped me off and then, without telling me, parked the car so he could be there as a support. He'd seen how upset I'd been after my experience the night before. I'm crying even as I write this, because that was a real low point in my writing career, and David was there to guide me through it, as always.

Slowly the room filled up, until I couldn't count the attendees on my hands. Ten minutes later, I was thrilled to see an auditorium filled with people who wanted to learn *non*-traditional forms of getting their work 'out there'.

As I'm writing this, at my Godmother Pip's house in the rainforest at Kureelpa, the whipbirds calling to each other all around me, I had to stop to wipe away the tears at the memory of that day. Pip came over at that moment to look at the money and bank books, and to ask me what I was writing about. After I explained, she expressed surprise at my lack of courage, given the mother I'd had as a child.

"Your mother used to sit doing sketches of people at markets for $5, sometimes waiting hours between clients. She persevered because she believed in her craft, and the crowds soon came."

"She had the courage to face her own insecurities and do what she wanted anyway. Now look. She turned those early market days into a successful career as a portraitist, and that was all because she had courage and conviction. Where was yours?"

Good point, well made. It took a few years and over a thousand people to give me the courage to do it again, I'll admit. When the Under the Lino (UTL) team suggested I write a book about this experience, I agreed, but knew that it would be a difficult journey. Under no circumstances would I be asking David to bankroll this one, though. It was time I stood up on my own two feet, with the raw courage and stubborn determination of my amazing mother.

And besides, how could I *not* write a book about this journey, with so much support coming from the UTL Team? All of the stars had aligned! Now, all I needed was for people to put their cash on the line. They needed to trust me with a $20 investment, which was a big ask considering they had only known me for a couple of months. Online.

Writing a book that has no ending in sight is a daunting process, especially when information is coming from so many sources, every day. When I told my friend, Mark, that it was like swimming up a waterfall, he likened me to a salmon. So, for most of this book-writing journey, that's what I've been. A crazed salmon, swimming upstream against a torrent of information and communication.

I have loved every minute of this journey, but if we'd all just decided to stick with a webpage, it would have been so much easier! The three enemies in the book-writing process have been Time, Distraction and Content. Masses and masses of content.

*

When I was a new Mum, and David was recovering from a severe illness, I turned to writing as a way of debriefing. I journalled all my sad and negative feelings, which was helpful to a point, but I still felt very alone.

Not only did I lose my sanity for a while there, I lost my sense of being an intelligent human with a will and a purpose other than feeding my family and caring for my husband.

I wrote about the funny, crazy and terrible moments of parenting, life with small kids and everything in between. I lost myself in the writing, threw all my passion into those words, and when I started sharing these stories online, other Mums loved them! I was getting published all over the place for providing interesting, heartfelt pieces of work that spoke to parents all over the world. It was very exciting to suddenly have hundreds of women writing to me sharing their similar experiences.

I went from being an isolated stay-at-home Mum to suddenly having long and deep conversations with parents about the highs and lows of parenting. It was addictive.

That's the trouble with addictions. The more I talked to other people, face to face, and online, about parenting, the less parenting I was actually doing. I would go to the park, meet all sorts of people and have great chats with them, ignoring the pleas and demands of my children when it was time to actually care for them.

I had very strict bedtime rules for the kids because I did all of my writing at night, when they were sleeping. If they got up for 1. A glass of water 2. To go to the toilet 3. To get a tissue 4. Another glass of water or 5. To say they couldn't sleep… I would become the scary Mummy monster, and yell at them all the way back to their bedrooms.

This was not a good way for them to finish off their days, and it certainly wasn't walking the talk I was sharing with my readers. Five minutes after screeching at the kids, I'd be writing an article called "How to better connect with your Children." Not my finest hour, I can tell you. While I was writing BSFBM, I was all of the above and so much more. I alienated my family, and became someone I didn't recognise or like.

This time round, I made them (and myself) a promise. I would feed them (real food, not two minute noodles!), clothe them, hug them, bandage them, drive them around and support every single need, before school and after school. During the day was writing time, as were the evenings, but all the rest belonged to them. This time, they would come first and the book would come after.

Well, I've been pretty good and true to my word, apart from that time I made them spinach that I didn't wash properly, and we all had to eat cereal because dinner was crunchy... or that time I made them a perfect lamb roast, even setting the table like it was a restaurant, and proceeded to spray a whole mouthful of red wine all over their full plates when I discovered a fly had gone into my glass. Two minute noodles for dinner *that* night because we couldn't find the fly...

Now, as I edit the first draft, time is ticking and the pressure is on. We all know there's an end in sight and my family is watching me fill every waking moment with words. David and the kids have started getting their own meals, and making *me* cups of tea. They're quietly going about their business and allowing me time and space to do my best. We are finally working together as a team. For that alone, all of the work had been worth it.

NB I heard Will talking to David last night, asking him when I'll be returning 'back to normal'... so all that stuff about teamwork is just temporary, apparently. They really just want me all to themselves again and think that once this book is published, I'll become a stay-at-home Mum again. Boy oh boy, have they got another think coming!

Funding the Book

I have always loved a deadline. I work well under a certain amount of pressure because something in my brain holds me back until exactly the right amount of time to get the job done. Occasionally I am let down by technology (usually printer ink running out an hour after Officeworks has closed) but for the most part, I am always on schedule, delivering high quality work.

Without a deadline, however, my endeavours become long-winded, guilt-ridden chores, something I didn't want this project to ever become. Under the Lino has been special from the beginning, with the frantic pace that was set in the first 48 hours. We were researching into the wee hours of the morning and uncovering more information in those first few days and weeks than any tertiary research program.

I smile now at the comment someone made about turning the Facebook posts into a book, sentiments that have been echoed again and again with every new coincidence and synchronicity. I loved the idea of turning this community detective search into a narrative in some way, although we were, of course, doing that every day. Less than five months after I found the documents, nearly one million words had been written on this subject, by myself and the Under the Lino Community. That's ten novels worth.

It's all fine and well to take on the mantle of author for a story you know like the back of your hand – how hard could it be? Ha! My naivety allowed me to suggest that people could pre-order copies of a book I was convinced I could write. A book that seemed to have already written itself.

Experience as a self-published author was invaluable at this point, because I already knew what work was required, and more importantly, what the costs would be. Self-funding this project was not a possibility for me as a stay-at-home Mum who'd left paid employment six months earlier, but the urgency with which the story needed to be told was obvious. The story had captured the attention and imagination of thousands of people. Over 55,000 people had watched the Channel 7 News coverage online, not to mention those who saw it live on TV!

Hundreds of people were following the posts and feeds and articles. I didn't have time to look for publishers, or start a PhD thesis – I had to strike while the subject matter was hot.

Crowdfunding

Jobee *Hey maybe we can set up an #Underthelino GoFundMe to help with research costs for this story*
Jay *Why not harness all this effusive interest with a crowdfunding campaign towards the possible writing of a book on this case by our esteemed Caylie?*

Crowdfunding was a great idea, given that it's a reward-based program where people don't donate money, but pre-pay for a product, an experience or a service. In this case, it was pretty simple. If people gave me $20, they would get a book. Eventually.

Hitting up my networks to pre-order copies had been suggested to me when I wrote my first book in 2014. Community fundraising was still relatively new at that time, though, and *I* didn't trust the process *or* my writing, so why would I have expected anyone else to? Despite believing that people had actually read, and liked, my work, I still didn't believe in myself enough to get people to cough up before the product was available. Fortunately, my husband believed in me and we bank rolled the first print run ourselves.

Three years and a successful first book later, asking people to put their financial hooks into a story I hadn't even written was still a monumental leap of faith, a concern I shared with the UTL Team. Honesty has always been my policy, so I 'fessed up to the group that I was concerned about what I should do. If I ran the campaign, would they support me?

The response was deafeningly in favour of pre-ordering, so I took a few baby steps towards self-education. *Pozible.com*, a crowdfunding organisation, just happened to be running a free workshop the following week in Brisbane.

This was another coincidence that was not lost on me. I eagerly turned up alongside a large group of other hopeful creatives, all of whom had unique and altruistic projects that deserved financial backing.

The biggest issue any of us crowdfunders was going to have on our hands was finding the right crowd and convincing them to fund our projects. My cocky self had already counted the people I thought would be supportive of a book. I needed $16,000 to make the project fly, which was a significant figure, compared to some of the other budgets at the *Pozible* night. At $20 a copy, I'd need 800 supporters. I knew 200 people (personal friends and family) who would be first in line just because they loved me and believed in me. Great. 600 to go. There were over 1,000 followers on the Under the Lino Facebook page. Surely, half of them would be keen to see all of this written on paper? Only 100 more... A little bit of media attention might help there – I had already had calls from ABC Brisbane and Channel 7, so I was sure greater Brisbane would present me with the last few people to kick the project over the line.

Well. How wrong was I? Those tens of thousands of people who watched the Channel 7 story smiled, looked under their own floor coverings and moved onto the next news item. Raising people's interest to a level where they would commit money to a book that HAD NOT BEEN WRITTEN YET was very, very difficult.

My friends and family were all very supportive, and added it to their 'to do' lists, as I also do when things like this pop into my inbox. The urgency I was feeling was certainly not reflected, or even understood, by those nearest and dearest to me, let along the greater Brisbane community!

A very dear friend of mine stepped in at this point to reassure me that everything would be alright. Sally is a wonderful folk musician who sings in a duo, with Rebecca Wright, called *Gone Molly*.

Musicians are another group of creatives who have traditionally been at the mercy of recording companies, playing for coins at gigs in the hope of being the next 'discovery'.

Publishers and record companies are inundated with manuscripts and recordings from artists all over the world, so rather than being put at the bottom of a pile somewhere, Sally and Rebecca took matters into their own hands, knowing they had a following who enjoyed their music.

Their music and voices should sell a million CDs, yet, when they crowdfunded for their debut album, they struggled with the stress and pressure of the process. However, not only did they successfully reach their target, with money from the community, but *Gone Molly*'s album of the same name, recently won three Australian Celtic music awards: Artist of the Year, Celtic Group of the Year and Producer of the Year 2018! All because they had the courage, the self-belief, the talent and most importantly, the support of their community.

Not only did Sally reinforce what they taught me at Crowdfunding School, she gave me insight into her own personal experience as a classic example. She also called me every few days during the campaign, helped me by advertising it on her personal social media channels, and held off on making her pledge until half way through the campaign to give me a boost in the quietest time. She was also the first person to call me when the campaign ended.

The UTL members who supported the crowdfunding were absolutely incredible. They had been witness to my commitment to the project, and even though few of them had ever met me, they trusted me enough to give me money towards an idea. Some people might think $20 isn't very much money to commit, but for people on a tight budget, it's asking a lot. Plenty of us out there are watching our pennies, and it really rammed that fact home to me when I had people writing to me asking if I minded waiting a little longer until payday, or to tell me that they loved the project, wished they could help with the funding, but weren't in a position to do so. They sent me their love and support, which helped propel me forward with the book idea, knowing that there were so many people backing me.

Of all the stress involved in self-marketing and promotion, the worst part is the spamming.

I've done enough social media education to know that it's not cool to advertise your products to your friends and family more than once or twice. People who earn a regular pay cheque do not get on social media and ask me to go to their place of business and spend my money there. My friends who own their own business rarely promote their services on private channels. It's annoying!

I've never been a fan of networking amongst those I know to tout for business, but when you're a starving creative-type, your friends and family are your first (and often, only) audience. You depend on them in the early days to read your work, tell you it's wonderful and shout about it from the highest peaks so everyone in the world will want a copy.

The thing is, I didn't actually have a copy for them to read. What if they'd read my first book and hated it? Why would they advertise to their friends and families about a product that didn't exist yet? It was certainly a big ask.

Not everyone loved the crowdfunding period of the project, or the idea of turning this adventure into a book. Some were quite vocal about me getting people to do my research for no reward or compensation. And it was true – nobody is getting paid for this. But I hope that people have had their money's worth of joy and satisfaction by being involved in one of Brisbane's most exciting experiences in years.

The naysayers were (mostly) respectful, and in the end, we had to agree to disagree. I believed in this book, as did the majority, so the crowdfunding went ahead. I maintained transparency throughout, as is my way. Nobody would be walking in blind.

Caylie *Right, there's been a comment about this page and the crowdfunding suggestion and the possibility of a book about this project turning this page into a commercial venture and I want to set the record straight.*

I will be launching a crowdfunding campaign in about ten days to raise money for a book to be printed and a party for the Under the Lino researchers and supporters. It is a transparent process. You will be able to see what funds I'm asking for.

If you pledge $20, you will get a book. If I reach the target – I will write the book. If I don't, I won't. Simple. Books cost money to print and I can't afford to do it alone.

I'd love to tell this story and share it with you all. Yes, there's been a lot of 'free research'. You will not be paid for it, and if I reach the target, neither will I. You will absolutely be credited for it in the book though.

I am a writer and I can give you the gift of your story together with research notes to help you on your own personal historical journeys. If the book goes viral, I will make some money. Yes. But if I ask you to crowdfund for the first print run, I will make nothing. Writers rarely make money despite the time they take to write! I am doing this for you, because you asked for it and what a wonderful thing it will be for all of us to say we were part of it! Comments welcomed – yes and no votes! But be kind, please. I'm not made of stone x

How it all panned out...

First I had to develop the campaign – I needed a good story to share, tantalising graphics and visuals and a video of me pitching the book. I needed to prepare a plan for what I was going to publicise, as well as how and when I was going to do it. All media channels had to be used, at certain times when people were most likely to be reading, listening or watching. There were press releases and teaser trailers to really whet people's appetites.

And then, when all that was done I had to launch the campaign with 42 days to reach the target. As luck would have it, the campaign finish date was on my birthday. That was also synchronous...

It was an exciting beginning for the campaign – within two days, we had achieved 30% of the target amount. A lot of people were sharing the posts about it, many were pledging and several were asking questions about contributing offline in a 'safer' way.

We were all pretty sure that we'd hit the target in half the time we'd allowed for. But then, all of the Pozible predictions came true. We entered the abyss of doom, for the four weeks in the middle of the campaign.

Pledges were dripping in, and the target *was* getting closer, but not fast enough. Members of the group who had already made their pledges and really wanted this book, were asked to find more support. I had a feeling that not everyone in the Facebook group was getting the updates. Facebook's algorithms were not working in our favour and only about 30% of the team knew about the Campaign.

So I asked a few people to help me by private messaging a list of others in the group. Facebook worked out what we were doing and blocked us! We also got a few messages back from cross members who felt they were being spammed (sorry guys! My bad ☹), so I put a very quick end to this form of advertising. I hated asking people for their support and I *really* hated asking others to canvass supporters.

The campaign hit an all-time low for me when I got an irate message from a friend to say that she was sick of people asking for money for this and that, and to please take her off my spamming list.

I very nearly packed it in right then and there. I never wanted to be bothersome. I really thought everyone would want a copy, especially from our group and I was mortified to be 'cold call selling' to people, when all I wanted to do was have fun and find the owners of the bank books.

The book suddenly became a noose around my neck, and I started to hate the campaign. Spamming my friends, family and half of Brisbane was probably the lowest ebb for me in the tidal wave of adventure that I found Under the Lino.

Jeff OCT 25TH, 9:22PM *G'day, you are to be commended for the work being put into the "Under the Lino" saga. I do have some concerns about the amount of time and effort you are personally putting in. I have detected in your replies a degree of tiredness. The adrenaline flow can sometimes be disguising other symptoms. I respectfully suggest you take time for yourself to be just you. Forget about the project you're undertaking leave the phone at home and go and smell the flowers for at least 24 hours.*

It will unclutter your mind and maybe give you a new perspective on the project. I really am concerned Caylie about you burning the candle at both ends and I feel sure your other half secretly thinks so as well. Years of training though tell me I am close to the mark. All the best

Caylie You are very perceptive and quite right! Between writing, responding, marketing and begging, I am tired and getting anxious, although I do feel bolstered by people like yourself who can read between the lines. I can't tell you how much I appreciate your message Jeff. I went to art class tonight and haven't checked my messages for hours so am already backing off for sanity! It's a full time job just managing the page! But I love you guys and this project. I will have the day off devices tomorrow on your excellent advice. Thank you for caring about me xxx

It was at this time that my musician friend, Sally, called me to see how I was going. She was so caring and empathic about being in the middle of the crowdfunders' 'abyss of doom'. She said she'd be making her pledge soon, and would share on her networks – she and others had been waiting for the quiet times to make their pledges so it would bolster me up.

This was the time the media picked up on the project. We were about two weeks from the end of the campaign when Channel 7, the ABC Radio, and Brisbane News did stories about the mystery and the crowdfunding. My friend and history teacher, Glenn Davies, wrote a fantastic article for Independent Australia about the project, and all of a sudden, we were legitimate. I finally had some evidence that we were doing something cool and amazing, and was therefore able to use those articles to promote the campaign without feeling like I was spamming.

The community interest was phenomenal and genuine, and the last week of the campaign saw us get very close to the final target. The day before my 47th birthday, we still had $5,000 to go, but had raised over $10,000, which was a success in itself. I had a serious conversation with David about whether he could prop up the campaign with a couple of thousand dollars, and he said he'd see how it went on the last day.

Meeting my Local Councillor for Paddington, Peter Matic

Some of the group members had told me about the Lord Mayor's Suburban Initiative Fund for people in the Brisbane community who were working on ways to make our city a better place.

As I was desperately trying to raise money to cover the costs of publishing this book, any opportunities for funding were welcomed and this one had Under the Lino all over it. Time was ticking, though, and I had no idea what it was that I needed from my local council offices.

Before I started writing up an application, Darcy Maddock had suggested I go and visit the Paddington Ward office. Darcy and Peter Matic had done a lot of work together in the past involving the Toowong Cemetery, and he said he'd put in a good word for the project on my behalf. Councillor Matic was a well-known local face, and I'd met him several times at school fetes and community events, always finding him friendly and approachable. My friend Tara had once encouraged me to give him a signed copy of my first book for his wife, which resulted in an order of 40 copies for BCC libraries! Peter was a good bloke in my eyes.

When I rang the Paddington office, I spoke with Fiona and Carolyn, two of the staff members there, asking for a meeting with Councillor Matic. To my surprise, they were both aware of the Under the Lino phenomenon, and had been following the story at home! They were so welcoming, and happily arranged for a meeting – coincidentally, on my birthday, and the last day of the crowdfunding campaign. I was hoping it was serendipity at work again, and saw it as a positive omen.

Three weeks later, my hands were sweating as I walked towards the office, even though I'd just had a big pep talk from my husband over my birthday lunch. The campaign finished at midnight that night, and we still had to raise $4,500. David had always said he would chip in the last few dollars if we were short, but that big a gap meant we'd have to sell one of the children... Maybe both, depending on the sort of day they were having!

Of course, I took the bank books and money with me to the meeting, and on arrival at the reception desk, both Carolyn and Fiona greeted me like an old friend and were thrilled to see I'd brought the documents. They, of course, had their own ideas and theories, and when Cr Matic joined the party, he was quickly swept up in the enthusiasm and intrigue.

I talked him through the story, and gave him an update as to where I was at with the investigation as well as my plans for the book. Then he asked me the dreaded question.

"So, Caylie, what do you want from me?"

Argh! Such an open ended question! I used to be a sales rep, a few lives ago, and I was immediately reminded of the same tongue-tied, awkward moment that doctors used to give me, "So, Caylie, you've given me your spiel about this fantastic super-drug that will change the face of health as we know it. What do you want from me?" This was my big moment to call for the order – they had asked after all! But this was when I always faltered. Surely they should know to call up the pharmacist and place a recurring monthly order for 200 units of said super-drug! I guess that's like saying, *Surely my kids can see that the dishes need washing up*, but no, they still need to be asked… If only Councillor Matic had said, "How much do you need to get this amazing project off the ground?" as he pulled out the Council cheque book from his breast pocket.

What I ended up saying to him was that I wanted the BCC seal of approval on the project, permission to speak at council events and schools of his choosing, perhaps a blurb from him to introduce the book, with a logo for the back cover and maybe some help with a website? Even though my primary reason for being there was to ask for funding, I was not able to ask him for money.

As the kind Councillor listened to my requests, he started texting someone on his phone. I was pretty disconcerted about this, until he said he was texting his good friend, the Lord Mayor, asking if he would be able to match a Paddington Ward grant and give me $500. That was $1,000 towards setting up the Under the Lino Webpage! Once again, my normally chatty self was dry-mouthed, in shock.

I was so thankful I didn't have to ask, that he had seen the value of the project and was willing to put the Brisbane City Council stamp of approval on all we were doing! I skipped all the way back to my car, and called David to tell him the good news.

"Have you seen the current crowdfunding figure, Cayles?" he asked, after I'd told him the whole story.

"Not yet, I'm about to have a look. Why?"

"Go and have a look and call me back," came his cryptic reply.

As I opened up the Pozible app on my phone, it said that there was only $2,000 to go to reach our target. I was confused. Only an hour earlier, it had said $4,500. How could the amount have dropped so quickly? And then I saw that someone, who has asked to remain anonymous, had pledged $2,000. Our best friends had also supported the book with $500 just because they believed in me.

As the Brisbane City Council's pledge had to be earmarked for the webpage, we still had $2,500 left to raise. I sat in my car on a Paddington hill on my 47th birthday, with one more important decision to make....

Would I sell Will and Kitty on EBay or Gumtree?

In the meantime, several panicked people had realised it was the last day, and pledges started rolling in. Some of the UTL members were buying more copies of the book, even though they'd already pledged, because they were so invested in the project.

At 5pm on November 8, 2017, David walked into my office with the children, carrying a bottle of champagne and a birthday cake, covered in sparklers. He sat down in my chair and made the final pledge on the campaign to get us over the line. Unbelievable. Even as I write this, I can feel the tears pricking my eyes.

As a result, the community (my own nearest and dearest included in that) successfully paid for the book that you are now reading. Absolutely magnificent effort by everyone involved, and I can't say enough thank yous! I only hope this book has been worth the wait!

Shar *You know Caylie there are 2 stories... there's the under the Lino story, but there's also your own private story... this journey you've been on must be wondrous, thrilling, nail biting, frustrating and strengthening... Thank you for letting me be a part of this 5 minutes of your life.*
Kerry *It's a buzz to have been part of this most unusual and intriguing adventure. And Caylie, without your original Facebook posting and dedication and determination, what you found under the lino would have remained a story to be told around your dinner table, and this additional tale of life in Brisbane would never be shared to all and sundry. Last birthday you planted a tree, this birthday you've committed to writing a book, I wait with some anticipation on this Facebook page to hear what your next birthday will bring... Go Girl!*

When I shared the great news with the team, there were hundreds of people screaming and cheering for joy, congratulating me and each other, wishing me Happy Birthday and grabbing their own bottles of champagne! I had *not* been feeling the pressure all by myself – it felt like half of Brisbane was right there with me, watching the figure slowly climbing, egging others to get involved, and sweating out the final few hours. Community engagement at its finest.

One thing I did learn from this experience, though... I never, ever want to do crowdfunding again, and I can still feel the stress of that time in the tension of my neck as I write this!

Getting the Book together

Okay, so now I had all this money, and a blank sheet of paper in front of me. Well, not really blank. There were hundreds of thousands of words on the subject plus enough documents and photographs to fill three folders. This all needed to be sifted through, categorised and rearranged.

How was I going to write the story about the mystery, the history AND the community, in a creative and interesting way? All the new historical knowledge I've gained through the research has certainly changed my perspective on writing.

Knowing that Suncorp Stadium, forever in my mind known as Lang Park, used to be a cemetery, with only the headstones removed, gives me the creeps every time I go there to watch a game now.

It rained cats and dogs one night while we were watching a Reds game, and as the players slipped and fell all over the field, I had flashbacks of the movie, *Poltergeist*, where a family discovered that their housing estate had been built on an old burial ground. Skeletons started popping up out of the ground in their unfinished swimming pool when it rained, so I was imagining bones poking out from beneath the washed out field, ready to cause havoc!

Ross *Every time Wally Lewis slipped in a game at Lang Park, my mother used to say he'd tripped over our great uncle who was buried there!*

Whenever I travel along Coronation Drive, my mind flickers in and out of sepia. The road in front of me flips into an earlier version of itself, and I'm suddenly in a carriage, being pulled by a horse along River Road in 1859, on my way to a QLD/NSW Separation meeting at City Hall.

When I drive into the school grounds of Brisbane Boys' College in Toowong to pick up Will after school, and hear the bagpipers calling, I am transported back to the early days of Auchenflower, where the Scottish brogue was heavily sprinkled throughout the neighbourhood, when you couldn't walk across the fields without tripping over a Leslie, an O'Donnell or a McIlwraith.

As I watch the Milton State School children playing sport in Gregory Park, my mind wanders to a time when it was called Red Jacket Swamp, while its namesake, Augustus Gregory, was exploring Queensland as the Surveyor General in 1859.

Names and surfaces might have changed, but activities of daily life have stayed the same. I walk the same paths as Eleanor and Arthur Webster every day... I go to the IGA at the Baroona Road shops to do my daily shopping, known as Tipper's Corner in Eleanor's time.

I walk beside her ghost every few days, me with my reusable plastic shopping bags, and she with her basket. We catch the train at Milton Station into the RNA Showgrounds every year, just like Arthur did when he was heading in to work at Mayne Depot.

Same place. Same route. Same activities. Different names. Different time.

I know that Eleanor would have shopped at the Terrace Butcher, two doors down on Mutch's Corner, now a room filled with flood-ravaged meat-slicers and warped blackboards showcasing the smallgoods process from 1997 when it was last open as a butchery. Sadly, the sky-blue shop now sits as an eyesore because of its heritage listing, seated in a flood zone. The only time we've ever been inside was to help them clean it out after the 2011 floods.

Arthur and Morgan had the 1974 floods to contend with and I like to imagine them both helping their neighbours to clean out their houses while my father was walking through the ruins of his business on Breakfast Creek wondering what to do next. Brisbane has always needed a mud army.

I have spent a lot of time thinking and worrying about the story I should write, who to be loyal to? Should it be Eleanor's story – illustrating the hardships of women in the first half of Brisbane's 20th century – after all, Eleanor suffered the loss of a child, saw two world wars where many family and friends were lost, faced the Depression and several natural disasters in her local neighbourhood. It would be easy to paint a picture of a 1930s' housewife, whose husband worked long hard hours, managing the home and finances, as well as caring for her sole surviving child.

I wrote a little vignette about Eleanor a few weeks after the project first kicked off on Brisbane's warmest September day since 1943, when the temperature gauge hit 38 degrees.

As the sweat pooled between her breasts on what was to become Brisbane's hottest ever day, Eleanor knelt down on the kitchen floor. Her left knee slipped slightly as her damp skin came into contact with the Linoleum but she managed to steady herself against the cooker.

With one last furtive glance over her shoulder, Eleanor removed the loose scotia board and quickly slid a small blue book underneath the flooring, dropping the board back in place.

She stood up too fast, seeing pinprick spots dancing before her eyes. She wiped her hands down her apron as her vision cleared, only to be met with the steely glare of her husband, leaning against the kitchen door.

"What are you up to, woman?" demanded Arthur, his filthy blue Qld Railways shirt clinging to his wiry frame.

"What are you doin' home, Art? Why aren't you at work?" Eleanor clenched her jaw to maintain a casual tone.

"Too bloody hot... the stoker puked his guts up at Albion and some daft bugger in the office reckoned the rails are bucklin'! What a load of shit! I've pushed that engine up North in 117 flamin' degrees and the rails were fine. Need a new stoker who's not such a bloody Nancy boy, that's all. I'm off to the pub, nothin' to do here but sit in a pool of stinkin' sweat."

As Arthur shuffled down the hallway, still muttering about the 'bloody stoker', Eleanor smiled thinly, crisis averted. He hadn't seen her then. With a final look at the slight rise in the flooring next to the stove, she turned on the burner for a restorative cup of tea and a cigarette. She'd earned it.

Not everyone wanted a fictional account, and I've been aware that this experience should not be fictionalised. I've added some of my own visions in from time to time – when you dream in monochrome and sepia, and walk the same paths as the people who lived here a hundred years ago, you start to think like them. However, it's important for you, as the reader, to make up your own mind.

Over time, I've discovered that my original vignette was a little out of whack.

Firstly, Eleanor was known as Nellie to everyone who knew her. Secondly, Arthur called everyone Jimmy but beat anyone up who called him Jumbo, which is what he was called in secret by his workmates. Thirdly, Arthur was not a wiry chap who drank a lot – he was a huge bull of a man, who never went to the pub.

This hot day occurred just a year before Arthur and Eleanor's son, Morgan, moved back into the family home after a very public end to his marriage.

The more information I gleaned about this family, the better I came to know them, to understand them and to like them. Take Arthur Webster, for example.

If I'd made it Arthur's story, I'd be telling a tale of hardship, working his way up the ranks of Qld Rail from the age of 16, with a father who was a Station Master always peering over his shoulder. Cleaning and firing locomotive engines for the first five years, in the oppressive heat of Queensland was a tough start to his long career as a steam engine driver. I want to shed some compassionate light on a man who was universally disliked by his colleagues, and possibly feared in the family home. A chap who started his life on the front foot, with a brand new house and lovely wife when he was in his early twenties, two beautiful boys and a job that kept him in Brisbane as an essential servicemen while so many lost their lives overseas. To have all of that swept away from him after those happy family years with the death of his second child, Colin, at only 10 months of age.

No money, no job, no privileged background could have stopped gastroenteritis from ravaging Colin's perfect little body and nothing could have brought his Nellie back to him after she descended into the despair of a grieving mother.

Part of this story is about the Webster family and it includes a fair amount of supposition, suspicion and deduction. Eleanor is the most likely person to have hidden the bank books and money based on the fact that after her death, neither Arthur nor their son, Morgan, found the money or used the bank books.

Many questions have been asked about why Eleanor might have been hiding their money. I could easily paint a picture of Arthur being a tyrant at home, based on his behaviour at work. Domestic violence was certainly not uncommon at the time, and I could draw some very long bows about Morgan too, having read articles about him in a disreputable newspaper.

Eleanor was 72 years old when she died, however, showing no signs of moving out because of domestic violence.

The war had been over for 13 years, and it was nearly thirty years since the stock market crash, so the likelihood that she continued to hide money for those reasons was small.

Muriel White, to this day, has never been found, although there are suspicions that the account either belonged to Muriel Murphy, Eleanor's cousin, or was a fraudulent bank account, with the initials of Muriel White being the same as Morgan Webster's.

A fraudulent account was most likely used to deposit excess income to prevent paying income tax or avoid losing the pension.

Is it my place to be making conclusions about the facts that we know? The community has shared many choice pieces of information that should shake the ground of any reason and provide some doubt to most theories.

I've chosen to write mainly fact with a tiny bit of fiction, giving you plenty of opportunities to make up your own mind, because when you put down this book, neither of us will have all the answers we seek.

There's also a lot more involved in producing a book than just writing the words. Traditional publishers would have just taken the first draft of the manuscript from me, given me a small cheque to keep me fed, and two years later, a book might come out after they'd done the editing, the typesetting, the photography and cover graphics, the marketing and the PR. I would get a box of 20 books to give away to friends, be asked to turn up to a few events, and then sit at home and wait for the royalties to come in. Which they rarely do, even in the traditional publishing world.

Self-publishing is a whole other thing, as I've already alluded to. While I've been writing, I've been talking about the project to the media and working on stories for the website, beautifully developed by the wonderful Rebecca Hope from *Belle Design*. I've planned a few local historic events for the UTL members, like a visit to Boggo Road Gaol and the Shingle Inn Christmas party. Then there've been school visits and a few historical group presentations to prepare for and present. And I've been working with wonderful people to make the book look amazing! Phew!

Part 10

The Community Collaborates

A little help from my friends...

The UTL crew have regularly offered suggestions for related reading material, to help me get into the zone of the different eras and places I'm writing about. I never have much time to read but understand that it's really important to study the local history and to get some different styles and perspectives when doing a new type of story.

Instead of just *reading* all the material I could lay my hands on, however, I thought it was also important to *meet* the writers of all those fascinating words. After all, they're local Brisbane people, we have things in common, and I had nothing to lose by trying.

Meeting Matthew Condon

A few years ago, I heard Matthew Condon speak at a *Men of Letters* event. The letter he read out so beautifully really resonated with me as a Brisbane local and fellow writer. I got in touch with him at that point on social media and was delighted when he responded to my comments, even agreeing to meet up some time to talk more about the possibility of doing a Children of Letters gig. The stars didn't align for either of us at that point, so these thoughts and dreams floated off into the ether, as they do so often.

When a member from the UTL group suggested I read Matthew's *Three Kings* books about the Fitzgerald era in Queensland, as well as his book called *Brisbane*, I was about to discover that we were always destined to meet.

The day after I purchased Matthew's books, I was shopping at Woollies in Paddington. As I approached the veggie aisle, I saw a man who reminded me of Matthew walk past me. I honestly thought my mind was playing tricks on me, and was therefore too nervous to go up to him to check if I was right. I'd never met him close-up, and it had been two years since I'd seen him on stage – what were the chances it was him?

Those few moments of indecision, plus three random run-ins with friends in the cereal aisle, meant that my furtive efforts to find him in the frozen peas section were futile. He'd well and truly left the building by the time I'd found my courage, and I knew that I had just missed a great opportunity. The Universe had dropped a member of Brisbane's literary royalty into my lap, for goodness sake. Elizabeth Gilbert would have slapped me on the wrist for ignoring that massive sign!

Not one to accept failure easily, I hid in the toilet paper aisle and jumped on Twitter, sending Matthew a message saying I thought I'd just seen him at the shops; that I had a local history project I was working on and could I have a chat with him about it sometime? I explained that the Courier Mail was writing up a piece about it in a few weeks (to reduce any crazy fangirl stalker threat he might be feeling) and that I could use some guidance.

It turned out that it *was* Matthew Condon in Woollies. Phew.

"You should have said, 'Hello!'" he tweeted.

Yes, I should have. Sigh.

It all worked out in the end, though, because thanks to his generosity, we caught up on a long phone call, where I had pen and paper to hand, no frozen food in my trolley and time, plenty of time to listen.

I was so nervous when I first heard his voice on the other end of the line, I talked like a jackhammer about the project, barely drawing breath, but Matthew was calming and listened to my story carefully.

He had read about the bank books somewhere, so wasn't completely in the dark, but I told him the back story about the money, the mysteries and the community, plus the fact that there were many serendipitous occurrences that ought to be shared.

He was happily surprised to hear about it all, and said that, strangely, he was currently writing a book about the Whiskey-a-Go-Go fire and murders, the research of which had led him to a flat on Heussler Terrace, where John Andrew Stewart and James Finch were staying just before the fire.

They got life imprisonment, but had been seen sunbathing in the backyard of the house just before the event.

Wow. Just wow. He had proven my point perfectly! I knew an elderly man who lived in one of those flats and was able to link them up, much to Matthew's delight. Writers helping writers.

My big question to Matthew was, *How would you manage this story?* I told him that some people wanted me to write a creative fiction narrative alongside the historical facts, but that I was nervous about writing fiction about real people I had never met. I explained that I saw the story as three separate strands – The Mystery, the History and the Community, and to perhaps divide the book up like that.

He visualised the book being written with two or three strands that I could tie together with a narrative rope. Starting with David and I about to buy this house, standing young and keen outside this dilapidated house, wondering what on earth we'd set ourselves up for.

Then to share Arthur and Eleanor's parallel story for 1914. Young newlyweds: no kids, new house, good job, world at their feet, Arthur chuffed to have such a world-wise wife, six years his senior etc.

Matthew wanted to see me doing this entwined dance between past and present and likened this story to that of a colouring-in picture. Bit by bit the picture emerges and then the community input funnels in and I can flesh out the picture with the 'Hive Mind' of the UTL group.

I told Matt of my fears about slandering the family in any way. He said to keep it simplistic and present the facts from all angles to you, the reader, with no judgement or supposition. To let you make your own mind up. I would need to build a solid picture of the landscape – the lifestyle and surrounds, the news and events of the time. What would the Websters have been doing on a daily basis etc? I needed to build a world around these people.

Matt's own grandparents used to live in Beck Street, Rosalie, and he discussed their lives here, walking me through how they would have been going about their affairs in 1950s' Milton. His Grandad, for example, was a painter and a motorbike enthusiast, so he imagined him using the old petrol station (now a bicycle shop) at the bottom of Heussler Terrace to fill up.

We discussed the Community aspect of the project and I explained to him that some people wanted to know my relationship with the Websters. At first, I didn't really like them, because of the state of the house, but then as I learned more about Eleanor (the loss of her second son, life with Arthur afterwards, living through two World Wars etc.), I softened towards her. Matt wanted me to write about my evolution with Eleanor.

He convinced me not to let my fear of what people want of me upset my writing process, agreeing that this was a FANTASTIC mystery, but not to fire all my bullets at the beginning. I needed to compel the reader all the way to the very end.

Are you still here, dear reader?

Matthew gave me the courage to tell MY story, speaking straight to my core as a writer. I have been compelled to write about all that's happened to me throughout the process but wondered if you, the reader, would want that.

"Absolutely!" he said. "That's part of the pull of the story!"

Matthew's enthusiasm also encouraged me to reflect on the journey contemporaneously, and comment on the personal impact this event has had on my own life.

Twitter message 23/02/2018
Matt, I can't thank you enough for your mentor/phone session with me yesterday. I was feeling completely overwhelmed by the enormity of it all, but you absolutely nailed what I'm trying to achieve and now my heart is racing fit to bursting every time I write. Do you ever feel so excited about your work that you can't write fast enough for your thoughts?! Cx
Matthew Condon *Hi Caylie, yes! I know that feeling... I'm very happy to have been of some help to you, you clearly have all the material for a great story, but sometimes you just need a fresh eye to suggest how you might organise that material, let me know if I can help any further, kindest, MC*

Two weeks later, while watching my son play soccer, I was mulling over a conundrum relating to the Milton murders, featured later in this book.

As I went to grab a coffee at half-time, I nearly fell over Matt doing the same thing. After telling him that I wasn't stalking him, but was there as a parent, he laughed and said he was a parent, too, and not to worry. When he asked me how the writing was going, I took the opportunity to question him about my murder-related problem. A solid discussion pertaining to my legal options followed, finishing with a suggestion to get some professional advice. As I walked over to my car after the game, my son's former rugby coach (and soccer dad), Mark, stopped me for a big hug and a chat. Of course, Mark is also a lawyer. Go figure. Mark passed me onto his friend, Darren Robinson, who was keen to furnish me with more legal answers I required to assuage my concerns.

A phone call to another lawyer friend, Amanda, dotted the i's and crossed the t's on the subject, so I was then able to write the upcoming Milton murder chapter with confidence. Apparently the Universe chooses sporting grounds and shopping centres to match me up with the people I need to do the best job I can!

On the day before this book went to the printers, I attended a soiree at the Museum of Brisbane in Brisbane City Hall, hosted by the former Mayor of Brisbane, Sallyanne Atkinson (1985-1991). Sallyanne introduced both Matt Condon and Trent Dalton, who were there to discuss why Brisbane history is so important to talk about, write about and read about.

Matt said we rarely look at our rear-view mirrors into Brisbane's back story, but the more we do, the better our understanding will be of where we are right now. Both Matt and Trent shared stories of Brisbane's underbelly, and their personal experiences within that scene.

I asked a question at some point, and was delighted that both of them recognised me, and asked how the book was coming along. It was very exciting, as I sat there with Cheryl and Lorene from the UTL Team, to tell them that the manuscript had been completed that day!

Matt and Trent were genuinely pleased for me, and afterwards, we celebrated with hugs, a photograph and a book signing. I learned my lesson after the Woollies experience, you'll be happy to know.

Meeting Hugh Lunn

Many, many years ago, well before children, David and I went through a glitchy patch in our relationship when we ran out of things to say. We were rather fond of each other, so rather than looking elsewhere for good conversation, we decided to conduct a home-made survey which confirmed three things.

One, that the number of activities we did was inversely proportional to the amount of TV we watched.

Two, that the quality of our reading material was inversely proportional to the amount of TV we watched.

And finally, that the lack of intimacy in our relationship was *directly* proportional to the amount of TV we watched.

So we ditched the TVs – all three of them – in favour of a life worth talking about.

On the downside, as a child of the '70s and '80s who loved TV like a soul-mate, it was really painful for me to give it up cold turkey. I'm that person you want on your trivia team who remembers everything about crappy sitcoms and only dances to really bad '80s music.

On the upside, we immediately found time for creating art, building projects, playing sports, travelling, socialising and, of course, romance... We also started to talk again, because we were more interesting as people and to each other.

Don't get me wrong... there is a time and a place for unwinding with back-to-back episodes of *M.A.S.H.*, and these days, I'm the first one in line to binge-watch *Frankie & Grace* on my iPad (obviously when I'm not writing this book!). But when we were in our mid-20s, at the peak of our physical and mental agility, we knew inherently that there were better ways to spend our time.

Shortly after our divorce from the television, we decided to move overseas, where we worked and frolicked for the next ten years. This sojourn removed us even further from popular culture, and meant that, although we often missed the *Coronation Street* coffee-machine chat, we were able to start different sorts of conversations and have relationships with people who held similar adventurous, mad-if-you-don't beliefs.

I went to French classes, learned how to row on the Thames without falling in, outed my inner artist, became a slow, fat triathlete, got a teaching qualification, turned into a competent sailor, rekindled my love of the theatre, visited many new places, became a writer and made some of the best friends I've ever known. All because I stopped watching TV.

We came back to Brisbane for a holiday in 2001, and enjoyed seeing our family, friends and old haunts. The Gunshop Cafe in West End was always a favourite, and we'd arranged to meet good friends there for breakfast one day.

In addition to being an annoying TV trivia geek and bad dancer, I am also the pest who makes everyone stop having fun and eating food so I can take a photo of everyone having fun and eating food. I had a new-fangled digital camera, which was a bit like letting a child loose in a lolly shop. No event, person, place or thing was safe from my favourite phrase, "This needs a photo! Say 'Testicles!'" which always got a smile, regardless of the annoyance factor.

I needed a group shot this time, so I went over to the next table to ask if one of them would mind taking our photo.

"Excuse me?" I said, holding out my camera, hopefully.

One of the young men at that table immediately rolled his eyes, and said, "I'm just trying to have breakfast with my friends, if you don't mind."

I apologised, quite startled at the rudeness of this young chap and as they returned to their meal, I moved towards another table to ask *them* to take our picture.

As I handed my camera to another patron, the friends of the rude man started laughing like loons, while he went extremely red in the face. He quickly got up from his chair and came over to me to take the camera.

"I am *so* sorry," he said, completely chagrined. "I, um, well, I thought you wanted to take *my* photo."

"Why would I want to take *your* photo?" I asked him, perplexed. "I just want a photo of my family and me together."

Which is what that self-obsessed possibly-famous boy did, mortally embarrassed. I never did find out who that young man was... all because we didn't have a TV!

Fast forward to 2017, when the UTL crew started talking about the 1950s to help me get some Brisbane background for the book.

Frederico suggested that I read a book called *Fred and Olive's Blessed Lino* by a chap called Hugh Lunn, along with several other enthusiasts, who couldn't believe I hadn't read his work. Well, I had never even *heard* of Hugh Lunn, let alone read any of his books, which is sacrilegious for any kind of real Brisbane writer. I wasn't even born when *Fred and Olive's Blessed Lino* was published, for crying out loud!

On further exploration, everyone I asked in my parents' generation knew all about Hughie Lunn, and were happy to share their memories of him with me as if he were a family friend. I couldn't believe I'd never heard of the man.

I found Hugh's website more easily than I could find his books – it even listed many of his incredible journalistic achievements, to my chagrin. He even has his own Wikipedia page AND in 2009, Hugh was named as an Icon for the 150th Queensland anniversary celebrations! How could I have not known who he was?

When I met this delightful septuagenarian in a local cafe for lunch, it was just me with a man who knew Brisbane in the 1950s. I wasn't a fan girl, nor was I hiding behind rose-tinted nostalgia. 1950s Brisbane to me was a Kodak chromatic faux-memory cobbled together from pop culture, television and my father-in-law's musings.

The 1950s to Hugh, however, was a time of backyard shenanigans between the choko vine, the dunny and the mango tree. A time of Catholic school tempests and cheeky lads licking cream buns at his parents' bakery in Annerley.

After our initial introductions, Hugh started our conversation by saying there was no such thing as an ex-Queenslander, just a lapsed Queenslander!

According to the seniors in our community, there was once a time when the top three books in Brisbane bookshops were
1. The Refidex
2. Women's Weekly cookbooks and
3. Anything by Hugh Lunn!

Hugh spoke fondly about his life as a journo, and his travels with his great friend, Ken Fletcher, former Davis Cup Tennis champion. Ken played at Milton courts, all those years ago – the stadium there was used later as firewood.

He told me how his friendship with Ken had led to the meeting of Chuck Feeney, bringing the US billionaire to Brisbane at one time, where he gave over $100 million to Anna Bligh for medical research centres in Brisbane!

I asked Hugh about his relationship with lino and he told me that the story about Fred and Olive was about how his parents were able to get the old lino out of St Stephen's Cathedral, when they renovated the building, to use in their house. It was the forever known as the *Blessed Lino*.

We discussed my project, which he thought was very interesting. He urged me to read the *Mayne Inheritance*, but reminded me that it was speculative creative non-fiction that had a lot of holes in it. As you've read, I agree wholeheartedly.

When I asked Hugh to tell me about his view of the 1950s, he handed over three of his books and said, "Read them!" He refused to take money for them, and said he'd like to hear more of the stories from UTL as time goes by. That he'd be keen to come to the launch.

It was a fascinating meeting, and I liked Hugh very much, staying in regular contact with him to share stories and keep him up to date.

Nearly not meeting Professor Pearn

One cannot write any kind of story about Milton without referencing Professor John Hemsley Pearn.

When he's not being a paediatrician at the Lady Cilento Hospital in Brisbane, John Pearn moonlights as a local historian and author. He has written prolifically about Milton and Auchenflower, as well as publishing many books about Brisbane's history – medical, botanical and biographical.

While I was researching this book, my initial thirst for local historical knowledge was slaked by immersing myself in John's books. The most relevant, and my personal favourites, are *Auchenflower, the suburb and the name;* and, *Willingly to School: a Personal Memoir of Life at a Queensland State Primary School.* John is a past student of Milton State School, as are both of my children, so his words were very important to help me with time and place.

John is a former National Director of Training for St John Ambulance Australia, Surgeon General of the Australian Defence Force, and was a Physician to the Australian and New Zealand forces in the Vietnam campaign. He is also the founder and former President of the Australian Society of the History of Medicine. He currently holds the title of Professor Emeritus of the University Department of Paediatrics and Child Health, as well as being a Paediatrician at the Lady Cilento Burns Unit and Vascular Anomalies Clinic. Life certainly shows no signs of slowing down for this energetic septuagenarian!

John also gives his time and expertise freely as a volunteer for charities, which, luckily, includes people who find things under their lino! Tracking him down for an interview, as you can imagine, was bordering on the impossible. He was Queensland's Senior Australian of the Year in 2005, for goodness' sake! What chance did I have?

The day I said goodbye to the final draft of this book was the day the Universe, oblivious to tight book-printing schedules, conspired to get John and I together. I am forever grateful to our mutual friends, Matthew, Caren and Faye, for helping to bring us together.

John Pearn, who personifies the word, 'gentleman', has a penchant for interesting stories and connections with people in his community. David calls him a true Renaissance man, with all of his fingers on the historical pulse of Brisbane.

Not only did John call me when he heard about the Under the Lino Project, he dropped in to my house for a few hours to see the money and bank books, to hear the full story straight from the writer's mouth, and to share his thoughts on the matter.

After examining the Websters' documents, John suggested that there may be a water-mark on Muriel White's bank book, where a surname has been damp-sponged off the paper, with the name 'White' over-written. This came as a surprise to me, as nobody had picked up on this yet. His interest in numismatics (the study of currency and related objects) no doubt helped! John gave me the name of the President of the Numismatic Society of Queensland, actually calling him while I  sat there with my mouth agape. He laid the groundwork for further discussion, saying, "If Bernie Begley can't shine a light on these bank books, nobody can." Let's see what comes of that!

After we shared many stories of Old Brisbane, John and I realised we also had many things in common, including our work at the Royal Brisbane Hospital, our love of sailing and, bizarrely, his granddaughter, Eva… I had helped her create and publish her first book, *The Story of Pieta Flowyo*, three years ago. The synchronicities made the hairs on the back of John's neck stand on end, which welcomed him nicely into my world!

My family was also honoured to meet John when he returned to gift us with several of his wonderful books. As I watched him bond with Will and Kitty about their schools, with David over sailing boats, and with my Mum about their working careers with babies, I fell a little in love with this delightful Professor, dressed in his Scouting uniform. I mean, who wouldn't?

John's Milton State School class are meeting for their 65th school reunion this year and we coincidentally share a mutual friend who will also be attending…

Nancy Knudsen

Many years ago, David and I had a big adventure across the oceans on our sail boat, Steamy Windows. We'd had a close call with terrorism while we were living in London and as a result, decided to pack in our crazy working lives, and do a crazy adventure instead, suddenly understanding that there was more to life than being a hamster on the London wheel.

I learned how to sail (as David was already a sailor), we bought a 20-year-old boat that had already sailed around the world (so she knew the way), and off we went. For two years we lived aboard Steamy, getting our sea legs in the Med before making a perilous journey down the west coast of Africa towards the Canary Islands. Once we arrived safely (only just, but that's another story), we had about a month to get to know the islands and prepare for the three-week Atlantic crossing with 250 other boats, competing in the Atlantic Rally for Cruisers.

One day, while we were cleaning out the boat, we heard a knock on the side of the hull and popped our heads up through our respective hatches like nautical meerkats. An attractive lady with short grey hair was standing there, looking fit, tanned and ready for action at the drop of a flag. She introduced herself as Nancy Knudsen, and she, too, was crossing the Atlantic, on a vessel called Blackwattle with her husband Ted. She'd seen the Australian flag on our boat and just had to meet us.

We invited Nancy aboard, delighted to hear another Australian accent in this part of the world. Over a drink, we shared some of our sailing stories, and Nancy asked if she could write a feature about us for Sail World Magazine. Nancy moonlighted as a journalist, which was her bread and butter now she and Ted sailed full-time.

Nancy and Ted also had many amazing sailing stories to share, and in the following month, we spent many hours in their company trading yarns.

In November 2006, the large fleet of sailboats set off from Las Palmas towards the Caribbean, all going our separate ways very quickly. We only saw one other boat in the next 21 days, so vast is that ocean.

Three weeks at sea saw Steamy Windows arrive safely in St Lucia, with a little stowaway aboard... I had joyously found out that I wasn't seasick on the journey, but pregnant with our first child, Will, named for his fortitude!

Upon landing, there were great celebrations and many cocktails (mocktails for me!) to be drunk, all filled with ice that we had missed so desperately at sea! Memo to self, don't get pregnant before going to the Caribbean, where rum is cheaper than Coke.

After many hours sharing stories of various Atlantic adventures and mishaps, we heard the news that another Australian boat had suffered extreme damage on the crossing, and were struggling to make it to the end. Ted and Nancy, aboard their yacht, Blackwattle, were staying with them all the way, so when both vessels sailed into the St Lucia harbour after 23 days at sea, they were given a huge heroes' welcome – we were all delighted to see them safe!

Nancy went on to write a lovely article about Steamy Windows and our sailing journey. Our families were told to buy copies of Sail World when it came out, and shortly afterwards, we received an e-mail from David's father, Bob, saying that we'd been very fortunate to have met the delightful Nancy Knudsen.

According to Bob, Nancy was Miss Queensland in 1959, had been a weather girl on the news and best of all, she had featured in *Skippy*!! She even won a Logie...

We had said goodbye to Nancy by the time we knew this about her, and all credit to her that she never felt the need to mention any of this. We had met as sailors, as equals, and left each other's company as friends. As usual, I was none the wiser about the company I kept and, therefore, had no opportunity to become star struck.

12 years on and a lot of water under our respective bridges, Nancy and I have remained friends, sharing in each other's writing achievements and keeping in touch sporadically.

It was a huge shock, then, when reading one of Professor John Pearn's books about Auchenflower and Milton, to come across a photo of Nancy as one of John's classmates at Milton State School in the early 1950s.

I called Nancy immediately – neither of us realising that we had a school and a suburb as part of our shared history! I told her all about the Under the Lino Project, and some of the experiences I'd had, particularly the synchronous ones. Nancy was amused to know that she, now, was another! She had once even been interviewed by Hugh Lunn, just as I had interviewed Hugh myself!

Nancy recounted some of her time at Milton with me. She and her family had lived in Rainworth which was mainly open land back then. Her parents bought a newly subdivided block and built on it, like so many others at the time.

Nancy Knudsen *Milton State School is etched in my brain with a kind of PTSD intensity – headmaster Mr Oldham, huge, grey whiskered and brandishing a cane; sweat-smelly boys we partnered to learn the 'Pride of Erin' in dance classes, daily hand-digging of dusty holes in the ground to play marbles.*

1946, post-World War II and how 'politically incorrect' we were! Milton State School, at the age of six, was my second state school. The first was Mossman, in Far North Queensland (FNQ). My first memory there was the headmistress saying we 'should not throw stones at the Catholics.'

"What's a Catholic?" I said to another child on the way home.

"Over there," she said, and there they were! Children dressed in beige and chocolate brown.

I thought there were no Catholics in Brisbane because no-one wore beige and chocolate brown. Except my mother's friend Edith, visiting after school.

"Are you a Catholic Aunty Edith?" I enquired.

"No," she said, looking puzzled. "Why?"

"You're wearing Catholic clothes – but I won't throw stones at you."

Life can be very confusing when you're six and just arrived from FNQ.

So Milton School took some getting used to – dark brick and three stories towering into the sky. I thought it was Catholic too, because all the walls were painted chocolate brown half way up and then beige to the ceiling. The colour no doubt merely hid the dirt marks, but it certainly looked Catholic to me.

I also brought some other opinions from FNQ. I knew what a Dago was because I couldn't understand their Italian. My grandmother didn't like Dagos.

When I asked her why, she said, "Because they cook with garlic and eat bread that isn't white."

However, I had grasped the lesson. At Milton when I first saw kids eating brown bread sandwiches, I didn't ask them about if they were Dagos. I was learning fast.

At six, we were given slates and slate pencils to write our letters. Except for chorusing, "A like an apple on a twig. A says 'ah'," and so on down the alphabet, we had to maintain silence. As, apart from my parents, I had only a dog at home to talk to, this was a shocking imposition. However, if you got your timing right, the screeching noise of 45-50 children writing simultaneously on their slates well masked the whispering and giggling which whiled away the hours. We also had wet sponges to 'wipe the slate clean'. I blame the putrid acid smell of those sponges for the total demise of my olfactory sense neurons in later life.

After a few years, we graduated to notebook and pencil, then pen and ink. The pens were doled out every morning along with white ceramic ink wells jammed into holes in the desks, for 'cursive writing' practice. The skill involved getting the 'down-lines' fat and the 'up-lines' thin. (Teachers maintained that using a 'fountain pen' was cheating. I hate to imagine their horror at that fabulous Hungarian invention, the 'Biro'.)

My first sharp memory was of Miss Crawford. She walked around, ruler in hand. If you weren't holding your pen correctly, a sharp rap across the knuckles could make some children cry. Terrified, I paid great attention. No doubt she contributed to my excellent hand writing when I left school. (Sadly lost now, thanks to computers!)

We sat all day in straight rows at desks which took about four children, each with ink well and pencil slot. An aisle ran down the middle. We were placed in the order of our last examination results, with the child who had come 'top' in the back row, on the 'good' side and everyone placed after them in turn. Then the placing continued on the 'bad' side of the class. We had one teacher who called the children on the 'bad' side 'Commies', being short for 'Communist' – her euphemism for lazy. Being post-Second World War, much suspicion abounded about 'Communists under the bed'.

There were no special sports teachers. Individual teachers volunteered to lead the sport of their choice. Wanting to play tennis, I approached the volunteer tennis teacher, tiptoeing into his empty school room, where he was correcting papers.

"Sir, I would like to start learning tennis please."

He looked at me perfunctorily, then back down at his notebooks, "No."

"Beg your pardon, Sir?"

"No."

While I was still trying to work out what to do next, with crying up there as a good option, he pushed back the pile of notebooks and said, "You're Nancy Knudsen, aren't you?"

"Yes, sir." Uh-oh, he knows my name. Bad sign...

"Well, Miss Jacobs, your teacher, tells me that you could do much better than you do. That you're so busy talking and making a nuisance of yourself that you disturb all the other children."

"No, sir."

"No sir, what?"

"No, sir, I only disturb those who talk back sir."

"You are down around the middle of the class. When you come top in the next test, come back to me then and you can learn to play tennis."

I didn't come top in the next test, only second, next to Robin Walden, but the teacher called me out.

"Nancy, we have to play Graceville State School this afternoon. You're in the team. Here's a racquet."

"But sir, I haven't learned yet."

"Well, you'll learn this afternoon, won't you?"

I like to blame this story, probably unfairly, for why my serve remained atrocious for the rest of my short-lived tennis life.

I lived and learned through those days without harm in spite of the biases of the day. For all their methods, I never doubted those teachers had our best interests at heart and they loved us all... so they are funny, happy memories.

In October 2018, I shall be very proud to attend the 65th reunion of our Scholarship Class at Milton State School.

Under the Lino Milton Locals

There were, of course, many fabulous people from the UTL group who also had fond memories of this local area, and shared them openly with us.

Catherine *My family home was near Toowong Station, until it sold in the 1950s. The area was relatively sparse at the time, so most people would have known one another. Cullum's Grocers were on Grimes Street, near Milton Road, where the Deer Duck Bistro is now. Mrs Cullum was part Jamaican and a very generous and loving woman who looked after everyone. There used to be a hat factory where Toowong Village is now and a post office, with Patterson's Sawmill next door.*

My great-grandfather was mates with Archbishop Duhig – they played poker together. He was an electroplater and sold his business to S. Cook, who traded at Everton Park.

My great-grandmother had a shop in George Street and they were quite wealthy. Her grandmother had afternoon tea at the Indooroopilly tollkeeper's bridge in the 1950s.

We kids used to polish our great-grandparents' silver to get money for the Ekka! My paternal grandfather was a mining superintendent in 1924 while my grandmother was a bowerbird. One of my maternal grandmother's family members died in the London Tower and another died in a duel!

We had a house at Nundah that had a nook with a fireplace and my grandmother carved the mantelpiece surrounds. Another great-grandfather came from Edinborough and settled in Melbourne, where he married a 'native' i.e. Irish Australian, born here.

It's funny what we discover about our own families when we start to dig – prisons and brothels etc.

Chrissy *One of the things I love about Milton is how it keeps changing and reinventing. From very low migrant area in the '60 – '70s to the yuppie place in the '80s, and now in some ways, a family suburb again.*

Caylie *There have been a lot of changes, from worker's cottages and industrial areas to gentrification; from cemetery to night soil dump to Lang Park and Suncorp Stadium; from Rosalie as a poorer cousin to Paddington to the hub of ritzy restaurants and cafes it is now, with floods and swamps levelling out the playing field every thirty years or so.*

Ian *I am an old Marist Brothers Rosalie boy. It was a rough area in those days. We were in Copeland Street. It has been completely transformed now. It was a major four bedroom Queenslander on a massive 32 perches built in 1900 and a doctor's residence with a three room servants quarters underneath. The doctor used those rooms as a surgery and waiting room.*

The current incarnation is a major adaptation of the original building. It is a totally unrecognizable building. Coincidentally, the current owner who did the reno worked with my brother as an Air traffic Controller!

I have some old photos of the original house from the 1960s if you would like them.

Sadly my family enclosed the verandahs to provide accommodation for a tribe of kids and extended family. That was the way it was done in those days. My Mum sold the place in 1978 and couldn't get $28,000 for it! She settled for $27,750! There was no real demand for the Queenslanders until a few years later.

My Dad was the Alderman (Councillor) for the area for the Central City ward. The only interesting relics I can remember under the house were some aerial bomb fin assemblies from WW2 which people used as pot plant holders.

Copeland Street House 1964

Ian kindly invited my family and me to join him one Sunday at his home on one of the Moreton Bay islands. We had a wonderful day with him, exploring the island and hearing stories about Milton when he was a child.

Ian's grandmother lived at 14 Bangalla Street, Auchenflower until she died, aged 94. It had been raining when she back from McDonnell & East on the tram one day, and she caught pneumonia.

He recalled Tipper's Corner (now where the IGA on Baroona Road is) and Mutch's Corner, which housed a grocer and the Terrace Butchers, where Morgan's housemate, Warren, used to work (now the unused blue building on the corner of Heussler Terrace and Baroona Road).

Ian's mother used to buy her meat from the Paddington butcher, who also ran an SP bookie business on the side. She would give Ian money in two envelopes – one for meat and the other for the weekly bets!

One of Ian's first jobs was at Barnes Bakery, which used to be Arthur's Uncle Thomas Webster's bakery on Fernberg Road. As an adult, Ian wanted to be a blacksmith but post-war, his parents expected him to get a public service job. So he became a writer, researcher, producer, editor and documentary film-maker. He stumbled into television, ironically working for Blacksmith Productions.

Ian took us on a tour of his island, telling us all about its history and sharing stories about some of its inhabitants. Dr John Pearn, for example, as I mentioned earlier.

One of the local islanders, Hayley, gave us a tour of her hobby farm, surrounded by repurposed purple train carriages. She told us a story about her brother who'd found a load of florins under his house when he was renovating it. Upon further investigation into the house history, he discovered that it had once belonged to a bus driver, who had obviously been stealing money from the passengers! He went to court to gain ownership of the money.

Ian also lived next door to a rather sinister character in Copeland Street who makes his appearance later in the book...

Media and Marketing

Now, I need to tell you, I don't love cleaning. I am a clean person, and like to live in a clean environment, so don't get me wrong. I just feel like it's a massive waste of my time to actually do the cleaning bit. You can see what a pickle I'm in.

Many people who don't like cleaning may invite a cleaner into their home every week or two. That's sensible, and I used to do that too, when I was working in a paid job. We'll ignore the fact that I used to clean before she got here, and sometimes, would even clean alongside her, because it felt elitist to have someone doing a job I was quite capable of doing myself. But I was time-poor and it made sense at the time. Besides, I loved Christine and we became friends as a result, and I wouldn't take back that time for anything.

These days, I write full-time in a non-paying role, I am still time-poor but have finally found a win-win-win solution to my cleaning problem. I invite friends or family over for a meal.

Nothing motivates me to clean more than the threat of visitors. And I *love* visitors. My family and friends wouldn't care if my house was a mess, but *I* care. In a fit of nervous energy, I race around and do it all in less than two hours – time I don't usually have, but I manage to find it when I have to.

Because of the Under the Lino Project, I have had many new people visiting my home. Members of the team have come for lunch or morning tea, Webster and Murphy family members have been interviewed here, and of course, there's the media. My dear friend Lyn has called me a 'media tart' from the beginning, and she's completely right – as long as it's positive attention, I'm totally happy to talk to the media about anything I'm passionate about. They've never done the wrong thing by me and publicity for a writer is very important.

If you thought having friends and family were impetus enough for me to clean my abode, you should see me before the media comes over! It's the silver lining to my husband's privacy concerns... our lives may be on display, but at least the house is clean.

I have been very fortunate that the stories we are sharing online resonate with so many people, and that the media have decided to help out as well. This was particularly useful when we were crowdfunding for the book, and trying to get some legitimacy relating to what we were doing.

We also hoped that the media would help us find answers to some of our questions – perhaps some relatives would come forward; perhaps someone would be able to shed light on the face of Muriel White; perhaps the Commonwealth Bank would be encouraged to speak to us.

Who are the People in my Neighbourhood...?

Joining the Toowong Soccer Club was the best thing we ever did for our son, Will. Not only did it provide him with a wonderful outlet for his sporty, testosterone-fuelled body, it put our worried minds at ease after watching him lying underneath rugby scrums containing boys twice his body weight.

This new sport also led to some lovely friendships with interesting people, such as Arthur Palmer, whom I wrote of earlier, and who shared the chapter about Aboriginals in Toowong with us.

Each Saturday morning, we would turn up to watch the lads play, and have wonderful, rich conversations with other parents sitting with us on the sidelines, interspersed with, "Come on boys! Keep it up! Great work! Woohooo!" It's very hard not to get caught up in the game, but we were fortunate, with this team, to have enthusiastic parents who encouraged their kids, as opposed to some of the fisticuffs we'd witnessed at other events.

I had made friends with a lovely mum called Sharyn. We'd sit together in her folding chairs trying to keep warm in the winter sun, while the Dads talked technicalities about football nearby. Sharyn and I always had loads to talk about, and she was one of the first people I told about the money under the lino and all the ruckus it had caused on Facebook.

Each week, I would update her, in between shouting our encouragement to the boys, and we would work on the mystery with all the new information gleaned since we'd last caught up.

Now, Sharyn had mentioned to me at some point that she was a journalist, and I had sympathised with her about the work conditions for journos, hoping she wasn't about to lose her job anytime soon. No, she assured me that she was okay for the moment, and that was the last word on it.

A few weeks before the end of soccer season, I was sitting with Kitty in a GP's waiting room one evening, watching the *Channel 7 News*. All of a sudden, there was Sharyn. On the telly!

I've mentioned before that I am hopeless with well-known people in Brisbane because we don't watch free-to-air TV, and I could have fallen through the floorboards when I realised that Sharyn Ghidella was a TV News Journalist, and quite a well-known one at that, from all accounts afterwards.

I was so shy when I saw her next, feeling like such a backwater hermit, and confessed to her what had happened. She found it all very amusing, and as always, because we had become friends first, nothing changed between us.

Sharyn then suggested that her producer might be interested in the story of Under the Lino for a news feature. Well, that was pretty exciting, to say the least!

It all happened very quickly after that – a phone call came one Friday morning, giving me an hour to prepare for the television crew, so when Katrina Blowers from Channel 7 came to see me, I was as red as a beetroot from the massive clean-up I'd just done.

I also had a quiet word to Johnny, the cameraman, about 'no backside shots', which he was most amused about, but respected my concerns, for which I will always be grateful!

We didn't find any relatives from that segment, or answers to our questions, but we got a lot of community interest and the numbers in the UTL Facebook team doubled overnight. The more the merrier, we all agreed.

A few feature articles in the Brisbane Times (Rachel Clun), the Sydney Morning Herald (Amy Mitchell-Whittington) and a wonderful story in Independent Australia (Dr Glenn Davies, my dear friend from James Cook University) gave our group the courage and credibility to keep going.

The coverage also sent us several family members and opened up a whole new world for Brisbane's amateur historians.

Leanne Edmistone's feature article (What Lies Beneath) in the Courier Mail's QWeekend, 26 May 2018, gave a particularly wonderful account of the project, made even better by the fact that Leanne has followed the tale from the beginning as an active member of the UTL Team. She has now become a very close friend, and I love her to bits!

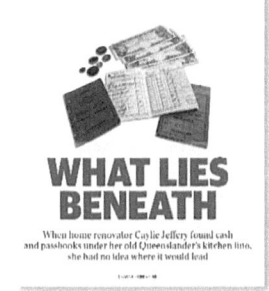

So much good has come from this project, with people all over Australia looking deeper into their local history, making friends with online counterparts and talking to their elders about their past. It feels like we're all coming out of hiding to bask in the sunshine of our ancestors.

Local School Visits

I have been doing author visits in schools for several years now, teaching kids that they, too, can become self-published authors. As the Writer-in-Residence at Milton State School, I helped over 250 children write, illustrate, edit and publish their own incredible works. Some of them even set up a shingle at home, selling one of their two books to their unsuspecting family members for $10! So entrepreneurial, so young. I love it!

One delightful student and voracious reader, Lila K, once wrote this poem for me after we'd finished our book project. It lit up my world and reminded me why I love working with children so much...

Creative as they get
Amazing, helpful and kind
You are the reason I push myself
Limitless heart you indeed have
I look up and find myself imagining
Everything I know about writing was from you

The Under the Lino Project has now taken me into schools as a history facilitator, sharing the Websters' mystery and Brisbane's rich history in a way that holds their attention like nothing I've ever witnessed before.

I've been to three local schools, filled with children who had grandparents originating from the area. Many had a story of their own to share, pertaining to an historical discovery or ancestor of interest – one girl's parents found old war medals stashed under a bomb casing, researched the owners and returned them.

The most interesting addition to my talks to schools has been the discovery of a link between the original landowner on my property in Milton and pioneer Australian explorer, Ludwig Leichhardt.

Ludwig Leichhardt

Portrait Ludwig Leichhardt 1813–c.1848
Courtesy of the National Library of Australia

Ludwig Leichhardt, for those of you who missed Year 5 Social Studies in Australia, was a German explorer and naturalist, most famous for his exploration of northern and central Australia.

He'd arrived in Sydney in 1842 planning to explore inland Australia, starting with the Hunter River valley north of Sydney to study the geology, flora and fauna of the region, and to observe farming methods. He then set out on his own on a specimen-collecting journey that took him from Newcastle, New South Wales, to Moreton Bay in Queensland.

During my research into the lives of George Leslie (who owned the land my house sits on in the 1850s) and his brother, Patrick (who pioneered the Darling Downs), I read a note at the bottom of an online obituary that said the Mitchell Gallery in the NSW State Library had evidence of some correspondence naming Ludwig Leichhardt and George Leslie as colleagues.

Leichhardt's first expedition was privately funded, and only supported by volunteers, when he set out from Jimbour Homestead in 1844, the most western outpost settlement on the Darling Downs. A memorial to John Gilbert, one of Leichhardt's companions on this journey, can be found on St James' Church, Sydney and says, "In memory of John Gilbert, Ornithologist, who was speared by the blacks on 29 June 1845 during the first overland expedition to Port Essington by Dr Ludwig Leichhardt and his intrepid companions."

George Leslie's bullocks assisted Leichhardt on his second expedition in 1846, which was supposed to take him from the Darling Downs to the west coast of Australia and ultimately to the Swan River and Perth. Sadly, they were forced to come back after only 800km was covered, because of inclement weather, malaria and hunger.

I know all this, because my children are both studying pioneer Australian explorers at BBC and St Peters, and Will came home one day to say he was doing his oral presentation on Ludwig Leichhardt. It was the same day I discovered that George Leslie was the first person to own the land upon which my house sits.

There's very little in my wooden chest from my Ascot State School years, but I did keep my Year 5 Social Studies folder for some reason. I pulled it out to show Will that I, too, had done an assignment on Dr Leichhardt, in 1980, when I was his age.

The State Library of NSW Website states: *There are at present on view to the public in the Mitchell Gallery, Macquarie Street, Sydney, several holograph letters, written by Dr Ludwig Leichhardt which were written by him in the years of his exploration in North Queensland. These letters are in a splendid state of preservation, and are easily read.*
Amongst the documents on exhibit relating to Leichhardt are the following:

Holograph letter dated November 14, 1846, written by Dr Ludwig Leichhardt to George Farquhar Leslie, of Canning Downs, expressing his thanks for the gift of four bullocks for his next expedition to North Queensland.

George Leslie and Patrick Leslie were members of the first group of settlers on the Darling Downs. Patrick Leslie pioneered the route from New England (New South Wales), in March, 1840, and he and his brother took up Glengallen Creek.

This original letter was presented to the Mitchell Library by Mrs. Alec Thomson, a grand-daughter of Patrick Leslie.

A call to the NSW State Library led to the provision of a scanned letter from Dr Leichhardt to George Leslie.

> Glengallan the 14th Novbr 1846
>
> My dear Sir
>
> I intended to call on you and to bid you good bye, as I past your station, but it was so late, that I found myself compelled to go on. I am exceedingly obliged for your kind present and I shall arrange either with Mr. Ingles or with Mr. Dennis about an exchange of the four bullocks. With my best compliments to your brother and Mrs Leslie and with my best wishes for your wellfare
>
> I remain
> My dear Sir
> Most sincerely yours
> Ludwig Leichhardt

Letter from Ludwig Leichhardt to George Leslie
Courtesy of the State Library of NSW Archives

Transcript

Glengallan the 14th Novbr 1846

My dear Sir,

I intended to call on you and to bid you good bye, as I past your station, but it was so late, that I found myself compelled to go on. I am exceedingly obliged for your kind presents and shall arrange either with Mr. Hughes or with Mr Dennis about an exchange of the four bullocks.

With my best compliments to your brother and Mrs Leslie and with my best wishes for your welfare.

I remain, most sincerely yours,
Ludwig Leichhardt

When I gave the children at Brisbane Boys' College (BBC) and St Peters Lutheran College copies of Leichhardt's letter to crumple up (to make them look old) for their history books, not only did it fit right into their curriculum, it tickled their imaginations and brought history to life right in front of them.

The Year 5s at BBC and the Year 4s at St Peters were also given a preview of the Milton murder story, which had them leaning forward, bloodthirsty and desperate for all the gory details. They all agreed that History lessons improved exponentially when they became gruesome, with most of them enjoying *Horrible Histories* on the ABC.

The BBC boys also loved that one of their classmates, Beau Palmer, was going to be mentioned in the book because it was his father, Arthur, who wrote about the Aboriginals of Toowong, and Sir Arthur Palmer who was Beau's GG Grandfather.

The Year 6 students at Milton State School weren't told about the murder, because we hadn't discovered it yet, but they loved that Morgan Webster had been a student at their school, and that the story revolved around their neighbourhood. Some of them even had relatives named Hill or White and went home to ask their parents about their own lineage.

Living history. Just what this project is all about.

My trip out to Pine Rivers State High School, to speak to the Year 8/9 HASS Extension class, was also illuminating and encouraging. Their teacher, Nicole Christian, is a member of the UTL Team, and together, we gave the kids a big hour of local history. We discussed the history of Strathpine – settled in the 1860s by the Scottish (those guys were everywhere!) for the Gympie gold rush, which was followed by the era of cane farms and rum distilleries. Queensland Rail named the suburb, Strathpine, in the 1880s, after which time it became an army base for aviation in WWII.

This tied in well with Arthur Webster's family ties to the railways. The discussion about the Brisbane Line in WWII had them all wondering what would have happened to them in North Brisbane if the war had been won by the Japanese.

The children I met surprised me with their critical thought processes and theories...

- Muriel White has same initials as Morgan Webster... are they the same person?
- Eleanor set up an account for Morgan to take care of him because she was going to die with heart disease.
- Morgan was a dodgy banker trying to look after his mum.
- Eleanor stole money from Arthur when he wasn't looking.
- Morgan or Muriel killed Betty Shanks (!!)
- Eleanor was keeping money from Arthur – so he didn't spend it on gambling or drinking
- Eleanor was saving money to leave Arthur because he wasn't nice to her
- Morgan very smart because of his scholarships and excellent Milton SS education so he would have set it all up
- Muriel accidentally left her bank book there and Eleanor was storing it for her but then she died before she could tell her
- Muriel Hill had a secret lover called Mr White and Eleanor was helping her keep it quiet
- Someone rubbed out the original name and put White there
- Teller ran out of ink and had to use another pen or the pen broke because in the old days the pens were fragile

- Someone asked how old they were when they died, looked at the bank books dates and noted upside down entries
- How did they die? Where did they die? Did the people at Montpelier Street not find out because Eleanor died just before she could tell them her big secret?
- Muriel White might have owed Eleanor Webster money
- Check local church records because they might have been religious and gone to church

I told the children they were history in the making, with their bright enquiring minds and creative ideas. They were obviously delighted to have had their opinions and thoughts about this mystery heard and accepted, so I think we can rest easy, folks – the next generation is doing just fine!

Finding out things difficult to share

Several people have shared stories during the last year, like Ian, where they've discovered information pertaining to their houses or family trees that has been difficult to process, and perhaps tough to share with their loved ones...

Diana *I spend a lot of time on the Trove website. I went there to help find the Websters at the start of this little adventure. As usual, I got side-tracked reading other articles and editing them. Found a relative in a place I never thought to look before. One thing that always strikes me when reading old newspapers is the sadness of some of the stories (like Morgan's). So many reports of suicides, accidental deaths, many at the workplace and murders. It makes me wonder why people talk about the "good old days" when they don't seem to have been all that good. Anyway, just want to ask, if you are searching Trove and find articles and notices of interest, please spare a few minutes to edit them if they need it.*
Steve *Quite right Diana, despite the problems we have now, we never had it this good!*
Diana *I have read at least 15 stories of farmers committing suicide, even as far back as the early 1900s. At least one of those impacted my family. The things I have found when reading articles from the past is eye opening to say the least. From the owning of 'nigger' slaves in W.A., to my own great uncle's letter home to his mother after being wounded at Gallipoli, to the lists of war deaths. I don't think those days were all that people remember.*
Vivianne *I have found out things about our family we had no idea about – like my grandfather being caught speeding on Kelvin Grove Road on his motorbike in the 1920s!*
Diana *I researched a family for months trying to find the connection and couldn't, so discarded it. Now DNA testing and family stories passed down on that side (that of course were never written somewhere for public consumption) has found the link to what had become a dead end. My ancestor was their ancestor's illegitimate son.* 😊

Shane *Interesting about old stories my ancestor's suicide made front page news when it happened nowadays not even mentioned*
Jay *Media has policies these days against the publishing of suicides. Theory says it might cause copycat suicides. But that is being challenged by therapists who believe it helps conceal the extent of the problem*
Rob N Suzanne *The Cemetery office staff are very helpful. That is how I found my long lost sister, never spoken about, who was buried there as infant of 6mths old with my cousin. These two babies were born and died around same time. No certificates were ever produced. Family kept this a secret for some 40 years 'til I started digging about doing my Family tree. I found that one was out of wedlock, hidden in closet never to be talked about... hahhahaha they can run but they can't hide.*

Brothels in Brisbane

Somewhere along the line, it was suggested that our house may have been working as a brothel (it wasn't). The fact that it had been divided up into flats was a red (light) flag to some people, so we entered into a discussion about what was going on in the sex trade during those years.

Cheryl, one of the team's most active members, got in touch with me to discuss her thoughts about Muriel White and the bank balances. We agreed that a face to face meeting was in order, so we could scrutinise the paperwork a little more closely. While we ate lunch, she decided to share a fascinating piece of her own personal family history with me.

I convinced Cheryl to write her story for us to enjoy, and to illustrate a point about why some houses were divided into flats. This is also a classic example of what could happen when one delves into one's family history, or, when one opens up the newspaper innocently on a Sunday morning...

My Ancestors' Secret Business
by Cheryl Palmer

Turning to the second page of the Sunday Mail to the feature article one morning, I was surprised to see photographs of my old family home in St James Street, Petrie Terrace, beautifully restored and looking magnificent, standing proud overlooking the city. I read with interest about the new owner's pride and love of his (my) home, which he had restored, and the research he had undertaken to find out its history.

It was a fascinating read for me, that is, until he declared that my old family home had been a brothel throughout its entire existence, right up until he purchased it in 1998, in a sad and dilapidated state.

How dare he say that? My great-grandparents and grandmother were not brothel keepers!

Originally a four-room cottage, built around 1883, my great-grandparents purchased the property sometime between 1889 and 1891. They proceeded to build over and around the small cottage and created a very large three-storey home.

My great-grandfather was a very well-known and successful businessman, whose craftsmanship can still be seen in many Brisbane buildings. He was also a past Master of the Freemasons, founder of The Burns Club, philanthropist and a devout Baptist. One would assume he would have been a role model in their era...

I indignantly phoned the new owner, asking why he'd made this claim. He invited me over for a chat and tour of his restoration work. After a lot of information exchange and copies of documents he had discovered, I was in half a mindset that this story may have some foundation. I discovered that they may have been leading a second life and with other means of income.

But brothel owners... seriously?

At some stage in the 1920s, my great-grandfather converted their large home into four or five flats, with he, his wife and my grandmother (then in her late 30s) living in one, and the other four flats rented out.

It turns out that the 'renters' were Ladies of the Night. A secret passageway was constructed which led to a window with red glass, and a ledge where a light was placed when they were open for business. The red window at the side of the house is out of place in the floor plan with its narrow passage way from the inside of one of the downstairs rooms.

He explained it was well-known by the old timers that, in WW2, a light was placed in that window which shone down to the American Army Base in Victoria Park, indicating that the 'girls' were ready for work. An elderly gentleman who also lived in the street told him a lot about the brothel.

This window and passageway still exist and can be seen from the street.

After he died in 1933, it appears that my great-grandmother and grandmother continued the business and the rent was paid into the Queensland Public Trustees Will account each week, deposited by my grandmother.

The difficulty I originally had with this, is that my parents and siblings also lived in flat number one and my great Aunt and her family lived in flat number two, when my great-grandmother died (I was nine days old at the time), so surely my parents must have known who was renting the other two flats?

The one thing that I do know is true, my mother disliked my father's mother with a passion but would only say 'she was a hard woman'. In 1950, after my great-grandmother's death, the trustees sold the home.

The twist is, my family home was sold to another enterprising older woman, who continued the business until her death in the 1960s. This has been confirmed by her grandson, who I have been in contact with. We had a laugh about our enterprising grandmothers. A large home, lots of spare rooms, not much different to taking in paying boarders. After my great-grandmother's death, did my ageing grandmother put the Trustees in contact with this prospective buyer?

From accounts of old residents, the property continued to be used for the same purpose until this new owner purchased and restored it, in the late 1990s. Hence the article in the paper that I was reading and my need to phone the writer about his absurd claims.

As researchers, we know to keep an open mind because not all is what it seems to be. Unaccountable funds often come from unsavoury activities.

This was a huge family story to discover and to have publicly aired as well. Finding out stories like this about one's family can be a fascinating journey of discovery, as long as nobody gets hurt during the ride. Throughout the UTL Project, most of us were hyper-aware not to turn any part of it into a witch hunt or make up stories where there was only speculation.

We often slid off the path sideways on a tangent, discussing what life was like in the hidden world of Brisbane back then, only to slide back to reality and move on with the research. Cheryl's great-grandparents sounded like very resourceful people, who found an untapped market before the days where Tinder and Grindr opened the bedroom doors to people who just wanted to have a sexual encounter, with no strings attached.

People may never find out the real stories of their past because of family shame or embarrassment. Three generations in might see it differently though, when times have changed, and indignancies have faded.

In Search of More Lino…

About a month into the UTL Project, I was whingeing to David about the lack of lino in my life as we drove over to East Brisbane to enjoy brunch with friends.

"I just wish I'd kept some for a photo shoot! Maybe I can find some at a house removalist's place or in a carpet shop skip? I could take the bank books and money to someone's old house and do a photo session?"

We arrived at Cath and Andy's house a few minutes later, and were delighted to be shown around *their* new renovation. They'd turned a small worker's cottage into a semi-modernised, double storey home, retaining many original features but injecting their personal touches into it, too.

As we climbed up the newly polished wooden stairs, I noticed something out of place leaning up against the wall halfway up. It was an old piece of lino, about a metre long and 20cm wide, cracked and stained. The design was still pretty and vibrant, though, in greys and pinks.

"What's that, Cath?" I asked, getting very excited and having one of my synchronicity moments.

"Oh, that's all that's left of the old lino flooring from the house. It's so pretty, and probably killing us all with asbestos, but I have a mind to frame it as a keepsake of the original house."

"Well, you won't believe this," I said, excitedly, "but I was just telling David in the car that I needed some lino for a photograph!"

Over brunch, we talked about the UTL Project at length. Cath and Andy are very well-read, interesting and intelligent people who enjoy a good story, so after coming up with various theories of their own, as people are wont to do on this project, they offered to loan me their lino to use for a photo shoot.

Have a look at the front cover… that's Cath and Andy's lino!

Kerry *Oh!! The lino on your pledge page was in my bedroom! The memories have just flooded back in an instant. I can see the whole room in my mind. Thank you.*

During my search for old lino, I'd read an article about a Melbourne photographer called Natalie Jeffcott, about the use of old lino in her photography. Natalie's webpage was covered in beautiful pictures of vintage lino, so I contacted her to ask where I might be able to find some for myself.

When Natalie answered the telephone, I immediately recognised her voice as belonging to a dear friend, who also lives in Melbourne. After we chatted about lino for a while, I asked her if she were any relation to my friend Melissa. Ha! She was her sister. Suddenly Natalie knew who I was – she had read about the Under the Lino Project on Mel's Facebook page!

Natalie then felt more comfortable to tell me about her own renovating project… a beautiful 1800s Victorian home that had once belonged to the original dairy in the area with its own beautiful lino.

I suddenly had an idea to ask Natalie if she could perhaps take some photos of her lino, and maybe do a cover for this book. After she'd spent some time reading about the Under the Lino Project, Natalie became completely lost in the mystery. She also happened to be coming to Brisbane for a conference, so next thing I knew, there she was, standing in my house, with her camera bag!

I whipped out Cath and Andy's old lino, and hey presto… we had a cover photo, thanks to Natalie's keen eye and photographic skills!

Meeting Magnus

Two days after I put the original post up about the bank books and money, Magnus Eriksson sent me a private message:

Hello Caylie – I'd be happy to help you find the original owners of the bank notes. There may be an interesting story around them as well. It should be an easy piece of research.
Cheers,
Magnus (House Histories page)

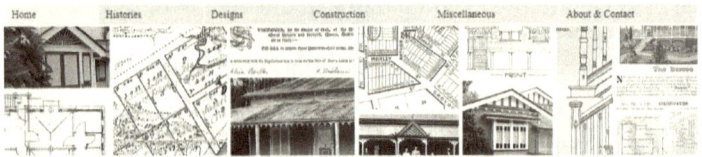

Imagine if I'd taken him up on that offer! Luckily for all of us, I got swept up in a tsunami of communication, and Magnus' message got lost in the deluge. He might have solved it all for us in a few days, and where would we be now?

I eventually did get in touch, however, after he recognised me at a local event. Our kids go to the same school (of course). We agreed to meet for coffee, ironically, at the same place Hugh Lunn and I had lunch, and I was able to get his story.

Hailing from Sweden, Magnus bought his home in Auchenflower in 2010. The house had a name, Clovelly, which piqued his curiosity. A massive research project ensued and he found all the relatives of all the owners as a result.

Magnus has sent us maps, and links, and words, and pictures, all of which have helped us piece this puzzle together. He's loved having a hand in such a wonderful project, but he was adamant that this project is not about individuals, it's about the group.

We discussed the community interest in this project and he agreed that television is passive and people with any sort of curiosity want to be active participants in life.

HouseHistories.org is a website where Magnus showcases 'Queensland's vernacular architecture and suburban history, with a focus on the south-east corner of the state. The topics are diverse and include local history, architecture, planning legislation, building materials and techniques – and anything related that sparks our curiosity. The geographical emphasis is on the Greater Brisbane Region but the information is relevant to all areas of Queensland and to some extent the rest of Australia.'

The work Magnus does on his webpage is 100% voluntary, as is mine, but the houses he's written about and the creative editing he's done on architectural pictures is incredible. His digital restoration of Cloudland will blow your mind

His final advice to me that morning was to send me off to buy a book by a chap called Andy Jenner, who is a friend and colleague of his, called *Building the Queensland House*, after we'd discussed our future dream projects.

When I found a copy half an hour later, at the Ashgrove Restoration Shed, I recognised the name of the illustrator. Do you remember me mentioning, way back in the beginning of the book, that my best friend, Clare, had died when we were just 17? Well, Andy Jenner was Clare's father's best friend, and Clare's father, John Braben, has done all of the illustrations for the book.

Until that moment, I didn't really believe in ghosts, I believed in synchronicity. I will tell you now, in public, that I rang my Mum straight away to tell her that one of the ghosts helping me on this journey was Clare.

Sealed Section

The Milton Murders

I told you on the back cover that there'd be a murder story in this book, remember?
Go and get yourself another cuppa, or perhaps a stiff scotch, and strap yourself in because this next bit is going to blow your mind.

The Milton Murders

Who doesn't love a good murder story? This is a mystery, after all, so why not throw some murder into it? The thing is, it has been important, throughout this investigation, to tell the truest account of the history and avoid any possibilities of slander, or misrepresentation. If we were able to find a link between events of the past to this house, then we would investigate, but if there were too many dead ends, we would drop what we were doing and move on.

MILTON WOMAN'S SUDDEN DEATH Police Investigate

Following the result of a post mortem examination made this morning, detectives have instituted investigations surrounding the death of Mrs. Beryl White, 28, of Heussler Terrace, Milton, which followed her collapse in bed at midnight.

Brisbane *Telegraph Saturday 16 April 1938, page 1 Trove*

For example, when we were sifting through records to find the identity of Muriel White, Brenda discovered that a woman from the area had been committed to trial for the murder of Beryl White (sometimes spelled 'Whyte'), who died in her home on Heussler Terrace in 1938. The coroner ruled death by septicaemia and pneumonia, after an alleged criminal abortion but despite a short period of incarceration at Boggo Road Gaol, the accused was acquitted and released back to her family.

Narelle *The lady who went to jail is my great uncle's mother and he is still alive. My sister and I lived with his brother who was married to my Nana's sister. She was acquitted until she was jailed again for another murder. My uncles were put in a home until she was released. The great uncle and aunt my sister and I lived with were lovely and so kind to us. His brother was a delinquent growing up. There's newspaper clippings of his antics.*

The names 'White' and 'Whyte' stood out to many of us, knowing that people often changed their names back in those days. This incident did, however, illustrate the sorts of activities that were going on behind closed doors in the neighbourhood at the time.

Sydney Herald
30 Jun 1968 TROVE

The Copeland Street murder was similar. Several members of the group mentioned that there'd been a murder just up the street, and went off to investigate what they could about this.

Michelle *Copeland Street is where the murdered miner's mother lived. She died in 1968.*
Narelle *Yes. The clipping says he lived with his mother and another man. Maybe this man was the one who they suspected of his murder.*
Michelle *He was over for her funeral and staying in his mother's house.*
Caylie *Oh that's so sad! He was killed while visiting for his Mum's funeral? One wonders what went down in the house before the murder... tensions running high with grief and loss?*
Narelle *There's a murder file on Qld State Archives site. It will be closed for 65 yrs*
Michelle *A thought that's been going through my head is how do newspapers and television shows goes access to some old records... is it Right to Information (RTI) or research exceptions... have you looked into what might be available those ways? Obviously it will depend on what's in files.*
Michelle *Yes. Used to be FOI.* www.rti.qld.gov.au/right-to-information-act/about-right-to-information

Then, one of the members of the group, who'd lived in Copeland Street sent me this...

I remember it although I was living in Maryborough at the time. Jimmy was the step-brother of the deceased and was devoted to his elderly mother who owned the house. They were very reclusive, although liked in the neighbourhood. When the mum died, the deceased, who had never been near them for years, came out of the woodwork demanding his share of the house which Jimmy used to maintain spotlessly. It was a neighbourhood showpiece. Apparently there was a violent argument between the brothers, and the step-brother visiting was murdered. Jimmy tried to make it look like an accident. My late uncle, who lived next door, gave evidence on what he heard etc. I think Jimmy did life for the murder and overall it was real tragedy. No idea whatever became of him. I liked Jimmy.

So many sad stories from those times, but none of them had any relevance to our mystery, until Chrissy came for a visit. Chrissy had come all the way from Doomadgee, where she was working at the time, to have a wander down memory lane – this used to be her neighbourhood.

Born 1965, of Scottish heritage like so many people who'd lived in this neighbourhood, Chrissy was a student at Milton State School from 1971-1976, and had lived in the aforementioned Copeland Street, which feeds into Heussler Terrace at the top of the hill.

Chrissy and I shared stories about the area, mentioning that in 1967, there was a murder on the grounds of Milton State School. It was a few years before she attended, but the children continued to talk about it for years to follow. The usual overinflated horror stories that kids love... *Blood was splattered everywhere! Don't ever use that toilet! I dare you to go in there! Who can stay in there the longest? You can still smell the blood on the walls...*

Mark *I went to school at Milton State and remember that story. There was a hole in one of the doors... rumours were it was a bullet hole. It really did have a bad vibe.*

As it had no obvious relevance to the project, I made a small note of it as an interesting side-story, and thought no more about it for several months. It certainly created a buzz in the team when I mentioned it, so when I came across the note again while researching for this book, I thought it might be fun for those with an interest to look into it, so I could write up a story for the webpage.

Caylie *Who wants to track down a Milton murder that happened around Milton State School in the late '60s?*
Nan *Jack Sim of* Brisbane Ghost Tours *would probably be able to tell you all you want to know. There are not too many Jack doesn't know about – historic and present day.*
Caylie *Nan, you are a rock star! Jack just wrote back to say he could shed light on this subject so I'll meet with him soon to interview him! http://brisbaneghosttours.com.au/contact/*
Ian *I lived next door to a lady in Copeland Street up the road. She had a boyfriend who was a real nutter who murdered a girl with a bayonet in the park (Gregory?) next to the Milton State School in about 1970. Got life for it from memory.*
Narelle *Is this what you're searching for?* **Trove: Big hunt for wounded killer of woman – The Canberra Times 1967**

We found a few articles that described the events surrounding the death of a young woman in Milton, giving only sketchy details, because they in were Canberra newspapers. *Trove* still didn't have Queensland newspaper stories for the late 1960s uploaded, but the articles we did find gave us the names of the murderer and the victim. Narelle also discovered that he'd been jailed for life, which, based on the dates, meant that the accused could have been released by now and may be living in the community. This is where things got tricky.

We were now looking into an event that might have negative repercussions on people's lives if they were to read the details. Information we gleaned showed that the accused was indeed still alive and married to a woman with the same first and second name as the victim. Given I had no reason to believe, at the time, that this event had anything to do with my house, I decided to delete the whole conversation and leave it well alone.

Caylie *Hi everyone, I recently put a post up asking if anyone knew of a local murder in 1967 near Milton State School. Evidence has been found on the subject, which was very interesting, but I have deleted all posts relating to it because the people to whom it refers are still alive. In the interests of privacy, I won't be mentioning the topic again, and urge everyone to continue on the well-worn paths of other topics in this group. Thank you all for understanding, and to those of you who worked to source information on this topic.*

The following day, my daughter, Kitty, was helping me pin up the Webster and Murphy family trees on a wall in my office. I'd been struggling to keep up with all the names on my small screen, so I printed them off, which then provided Kitty and I with a cutting-out activity for the afternoon. I would call out a name on my list, and she would hand me the corresponding name to pin in the correct place on the wall.

After about a hundred pins, I noticed one of the names was familiar... someone on the family tree had the same unusual surname as the Milton murderer!

Later that afternoon, I started a small investigative group with some of the women who had shown an active interest in researching the murder when I first mentioned it. I had a strong feeling that the murderer was somehow linked to this house.

25 FEB 2:49pm I named the group Gregory Park Detectives.

Caylie *Hi ladies, as you know I had to delete the thread about the Gregory Park murder. I am going to continue the investigation and would love your assistance, if you're keen.*

Today I've been pinning up the family tree for the Websters and Murphys on a board so I could get a better picture of it all. A family member was married to someone with the same surname as the accused!

Not everyone agreed that we should continue, with one of the group saying that the man had done his time and by all rights, should be left alone. I thought it was important to find out if there was a relationship, but I appreciated her point of view and made a promise not to sensationalise this event, after she left the discussion.

Caylie *If there's no relationship, we'll shut it down for good.*
Chrissy *Wow, never occurred to me that this crime could be connected to our mystery. I mentioned it as part of Milton's amazing history.*
Michelle *Just a quick look and the family tree surname is slightly different to the murderer... so may not be any connection at all.*
Narelle *Many Germans changed their surname spelling. In my own family they changed from Weisse to Wise.*
Kym *It would be amazing if this family had something to do with your Lino family, but you do get some strange coincidences in life.*

We worked hard to uncover a relationship between the murderer and the family who lived here, and were finally able to trace him to someone related by marriage to a family member in the UTL tree. This immediately made it a story worth investigating, as far as I was concerned.

Narelle *I have found the link! The man is related to someone who married into the Webster/Murphy family. There is definitely a connection as I built the tree for the accused from 1930-1995. It eventually lead me to a tree with our family member.*

We researched using electoral records and Ancestry.com, and knowing we could only access some digital newspaper records through the State Library of Queensland, I went there on a mission one afternoon.

Caylie *A few hours at State Library today...*

At this juncture, we were able to get a proper sense of what happened after reading the articles thoroughly and discovered several pieces of information that were absolutely mind-blowing.

Firstly, the murder victim was a young woman who'd been living in Annie Street, Torwood, which was where Morgan Webster's fiancé, Gladys Hack, had lived before they married.

Secondly, a blood trail from the scene of the crime went from the school grounds into Rosalie, where the murder weapon (a bayonet) was thrown under a fruit shop gate. The trail then continued around the block of the school, along Haig Road and up Heussler Terrace. The blood trail stopped at this house, before going back down to Baroona Road, along Park Road to Coronation Drive, and then into Roma Street, where an injured man was picked up by an ambulance and taken to the Royal Brisbane Hospital for treatment. He was later arrested there, and charged with the murder of the young woman.

Thirdly, the bayonet was discovered by a fruiterer, Ted Morcombe, early the next morning inside the entrance to his fruit shop.

Finally, Ted Morcombe's children followed the blood trail and were the ones to discover the body of the murdered woman. The names of the children were Perry, Bruce, Lindy and Scott. A little more digging, after a researcher recognised the name of one of the children, had us realising that the Morcombe family who discovered the murder weapon and the grisly scene of the crime, are Daniel Morcombe's family.

Daniel's grandfather was the fruiterer, his Uncle Perry was 16 at the time, his Aunt Lindy was 12, his father, Bruce, was eight and his Uncle Scott was five.

What on earth were we going to do with this? It honestly stopped us in our tracks when all we really wanted was to delve so much further into this story. We had made a connection between the killer and this house, with a family tree confirmation and a blood trail. It's possible that he came here, injured, wanting assistance from people he knew...

But the Morcombes? Hadn't they been through enough, without me opening up this can of worms for them?

At this point, I decided we should leave the investigation alone; that there was no point bringing up old memories for this family who had been through so much. The researchers agreed, and we let the discussion trail off. Over the next few days, my conscience and my curiosity waged a furious battle.

I really wanted to tell a murder story, I'll be honest. Despite my promise not to sensationalise this tale, the writer in me felt this new information was absolutely fantastic! Everyone wants to hear a good murder tale, and I had enough related to the Webster/Murphy connection to be able to put it in this book.

But throwing the Morcombe family into the mix was too much – my conscience was winning.

My friend Brett, who works closely with the media, strenuously disagreed, after I shared my conundrum with him one day.

Not only did he suggest I contact the Morcombes to interview them, he wanted me to contact the accused for a chat! If the thought of approaching the Morcombe family was abhorrent to me, any notion of contacting a convicted murderer was absolutely out of the question! That's when I decided to phone a friend. Kim would know exactly what to do.

Kim Skubris

When my daughter first started school, it was a nerve-wracking time for both of us, even though her brother had been at school for a year, and I'd made some lovely parent friends. Kitty and Will are only a year apart at school, which was quite rare, given that most sensible parents wait at least two years before jumping back into the reproduction pool. As a result of our poor timing, I was required to get to know a whole new class full of parents.

One of the first mums I met was Kim Skubris. I only knew her by her first name at the time, and again, because we didn't have a TV, I had no idea that she was a Channel 7 journalist. She was just bright and bubbly, welcoming and friendly, and I liked her immediately. She also loved my Kitty and was always so kind to her, especially when she was sad. I automatically fall in love with anyone who treats my children with respect and love, so Kim was a shining light in our lives from the start.

Kim and I have remained good friends over the years, attending several parent functions together at Milton State School, and some charity gigs. She had shown a genuine interest in the Under the Lino Project, having renovated her own home and discovering historical artefacts like horseshoes, which she proudly displays in a 'u' shape in her home. Earlier in the investigation, she even asked her producer at Channel 7 to do a story about my experience and was just pipped to the post by another journalist from her station – work was already underway to do an interview.

Kim was adamant, however, that she would help me in any way I needed for the remainder of the project, for which I was so thankful. Neither of us would have guessed how I was going to call in that favour from her in the future.

One of the things I admire most about Kim is the passion and drive she displays towards the Morcombe family. She was one of the first journalists on the scene when Daniel Morcombe was abducted in 2003 on the Sunshine Coast. Kim has built, and maintained, a very strong relationship with the Morcombes, supporting Daniel's parents, Bruce and Denise, as they started the Daniel Morcombe Foundation.

I personally met Bruce and Denise at a *Dance for Daniel* event, and cried many tears for those incredible people who have done so much for our children and community, in the devastating wake of losing their son.

My brilliant idea was to ask Kim what to do. She, of all people, would know.

"Kim, I wonder if you'd mind meeting me for a drink soon to discuss a sensitive topic relating to the money I found under my lino?"

"Of course, honey, when and where?" was her reply. No questions asked and no judgements, which she later told me was par for the course of her normal day – she had people wanting to share stories of all kinds with her, so mine was not an unusual message.

Kim and I met at a local café to discuss the situation. I built up the story for her from the beginning, outlining the details of the murder, the link to the family tree, the blood trail etc. The café, ironically, was directly over the road from where the bayonet was found, and I had the dramatic moment of being able to point to Crookes & Jenkins' Dental premises and tell her that a fruit shop used to be there; that the fruiterer found the murder weapon and his four children had followed the blood trail and found the victim's body.

Pause…

"Kim, the name of the fruit shop owner was Ted Morcombe."

Pause…

"Ted's children are called Perry, Lindy, Bruce and Scott."

Pause...

"Ted was Daniel Morcombe's grandfather."

I was so nervous, thinking she might be mad at me or disappointed that I was even considering asking her what to do? Maybe I just should have known the right answer all along. I watched Kim's face as she put two and two together – a mixture of emotions crossed it, as it had mine. I could see her donning two hats – the journalist hat, desperate to get the full story, and the protect-the-Morcombes-at-all-costs hat of reverence and care.

I was also a little tearful as I shared this story with her, as it was an emotional moment for me – finally being able to tell someone about the whole tale was akin to visiting the confessional, as well as the exciting possibility that I would get some real insider advice on what to do next.

"Right," she said, "that's absolutely incredible, for a start. I love that you want to protect the Morcombes, and are seeking advice before turning this event into a media circus. Nobody would want that, and we all know that the media would love this story."

She thought hard for a minute.

"You know, Bruce is a really pragmatic man who has seen every angle of the media and faced much tougher things than this. I reckon I should put it to him and let him decide. I'll call him tomorrow."

And that was that. Decision made – she would ask Bruce, and if he said an unequivocal, "No way!", then I'd shelve all the information I had and forget I even knew about it.

But he didn't say, "No Way", did he...

Bruce Morcombe said to Kim, "Oh, I'd asked one of the Courier Mail journos if they could try and dig up any of those articles for me from 1967, but they never got back to me. Could you get Caylie to email them to me, and of course I'll talk to her, if she's the kind of person you say she is. Feel free to pass on my number."

Kim said they'd discussed the matter at length, and both agreed that it was best to keep things out in the open, rather than being approached by the press later in the day for comment about something they'd known nothing about. Bruce was also keen to know what had happened after that day – he was only eight years old at the time, and had hazy memories of the aftermath.

Kim also suggested that she could interview the man who committed the crime, if I wanted her to, but I was horrified about this possibility, despite the fact that she does this sort of thing for a living. Time to leave that chap alone. He's done his time, there's no need to rehash it for him.

The offer still stands, and if I thought it would make any difference to finding Muriel White, I would take her up on it. For now, it was only ever an interesting aside, which shows that our community is indeed very small and very generous.

Bruce Morcombe

On March 23rd, 2018, I called Bruce Morcombe and introduced myself as Caylie Jeffery, Kim's friend, who is writing about money under the lino and murders in Milton...

Bruce, as I'd remembered him from events I'd seen him at, was friendly, interested and happy to discuss that time with me.

"It's a real blast from the past," he said. "Thanks for sending the articles through to me. I shared them with my siblings, and it really took us back. That photo of us is pretty happy – but it was taken that morning, because I was still in my pjs! Of course."

"I remember Dad's fruit shop, it was just up from Mogo, the Japanese restaurant on the corner of Baroona Road, over the road from the school. There was a newsagency and a servo down at the village, and I used to deliver newspapers around the area."

Bruce recalled that his family had lived in the house behind the shop for about 4-5 years in the mid-'60s, after which time they moved to Bardon. All four children attended Milton State School.

He described finding the blood trail outside the shop...

"There were lots of drops, and it went a long way along the footpath on Baroona Road. We followed the blood, and then my oldest brother, Perry, said, 'There's a body over there!' pointing into the school grounds. Well, we couldn't run home fast enough!"

"There was wire mesh in front of the fruit shop gate, and I remember the police doing a re-enactment, reaching underneath to see how far the weapon would have gone. We had a German shepherd dog, who was supposedly guarding the shop, but nobody heard him."

"You've also got to remember that I was only eight at the time, and my brother Perry was 16, so he's really the one to talk to. Perry gave evidence in court during the trial and I remember that the police picked him up from school in a police car to take him. It was a huge responsibility for a 16 year old."

I explained to him all I knew about the circumstances of the murder, including who was involved and what happened after the fact. He was surprised to hear that the perpetrator was still alive, and laughed when I told him Kim wanted to interview him.

"She should go in saying, 'You're potentially the heir to a fortune found under the lino!' and he'll tell her whatever she wants!" he laughed.

Bruce and I signed off after a lovely and easy conversation where we agreed this was a good story to tell, and he gave me permission to tell his part in it. He also asked his brother Perry to get in touch with me if he was interested in discussing the event.

Perry Morcombe

I met Perry Morcombe in Rosalie for a coffee on a rainy Sunday afternoon, soon after I'd talked with his brother, Bruce. We recognised each other immediately and after a few minutes of greetings and ordering coffee, we stepped back in time to 1967 Rosalie...

"It was a Sunday morning," he remembered, "and I woke up early. Our German shepherd, who was supposed to guard the shop at night time, had slept through the night, and missed anything of interest. Obviously, the dog used to watch burglars come in and out without batting an eyelid! Dad found the 'dagger' when he went to open up the shopfront. It brought pictures to my mind of pirates, at the time."

Perry's father, Ted, had found a nine-inch bayonet which had been used as the murder weapon. There was a full height mesh grille gate in front of the shop, and the children came out the front and found the trail of blood leading to the gate.

"Blood stains were very clear in front of the shop. The fellow had walked quite far with all that blood loss."

Being the oldest brother, Perry took his sister, Lindy, and younger brothers, Bruce and Scott, for a walk to follow the blood trail.

From our vantage point at the Bungalow Bar in present-day Rosalie, Perry and I were able to look directly at where the old fruit shop used to be – the building is now my friend Nicki's dentistry practice. I'd only bumped into Nicki at Toowong Village the day before, where she'd asked me how the book was going. She'd already bought her copy and wanted to know when it was going to be done... I laughed and told her all the right things, considering she was one of my many employers! I look forward to the phone call I get from her when she reads this line and finds herself and her dental practice in this story!

Perry and I decided to do a walking tour of the scene from that day. We stood outside the building that had been his home and his parents' fruit shop all those years ago, and started to retrace the steps.

On that December '67 Sunday, the Morcombe children walked to the corner and crossed the road to get to Gregory Park. They followed the trail along the footpath until they were just near the current public toilet block, which is when Perry saw the body across the field. He questioned what made him look up and into the school grounds at that point, because they were all looking down intently at the ground.

He saw what looked like the body of a pirate on the ground in the school assembly area (outside the current music room). He shook his head at that, saying he must have had pirates on the brain at that time, or perhaps the dagger had planted swashbuckling thoughts in his impressionable mind!

He and his siblings raced back to their house to share the news with their father, who went down to the school by himself for a look. He then came home and called the police.

Soon after, the police and media arrived – Perry and his family had a good laugh about their picture in the newspaper, because two of them were still in their pyjamas, as Bruce had also mentioned to me.

The police interviewed both Perry and his father that day. Perry attended Toowong High School at the time, and remembers being in Year 12 when the trial came up in 1968. He has no recollection of being harassed by the defence counsel, remembering it as more of a Q&A session.

I asked him if he ever thought much about the victim, and he admitted to not really understanding much about sex at that stage, let alone rape. I told him what I knew about the case, which seemed to put a few things straight in his mind about the events that November weekend.

As we walked the path that Perry and his siblings had walked, I had more of my sepia moments – only more chromatic this time and from the looks of him, Perry was feeling the same. Visiting the past so physically can be quite disturbing, and I was hoping this wasn't too much for him to cope with as I watched him disappear back to the events of that day.

Walking across the oval towards the school grounds, I was shocked to see a familiar figure standing in our path. It was Kim Skubris.

I felt really confused for a second, thinking I must have made a time to meet her and forgotten, but when she saw my look, Kim explained that she was there playing cricket with her family. Extraordinary coincidence, as had become the norm with this project! Kim had met Perry once before at a *Dance for Daniel* function, and she was thrilled we'd had a chance to meet and discuss the events from so many years before.

We let her get back to her game while we continued on our journey towards the school grounds where the body had been found. The gates were locked, as well they should be on a Sunday afternoon, and so we weren't able to get any closer, which was disappointing for us both. Just at that moment, however, a head popped out of one of the doors in the closest building, and there was my son's Grade 1 teacher, Shannon, doing some work in her classroom. We exchanged surprised greetings, and after I introduced her to Perry, she unlocked the gate and invited us in to look around.

It felt as if an ethereal red carpet had been laid out for us all afternoon – it was all just so easy. Fancy the Morcombes' old fruit shop being my friend Nicki's business now; fancy Kim being in the middle of our path as we walked the old memory trail; fancy Shannon being there just at the right moment when we needed the gate unlocked.

The Universe was listening that day, or there were ghosts helping out, that's for sure! I remarked upon this to Perry, who agreed that ghosts were often at work. He said the rain was also significant for his family.

"At the last *Dance for Daniel* event, your friend Kim was the MC. She started off the night saying, 'It rained on the morning of Sunday 7th December 2003', which upset me because I knew that because of that early rain, Bruce and Denise's boys were unable to pick the passionfruit on their neighbour's farm as early as they'd planned before their parents left to go to Brisbane for a work Christmas party. They were actually meant to go with them, but for the fruit-picking. Had they gone to Brisbane, Daniel would still be here with us today. Hardly anyone in the room would have noticed the significance of those few words about the rain. It's actually Denise who always notices rain at special times because she knows Daniel is there with her."

It rained that afternoon while Perry walked me through the village – if any ghosts were helping us that day, I'd like to believe one of them was Daniel.

It was a pleasure and a privilege to be invited into the lives of the Morcombe family; a time and an event so long ago in their memory, with so much pain and suffering in between.

One of my main aims for this project was to do no harm. Only positives must come from all that we're doing, and by being so careful with the Morcombe family, it all panned out really well.

Perry is now an active member of the Under the Lino Community, offering to help wherever he can (he did the massive job of proof-reading this book!) and for that additional assistance alone, I am eternally grateful.

Jack Sim

When we first started looking into the Milton murder, one of the UTL members (Nan) suggested I get in touch with Jack Sim as he would probably know all there was to know about the crime. I'd never heard of Jack, so I had a little look into who he was and what he did.

It was common knowledge, to nearly everyone but me, that Jack Sim is the eyes and ears of the dark waters of Brisbane's historic criminal world. He's had radio shows, he's written books, he runs ghost tours, and is the Managing Director of the Boggo Road Gaol Tours. And that's just for starters!

More than impressed, I contacted Jack, and was delighted that he responded with a message to say that yes, he had information for me, and that we should meet at Boggo Road.

I am not a big fan of jails, to be honest, and the only one I've ever visited was Robben Island Prison in South Africa, where Nelson Mandela was jailed for 18 of his 27 incarceration years – a humbling and haunting experience. I'm as morbidly interested in crime as anyone else, I suppose, but I am fearful of prisons. I don't like doors that lock so soundly, so finitely. So when I turned up, with my trusted recorder and notebook, at Boggo Road, I was considerably unnerved by the solid brick buildings, coils of razor wire and rasping metal gates, despite the fact that the jail hasn't been operational since 1992.

Imagine my consternation, then, when I first met Jack Sim – a burley bloke in a khaki uniform, with a big bushranger's beard and a grip that swallowed up my hand when we shook.

I'd assumed we would just sit in his office or go to a local cafe for lunch, but no, he took out a prison guard's set of keys on an enormous metal ring, and proceeded to unlock gates. Then, with what I thought was an unnecessary amount of clanking and clattering, Jack locked the gates behind us. He'd assured me that all tours were over for the day, and we had time to chat. Alone...

When we were well and truly locked inside, my heart rate had gathered speed and I was feeling a little uncomfortable, which is something that Jack Sim excels at – it's his job to make people feel ill at ease, on ghost tours, in his books and inside the walls of Brisbane's most infamous prison.

After the dim and dingy interior of the main building, I thankfully found myself in a sunny quadrangle (*on the inside, the sun still shines...* Ha ha sorry, couldn't resist!), with a covered area in the centre – something that had been added for the guards to shelter under on sweltering Brisbane summer days. We sat opposite one another on a bench, and proceeded to talk like we'd always known one another, about the seedy side of our city.

Jack gave me a brief rundown on the prison's history, while I looked around at the prison yards and tiny cells, imagining far too vividly what life on the inside might have been like. *The Shawshank Redemption* is one of my favourite movies; I used to hide behind Mum's armchair as a child to watch *Prisoner*; and I totally binge watched *Orange is the New Black*, so I felt like I was somewhat of an armchair expert of prison life. I had no idea, really.

Boggo Road Gaol was a notorious Queensland prison, located on Annerley Road in Dutton Park, on the south side of Brisbane. The heritage-listed site houses the only surviving intact gaol in Queensland that reflects the penological principles of the 19th century.

Originally built in 1883, more than 500,000 people had passed through the gates as prisoners, guards, or visitors, before it was closed in 1992.

Despite my earlier consternation, I found Jack Sim to be incredibly easy to listen to, with his amazing wealth of macabre knowledge.

He discussed the history of Brisbane as being relatively short compared to the rest of the world – in Jack's words, "digestible", which I liked a lot.

"It's convoluted enough to be really interesting, but not too much that you lose track," he explained.

Jack has always been interested in the dark and the creepy, the sinister and the horrible. He's my age, both of us growing up in Brisbane during the '70s, and while my history teacher was putting me to sleep, Jack was getting belted for asking questions at school. Six-year-old Jack's experiences with abusive teachers negatively impacted the way he thought about certain areas of his education, just as my soporific teacher turned me off history until only nine months ago when I re-discovered the money under the lino.

It was very clear to Jack, from a young age that history is written by the victors – the rich and the powerful and the famous. This was the prevailing wind of history in Brisbane during those times. Coming from a working class family, he became more interested in who built these places and who was locked up in them, rather than what dignitary has designed it, and who became wealthy as a result of it.

Jack remembers Brisbane's stories being told, in his childhood, through gossip, innuendo and rumour. The dinner time entertainment often involved conversations about the underbelly of Brisbane. Family gatherings on weekends would include lots of talk about current affairs – murders, robberies, local stories of interest and if people didn't have the full facts, they just made them up!

I also grew up in working class Brisbane, on the wrong side of the tracks to the wealthier adjoining suburbs, a close observer of the underbelly but attending school with the elite, as a poor child from a multi-racial family with divorced parents. My ears have always been open to a good story, because my life has been full of them. I like the psychology behind WHY people do things and Dark History will tell you why *and* how, in a way that titillates the senses to make you think about where we fit in the scheme of things.

Jack and I spoke for some time about matters involving the Milton murder. He generously gave me some crucial mentor's advice about writing safely and considerately about people who have served their time. He has been on the wrong side of some serious threats because of what he writes about, and he advised me about sensitive ways to manage these subjects.

When writing about crime and murder, he warned me that it's serious and important to get the facts straight. There are relatives and family members who can sue so he recommended I get defamation insurance if I was planning on mentioning names. A story he co-authored about a 1926 'lifer' from Boggo Road, together with his edited Betty Shanks book, had resulted in death threats, so he was very concerned for me.

Defamation is a concern because the Prisoner Rehabilitation Act of 1996, established when Wayne Goss was Premier, says that one cannot technically name someone in a public realm if they've served their sentence – they have a right to anonymity under the Act – the same legal advice I'd received from my lawyer friends, Mark, Darren and Amanda.

Which is why I haven't mentioned the name of the accused or the victim in this book. I want to be ethical and I am not insured like reporters who work for big publications. Victims and the families of perpetrators of crime have the right to anonymity. Self-editing is important. People are very judgemental. Legally, I can't obtain a criminal history about them. But in the digital age people think everyone has the right to a person's criminal history.

For example, I have the Wills and post-mortems for many people involved in this project... I can't publish them but I can discuss what I've found as it relates to the mystery and history. There is too much digital access to information these days, with little protection for people who have served their time. People exploit others, and carry out biased activity, so these laws are there to protect people, particularly children and families. State Archives have long periods, up to 100 years, where information is not available to the public until it's assumed that those it pertains to have passed on.

*

This is where the story about the Milton State School Murder ends, I'm afraid.

It is highly probable that the perpetrator was related to the family who once lived in my house, if only by marriage. It is also possible that he came to the house after he committed the crime because he knew someone who lived here and wanted their help after his injury. I like to think that if Arthur or Morgan did answer their front door in the early hours of that terrible November morning, they closed it again quickly and went back to sleep, safe and secure in their beds.

I have chosen to keep the identities of the accused and the victim anonymous, because that's the right thing to do, and it's not important for this story. I have intentionally left the newspaper sources off the photographs to protect those still alive who may be affected. If you want to find them, the articles from the paper are all on public record. Just be careful what you do with the information when you find it. That knowledge will not tell you who Muriel White is, why the money was hidden or why there was so much of it.

Why have I just told you that story then, if it didn't answer any questions about the money I found in my house?

Well, apart from the fact that it showcased the process we went through to discover what we did, it describes the incredible links we confirmed and some amazing synchronicities. It has been a fascinating journey for several members of the UTL Community, because of a chance remark by Chrissy, who used to live in Milton.

And besides, who doesn't love a good murder mystery...

I would like to dedicate this chapter to the Morcombe Family. Their kindness and generosity in sharing their story, as well as Perry's ongoing assistance with the project, has been greatly appreciated.

The Daniel Morcombe Foundation

The Daniel Morcombe Foundation's objectives are to educate children regarding their personal safety (including abduction); to assist victims of crime, particularly where crime involves children; to remember Daniel with suitable child safety community awareness events and to support the families of Missing Persons particularly where it involves children. The foundation cannot operate without financial support, however, and welcomes donations, which are tax deductable.

https://www.danielmorcombe.com.au/donations.html

In Conclusion...

My favourite fable as a child was the story of *Stone Soup*.

It's about a peddler who arrives in a village where the people are starving, and sets up a pot of water to boil in the village square. He places a stone inside the pot and waits. One by one, the villagers come out of hiding to add whatever they have to the soup – not enough to feed their family, but it might make a stone soup taste a little better. Eventually, there's a large enough pot of tasty soup to feed the whole village...

My mother read it to me from one of her old Aesop's Fables books, and whether it was the time she gave me, the meaning behind the story, or a mixture of the two, this one has always stayed with me. I'd like to give you a revised edition, as my final word.

The Empty Journal
by Caylie Jeffery

There was once a writer of very few means, who was a great traveller. She spent her life roaming the lands, meeting all sorts of people, sharing their food, their culture and their company, telling stories of her travels as payment for her keep. The woman carried only a burlap bag with a journal, a pen, a copper kettle, two mugs and some tea leaves.

One day, she came to a place where the lack of intellectual stimulation had plagued the townsfolk for many years. She knocked on their doors, asking for food and shelter, in return for her stories. The people shunned her, as they had become wary of strangers, and, worse still, of each other. They stayed inside their houses, worrying about the state of the world, watching smartphone zombies walking the streets, desperate for decent conversation but all the while, keeping their knowledge, memories and history to themselves. They were very bitter about the way things were.

The woman was saddened by the plight of these people, and decided she would help them. In the middle of the town square, she made a large fire and sat on a stone wall, watching the flames reduce. The people peeped from behind their screens and closed curtains, curiosity getting the better of their wariness.

"What was this stranger doing?" they all wondered.

The writer collected water from the town well in her copper kettle, and set it upon the embers. While the water started to warm, the townsfolk saw the woman place two empty cups next to her. As she perched comfortably on the wall, with her journal opened up on a blank page, the people slowly came out of hiding and asked the woman what she was doing.

"I understand that the people of this town have lost sight of their history, that you are starved of stimulation and good conversation, so I am making you all a hot cup of tea and a place for you to sit with me for a while. By nightfall, I can guarantee you will all have unearthed some memories, restimulated your minds and grown smiles on your faces!"

How the townsfolk laughed and scoffed.

"Cup of tea? Place to sit?" they cried. "How will that reveal our history and ignite the memories of our people? You are a crazy woman! Go back to where you came from and leave us alone!"

But the woman just smiled, and kept on looking into the fire, pen poised in the air. After a little while, one woman left the square to go back to her home, an idea brewing in her mind. She returned holding a single photograph.

"Madam, it's not much, but it's all I have left to remember my brother. It won't bring him back from the war, but you might fill a page of your book with some of his story."

The writer thanked her warmly with a smile that lit the woman's heart, offering her a seat on the wall, and a cup of tea. As the woman sipped her tea, the writer asked her questions about the man in the photograph. The woman stared into the flames of the fire and began to talk. The writer listened keenly to her answers, and started to write as the woman was transported back to another time, a different place in her mind.

A man left the crowd, only to return a little later with a chess board and his own cup.

"I heard what you were saying about your brother," he said to the woman. "I knew him as a soldier, and I have a chess board that he once gave to me when we were in the army together. Perhaps you would like to hear about our time as friends," said the man, humbly.

The woman took the chess board, with a bow of gratitude that reached into the man's soul, and as they began to set out the pieces, he told her stories of her brother that she'd never heard before. The man was proud to have been able to help, and enjoyed remembering the years he'd spent with his old friend. As the pair shared stories, the writer's pen moved quickly across the page.

One by one, the townsfolk went home and returned with their meagre offerings – an old recipe book, a wooden toy, a few coins, some letters, a diary – all they had left of their history to share. Each brought their own mug and was given tea by the writer before she continued to write. One by one, the townspeople started to look at each other's offerings. They began to make comments, and ask questions. Words and laughter filled the air like butterflies, newly hatched from their solitary cocoons.

By the end of the day, the writer was tired but the journal was full. The people who had gathered had shared their memories and their stories with her, and with each other.

There was great anticipation of the wonderful volume to follow, which would contain all of the tales from the day. Neighbours who rarely saw one another now sat together, drinking tea and laughing with the joy of shared histories. They began to share ideas about how to solve the problems of the town, each person telling of their skills and what tools and knowledge they had that could help the community.

While the people drank and talked and planned, the writer refilled their cups, washed out her copper kettle and placed the book in the middle of the table as a gift to the townspeople. A reminder to them that shared memories bring joy, revive history and relieve solitude; and that when people work together sharing skills, tools and knowledge, they can achieve great things.

*

When I first shared that picture of the money and bank books, I had no idea that I was walking into such a hungry community. One by one, the Under the Lino members threw what they had to offer into my stone soup, and by asking the right questions, sharing research methods, experiences, photographs, articles and anecdotes, we have created a wonderful cooking pot of stories from the people and places of yesteryear to share with the world.

This book is my gift to the people of the Under the Lino Community for their hospitality and support, their kindness and their knowledge, their memories and their history.

I hope you've enjoyed the journey of our travels throughout this extraordinary historical experience.

Perhaps you could use this as a golden opportunity to begin your own research, and start writing down some of your memories. Because your history is just as important and interesting as everybody else's and your stories should be recorded.

Yours in story-telling,
Caylie xxx

Now it's your turn...

Here are some Helpful Research Notes to get you started with your own house or family history!

Appendix 1
Doing Your Own House Research

The Queenslander Part 2
by Magnus Eriksson

If you're lucky enough to be the temporary caretaker of a vintage Queenslander house, then you've probably wondered about all the people who owned it and lived in it before you. A house built in the late 1800s, assuming a generational cycle of 25 years, can easily have a history of six or more resident families, each raising their children, watching older generations pass away, and living through the full spectrum of joys, triumphs and tragedies. With the growing repositories of digitised historical information available at our fingertips, these stories can be uncovered and brought into the present. If you embark on such a project, you will find that it provides a fascinating perspective on global and local history, and the inescapable cycles of human existence. It's comforting knowledge, in a very profound sense.

You will also realise that there is no such thing as dull history. In my hobby of house history research I have investigated hundreds of houses, and some in very great detail, and it has never been boring. As you go deeper into the past you will resurrect characters of the early 1900s, and for older houses perhaps their colonial-era builders and inhabitants. Who were they? Why did they come here? What did they do for a living? What organisations were they part of? Did they make the news – for good or bad reasons? By virtue of the butterfly effect, the early inhabitants of our state had a tremendous impact on its future trajectory, no matter how humble they were in person. And in many cases, these people live on, in the hidden fabric of street names, organisations, subdivisions and the suburban infrastructure that surrounds us.

The second reason why you should research your house is more along the lines of an obligation, to identify and preserve important historical data.

The precise construction date of the house will be an important determinant for its level of protection under city plans, and if its construction or history is notable, it may warrant inclusion in council or state heritage overlays. The chances of the latter may be small today but will grow as time goes by. And as the quantity of online information multiplies, this type of research is becoming more accessible every day. So, there's really nothing stopping you – just turn off the TV and go to it.

There are several on-line guides on Queensland house history research, including my own website www.househistories.org. We won't cover the details here, but I would like to offer a few pointers for a successful project.

First, the research should start with sourcing the historical Title Deeds for your property. They will cost you a little bit of money, but they will greatly facilitate the work and uncover information about owners, transactions, subdivision and other details that cannot be found elsewhere. I would advise that you source all the deeds going right back to the Deed of Grant of Land, which documents the sale of land by the government to a first private owner. That way, you won't miss any phase of its history. The House Histories website contains instructions for how to source and interpret the title deeds.

Once you've established the owner's names, you will want to uncover their biographies in as much detail as possible. Most of this information can be derived from two sources – genealogical databases, and the National Library Trove collection of historical newspapers and other documents. The Ancestry.com database for example is very extensive and easy to use, and you will quickly learn how to navigate Trove.

In Queensland we have a unique challenge when it comes to House History research – namely that these sturdy buildings tend to move around. This has been happening for a long time, and in some cases a house may have been relocated more than once. Unfortunately, information on house relocations is rarely kept in public archives, and there is no easy way of finding it.

I would recommend that you use your research to identify the owner of the house when it was sold, and then contact them directly to see if they have any leads.

Once you have the suburb or street of origin, you can use the Queensland Government Imagery website to study aerial photos from different years and see if you can spot your house in its original location, before it was removed.

Don't be shy to contact past inhabitants of your house. It's easy nowadays, using Google and social medial platforms such as Facebook and Linked In. They may have some very personal and useful memories to share, and in most cases they will be delighted to do so.

My last piece of advice is for the curious and obsessive personality types, such as myself and probably most of the contributors to this book. It's more of a warning than a tip. Once you go down the rabbit hole of research, and you start resurrecting the long-forgotten owners of your house, their families and life histories, it can be very hard to stop. In fact, it can become quite consuming and lead to all sorts of weird and wonderful projects. History is infinitely long, broad and fascinating, and it can suck you in like nothing else.

So, if you are the owner of a traditional Queenslander house, please cherish it and regard yourself as a custodian of something that is likely to remain long after we've all passed. Your history will be another page in a long chronology extending into the future. These houses were uniquely adapted to the Queensland climate, and are very resilient given good care. Most of the older, low-set colonial-era houses are susceptible to termite and water damage, and those modern houses being built around the corner, with synthetic laminates and nail guns, won't last more than a few decades. But the traditional Queensland-style house will remain.

And as Andy Jenner states in his excellent book, *Building the Queensland House*, "...there can be no true Queensland without it."

Appendix 2
Sites Used in the UTL Project

Ancestry.com
Australia and New Zealand's leading family history website, offers members access to one billion searchable Australian, New Zealand and UK family history records.
ancestry.com.au

Australian Bureau of Statistics
The ABS is Australia's national statistical agency, providing trusted official statistics on a wide range of economic, social, population and environmental matters of importance to Australia.
abs.gov.au

Australian Society of Archivists
The peak professional body for archivists in Australia. It was formed in response to the growth of archival, recordkeeping and heritage preservation services in Australia, and the increasing demand for archival and recordkeeping skills in community organisations, corporate entities and government.
archivists.org.au

Australian War Memorial
Good for searching records of individuals in the army/wars, they sometimes also have the individual's full records and correspondence
awm.gov.au

Billion Graves
The world's largest resource for searchable GPS cemetery data. Most gravestones have been diligently photographed and cross-referenced so you can see most headstones and engravings without visiting.
billiongraves.com

Births Deaths and Marriages
QLD: **qld.gov.au/law/births-deaths-marriages-and-divorces/birth-death-and-marriage-certificates** and **qld.gov.au/law/births-deaths-marriages-and-divorces/family-history-research**
NSW: **bdm.nsw.gov.au/Pages/family-history/family-history.aspx**
VIC: **online.justice.vic.gov.au/bdm/indexsearch.doj**
WA: **bdm.dotag.wa.gov.au/_apps/pioneersindex/**

Brisbane City Council Archives
Researching your family house and suburb... Titles, postal records, building approvals, electoral rolls, newspapers. Building registers, detailed plans, aerial photos, rate books, Brisbane images
brisbane.qld.gov.au/planning-building/do-i-need-approval/restoring-researching-heritage-properties/research-history-your-house
House styles – Brisbane house styles 1880-1940 (library) and Heritage Pages on BCC website
brisbane.qld.gov.au/planning-building/do-i-need-approval/restoring-researching-heritage-properties/heritage-register

Brisbane City Council Grave Search
graves.brisbane.qld.gov.au

Brisbane City Council Libraries
Guide to researching your house: Water supply and Sewerage detail plans – Brisbane Images tab on BCC library catalogue- search for Detail Plan Key Map. Post 1940 Brisbane was photographed by BCC – over 3000 pics, include documents and plans. Brisbane Municipal Council formal building approval records from 1904-1925, tells Register of new buildings and how much house cost to build and buy. Pre-1925, responsibility for building approvals was shared by different local authorities.
library.brisbane.qld.gov.au/client/en_AU/BrisbaneImages

Church Records
See individual churches

Council Records
See your local city council

Defence Force websites
See individual sites

Detectives
Marianne Taylor, The House Detective
housedetective.com.au

Facebook Social Media Groups
Old Qld Album
facebook.com/groups/OldQLDAlbum/

Bygone Brisbane & Vintage Qld
facebook.com/groups/vintagebeaches/

Vintage Australia
facebook.com/groups/Vintage.aussie/

Queensland Genealogy
facebook.com/groups/1411974805727245/

Queensland Government Railways, Days Gone by
facebook.com/groups/QLDRAILDAYSGONEBY/

Fortitude Valley Revisited:
facebook.com/groups/13922502535/

Australian Genealogy
facebook.com/groups/talltrees/

Aussie Help for All Genealogy
www.facebook.com/groups/1424411964495247/

Family Search
Family Search is the largest genealogy organization in the world. Millions of people use FamilySearch records, resources, and services each year to learn more about their family history.
familysearch.org/

Find my Past
A family history and genealogy website, with millions of records covering Australia, New Zealand, Papua New Guinea and the Pacific Islands.
findmypast.com.au

Funeral notices
Newspapers

Genealogical societies
QLD: **gsq.org.au/**
NSW: **heritagegenealogy.com.au/**
Vic: **gsv.org.au/**
Tas: **tasmanianpioneers.com/resources.html**
tasfhs.org/
ACT: **familyhistoryact.org.au/**
NT: **gsnt.org.au/**
WA: **membership.wags.org.au/**
SA: **genealogysa.org.au/**

Heaven address
Online grave search: **heavenaddress.com/**

Historical Societies
history.org.au/

House Histories
How to research the History of your House
househistories.org/research-the-history-of-your-house

Museums Australia
museumsaustralia.org.au/

National Archives of Australia
The National Archives of Australia can best be described as the memory of our nation – collecting and preserving Australian Government records that reflect our history and identity. Has all World War records. Also includes some immigration records particularly from 1950s on, plus lots of other records.
naa.gov.au/
Census records: **abs.gov.au/census**
Trove: Trove helps you find and use resources relating to Australia. It's more than a search engine. Trove brings together content from libraries, museums, archives, repositories and other research and collecting organisations big and small.
trove.nla.gov.au/

National Film and Sound Archives
nfsa.gov.au/

Outward Passenger Lists from the UK
nationalarchives.gov.uk/help-with-your-research/research-guides/passengers/

Online search
Google and Social Media – use the person's full name, you might find a living relative

Post Office Directories
Post office directories, trade directories and almanacs are useful for tracing the location and movements of people and businesses in the past. A listing can confirm a person's address at a certain time, and may provide clues as to their occupation or year of death.

Directories usually contain alphabetical lists of occupants' names and addresses, but directory contents and their arrangement varied over time with different publishers. While some directories contain a single alphabetical index, others arrange lists geographically, under town or suburb names, or in street number order under street names.

Property search sites
Google these as they change regularly, and can be attached to Real Estate Agents

Public Trustee
Services include Wills, Enduring Powers of Attorney, Executor Services, Financial Administration Services, Real Estate Auctions and Unclaimed Money, and you can download copies of their brochures and other publications.
pt.qld.gov.au/

RSL Virtual War Memorial
rslvirtualwarmemorial.org.au

Records and Information Management Professionals Australasia
rimpa.com.au

Ryerson Index
A free index to death notices appearing in Australian newspapers
ryersonindex.org/

Schools and Hospitals
See individual organisations – often have an historian/archivist

State Archives
Queensland: **qld.gov.au/dsiti/qsa**
NSW: **records.nsw.gov.au/**
Victoria: **prov.vic.gov.au/**
WA: **sro.wa.gov.au/state-records-office-western-australia**
ACT: **archives.act.gov.au/**
Tasmania: **search.archives.tas.gov.au/**
NT: **nt.gov.au/leisure/arts-culture-heritage/search-the-nt-archives-service**
SA: **archives.sa.gov.au/**

State Libraries
Electoral Rolls, Family History, Historical photographs, Newspapers,
Queensland: **slq.qld.gov.au/**
slq.qld.gov.au/resources/family-history
John Oxley Library: This library contains unique Queensland resources including diaries, manuscripts, artworks, photographs, original maps and plans, and oral histories.
slq.qld.gov.au/services/library-spaces/john-oxley-library
NSW: **sl.nsw.gov.au/**
Victoria: **slv.vic.gov.au/**
WA: **slwa.wa.gov.au/**
ACT: **nla.gov.au/**
Tasmania: **linc.tas.gov.au/**
NT: **dtc.nt.gov.au/arts-and-museums/northern-territory-library**

Title Searches
Title deeds were a living document with history of owners, mortgages, caveats. If you are buying a house now from an original owner there will be an actual title deed. But you don't automatically get it – you have to request the old document from Titles Office (Dept. of Natural Resources Mines), and it will be converted to a computerised document. Aerials and detail plans; Historical Lands Title search goes all the way back to the land sales.
You can buy title searches and copies of survey plans and titles documents online, in person or by phone.
business.qld.gov.au/industries/building-property-development/titles-property-surveying/titles-property/searches-copies
The Department of Natural Resources and Mines (Level 13, 53 Albert Street, Brisbane)
qld.gov.au/housing/buying-owning-home/property-land-valuations/property-title-searches
Go in and visit them for historical searches or visit them online
dnrme.qld.gov.au/titles-valuations

Unclaimed Money
Unclaimed money is money from lost bank accounts, shares, investments and life insurance policies. This money becomes lost when you move house and forget to update your details with a financial institution or company.
moneysmart.gov.au/

Writers Centres
QLD: **qldwriters.org.au/**
NSW: **writingnsw.org.au/**
Victoria: **writersvictoria.org.au/**
WA: **writingwa.org/**
ACT: **actwriters.org.au/**
Tasmania: **taswriters.org/**
SA: **writerssa.org.au/**
NT: **www.ntwriters.com.au/**

Websleuths
Online detective forum
websleuths.com/forums/

In Humble Appreciation...

Being able to include so many members of the community in this whole experience has been my favourite part of writing this book.

People with a love of Brisbane, and our short, but rich 'settled' history; people with a penchant for the Queenslander (and the linoleum within), having either lived in one, renovated one or visited relatives in one; local Milton residents from now, and 'ago'; people who just love a really good mystery story; and people who came on the journey just because we invited them.

So many have lent their professional expertise, their personal experience, their family memories, their research skills and their enthusiasm to get us to this point. They've enhanced the lives of so many people as a result – mine most of all.

I am terrified I'll forget someone, and there's not enough paper in Brisbane to thank everyone personally, but I must pay tribute to the following people for all they've done to make this happen. My deepest thanks goes to:

My Under the Lino and Old Brisbane family for your skills, passion, fortitude, enthusiasm, humour, curiosity, love and kindness. You weaved your stories into our fascinating local history, and therefore, became an integral part of the fabric of this wonderful community project and each other's lives, especially mine.

Lyn Cox for keeping me honest, always telling me the truth and being my strongest pillar of support all the way through.

Hamish Elliott for all your research efforts on the project, for inventing the Under the Lino Facebook group (I told you we'd get to a thousand!) and for sharing moderating duties.

Greg Davis for providing the awesome Old Brisbane Album platform that has always supported the UTL community and letting me post on there regularly!

All of the Incredible Fundraisers who supported the production of this book by pre-ordering a copy! This actually happened because of you! And Elliott Chapple and Lily Nishiyama from Pozible.com! And these major financial contributors: David, Will and Kitty Jeffery, Nicky and Kim Lynch, Alex and Catherine Fernandes, Mark, Melissa, Ella and Thomas Gjerek, Alicia Jeffery, Allison McDonald, Andrea McLeod, Annette Dell, Barry Markwort, Brenda Koster, Brendon and Amy Brodie-Hall, Bron Wolter, Bronwen Jones, Caitlin Enriquez, Carol Palmer, Carolyn Murphy, Catalin and Cristina Draguceanu, Catriona McNamara, Cherri Ryan, Cheryl Palmer, Cheryl Smith, Christine Murphy, Christine Hegerty, Claire Faulkner, Darcy and Lyn Maddock, Dominic Peterson, Emma Lakin, Fiona Robertson, Gail Creighton-Davies, Gareth Cole, The Goan Family, Greg Tuckwell, Helen and Kevin Diehm, Jacey and Quentin Wheelwright, Jackie Sears, Jacqueline Davis, Jade Goulding, James and Anna O'Brien, Aleisha Godfrey, Jane Harding, Jane and Kim Malcolm, Janelle Duncan-Davies, Janet Nash, Jazz and Jackson MacCotter, Jim Larsen, Jodi Robertson, John Winterburn, John Allan, Julie and Kevin O'Sullivan, June Grant, Karen Culshaw, Karen King, Kate Gegg, Kate Lyons, Katrina Fogarty, Katrina O'Malley-Jones, Ken Ingram, Kenneth Glavimans, Kerry Beeton, Lachlan Dreaver, Libby Versace, Linda Mansell, Lorene Richards, Luke Simpson, Mark Seeto, Melissa Griffiths, Melissa and Mark Haddad, Nadine Jensen, Nancy Blindell, Nick Parr, Nicole Christian, Nicolie Jenkins, Nina Moss, Olga and Angelo Pennisi, Philippa Stanford, Pip Stace, Rachael Banks, Rebecca Masoud, Rhonda Gibson, Richard and Bronwyn Dunks, Richard, Alice and Priya Fernandes, Roslyn Mullen, Samantha Wheeler, Sharon Walker, Sharon Ward, Sharyn McErlean, Suzy Moss, Tracey and Shane Ford, Tracey Jeffery, Tracy Malone, Tracy Donegan, Tricia Naylor, Valerie Rees, Gladys & Neville Roach, and Joanne Melton.

The Webster and Murphy Families (past and present) for sharing your family stories with us all so generously, for coming to visit and for your friendship.

The Unwavering Research Team: Claire Faulkner, Cheryl Palmer, Lyn Cox, Brenda Koster, Michelle Hill, Kym Whitehouse Brockwell, Narelle Honeyman and Chrissy Benedetto.

The Super-Honest, but Ever-Caring Beta-readers, Proof Readers and Editors: Perry Morcombe, Claire Faulkner, Cheryl Palmer, Lyn Cox, Michelle Hill, Brenda Koster, Bronwyn Wallman, Daphne and Dom Gonzalvez, Sue Fernandes, Virginia McMillan, Mark Seeto and Mark Cryle.

The Creative Geniuses (responsible for logos, family trees, photographs and cover designs): Caren Crawford, Daniel Jarick, Natalie Jeffcott, Nicole Christian, Emily Harper, Allison McDonald and Leanne Carkeet's Wednesday night art class.

Dr Glenn Davies for 30 years of friendship, your supportive words and your passion for the History of this great country.

Lord Mayor Graham Quirk and Brisbane City Council Staff for your ongoing support of the UTL Project and Website funding.

Councillor Peter Matic, Fiona and Carolyn at the Paddington Ward Office for believing in this project and our community, and for supporting the website so generously.

My Literary Advisors: Cherri Ryan, Brett Lethbridge, Mark Gjerek, Justine Gannon, Samantha Schraag, Katie Woods and Pip Stace.

The Morcombe Family for your openness, generosity and candour.

Kim Skubris for your passion, enthusiasm and encouragement.

The Morrow Family for sharing your part in this story and offering me such friendly hospitality.

The Contributors of Special Stories, Important Information and Articles for the Book: Magnus Eriksson, Miles Sinnamon, Arthur Palmer, Cheryl Palmer, Jack Sim, Hugh Lunn, Matthew Condon, Trent Dalton, Nancy Knudsen, Glenn Davies, Chrissy Benedetto, Megan Nash, Adrian Gibb, Vivien Harris, Ross Webster, Steve Webster, Darcelle Hegerty, Warren Allen, Di Harte, Kay Dieckmann, Dan Flannery, Edwin and Gloria Murphy, Bobbie Edes, Belinda Smith, Ian Rowland, Phill Cole, Narelle Honeyman, Allan Taylor, Mark & Louise Kudeborg, Darcy & Lyn Maddock and the staff at Toowong Cemetery, Melissa Biedak, Ivan McDonald, Stephen Clarke, Matthew Wengert, Margaret Henderson, Professor John Pearn, Nicole Christian, Ross Palm, the Adsett and the Strachan families.

The Students and Teaching Staff (Classroom, Library and Head Office) at Milton State School, Brisbane Boys' College, St Peters Lutheran College and Pine Rivers State High School – for your amazing historical creativity & contributions!

Queensland Rail Contributors: Janelle Duncan Davies, Greg Hallam, Noel Condon, Rowland 'Gillie' Williams, Brian 'Sully' O'Sullivan, Norm Duncan, Rob Shiels, Xao Thaow, David Hampton, Merle Heiner and Murray Barker.

Rebecca Hope for your incredible design of the UndertheLino.com.au website, and regular assistance.

The Media who have supported everything about this project: Leanne Edmistone, Sharyn Ghidella, Rebecca Levingston, Craig Zonca, Rachel Clun, Maylee Flannery, Amy Mitchell-Whittington, Kaye Mobsby and Those Two Girls.

My Legal Advisors: Franki Simmons, Mark Jenvey, Darren Robinson, Amanda Karpeles, Jack Sim and even you, José 'Webster' Sarmiento... Fancy pretending to be a Webster at the BSHS reunion! Thanks for the early police advice on what to do with the money.

My Home Team: Melissa, Christine S, Christine B, Sally H, Mat Sullivan, Tara, Pip, Jane, Olivia, Jacey, Quentin, Natasha, Ian, Amy, Brendon and Lila.

My Dearest Friends from BSHS: Mandy, Fiona, Flora, Vanessa and Rhonda – if you hadn't kept in touch with me before that reunion, this would never have happened! This blank bit here is for you, Stan Thompson ⟶

Ben Aitchison and Michael McDermaid from Paradigm Print Media for printing this fabulous book for us all!

Cath and Andy Ross for lending me your piece of old lino and your enthusiasm for this project!

Pip Rhodes for your unconditional love and hospitality when I needed to write this book in peace.

David for stepping back and letting me do this, always ready to catch me should I fall. I forgive you for falling asleep while I read you bits of the book. I love you more than Wonder Woman, I promise.

Will and Kitty for listening when I rambled, for forgiving me when I grumbled, for all those cups of tea you made for me, and all those meals you made for yourselves. I love you more than Thor AND Wonder Woman put together.

Mum for supporting me through all my crazy projects and for the fantastic life you've given me. You *are* a Wonder Woman.

Last, but not least, a quiet whisper of thanks to my Universe and the ghosts of those who have gone before us.
I know you've been helping us, too.

Now, I'm just off to have a Quick-Eze, a Bex and a good lie down... Thanks and love to you all, Caylie x

How to Help an Author!

If you've enjoyed reading Under the Lino, here are a few things you could do for me...

1. **Buy copies for your friends and family** www.underthelino.com.au/book
2. **Write a review on** www.facebook.com/underthelino/ and www.goodreads.com/book/show/41751170-under-the-lino
3. **Promote it on social media...** Take a photo of yourself reading Under the Lino, or a picture of the book, and post it on Facebook, Twitter, Instagram and LinkedIn. You could also write a recommendation with a link so others can purchase it.
4. **Have me speak to your company, club, school or professional association.**
5. **Read it for your book club.** I can also come and visit your book club or do a brief Skype chat during the meeting.
6. **Feature the book in your blog, podcast, or newsletter.** If you (or a company you run) has a blog, podcast, newsletter, YouTube channel, or other content stream, perhaps interview me for it, or write a review of Under the Lino (and include a link so others can buy it if they're interested). I will totally appreciate the shout-out and exposure to a new audience.
7. **E-mail your stories to** underthelino@hotmail.com about personal discoveries or your own historical research so I can share them on the website.
8. **Share articles you enjoy from the website with your networks.**

Thanks so much for your support!
Caylie xxx

www.ingramcontent.com/pod-product-compliance
Lightning Source LLC
Chambersburg PA
CBHW030429010526
44118CB00011B/558